Helping English Language Learners Succeed in Middle and High Schools

Faridah Pawan and
Ginger B. Sietman, Editors

Collaborative Partnerships Between ESL and Classroom Teachers

Debra Suarez, Series Editor

Teachers of English to Speakers of Other Languages, Inc.

Typeset in Chaparral Pro and Avenir
by Capitol Communication Systems, Inc., Crofton, Maryland USA
Printed by United Graphics, Inc., Mattoon, Illinois USA
Indexed by Pueblo Indexing and Publishing Services, Pueblo West, Colorado USA

Teachers of English to Speakers of Other Languages, Inc.
700 South Washington Street, Suite 200
Alexandria, Virginia 22314 USA
Tel 703-836-0774 • Fax 703-836-6447 • E-mail tesol@tesol.org • http://www.tesol.org

Publishing Manager: Carol Edwards
Copy Editor: Tomiko M. Chapman
Additional Reader: Sarah Duffy
Cover Design: Tomiko M. Chapman

ISBN 9781931185462
Library of Congress Control No. 2007909555

Contents

Series Editor's Preface v

Dedication ix

Acknowledgments xi

1. Introduction 1

2. Integrated Curriculum 5
   Faridah Pawan and Brenda Ward

3. Language 31
   Susan Jenkins, Mark Nigolian, Mary Kay O'Brien,
   Elizabeth O'Dowd, and Linda Walsleben

4. Standards 59
   Heidi Goertzen

5. Assessment 85
   Trish Morita-Mullaney

6. Assessment of English Language Learners
   With Disabilities 103
   Michael W. Dunn and Trenia Walker

7. Community 117
   Thomas H. Levine and George C. Bunch

8. Culture and Advocacy 141
   Raquel Oxford

9. Extending Collaboration Into the
   Foreign Language Context 163
   Sally Hood

Glossary...187

Contributors 193

Index 197

Series Editor's Preface

Debra Suarez

Cultural and linguistic diversity in the U.S. student population represents a challenge for all educators. The number of school-aged speakers of a language other than English continues to grow. In the early 1980s one in ten school-aged children was from a non-English speaking background. By the early 1990s, the number increased to one in seven (Macías, 2000). During the 1994–1995 school year, the total reported number of limited English proficient (LEP) students in U.S. public schools was just over three million (NCELA, 2006a). A decade later, during the 2004–2005 school year, there were 5,119,561 LEP students, representing about 10.5% of the total U.S. public school enrollment (pre-k through grade 12), and a 56.2% increase over the 1994–1995 LEP enrollment (NCELA, 2006b).

These figures are especially poignant when it is noted that over the past 15 years, LEP student enrollment has increased at nearly seven times the rate of the total U.S. student enrollment (NCELA, 2006a). Further, the nation's LEP enrollment is principally concentrated in the elementary school grades, and the highest numbers are in kindergarten through third grade (NCBE, 2000). These enrollment patterns in the early grades further ensure that this challenge will continue for the coming years.

The student population increasingly comprises ethnic minorities of color, immigrants, non-Europeans, and speakers of languages other than English. The teaching force, however, continues to be predominantly Caucasian, European-American, middle-class, female, U.S. born, and monolingual English speakers (Banks, 2001; NCATE, 2002; Sleeter, 2001; Taylor & Sobel, 2001). It is most probable that teachers will inevitably teach in classrooms where the cultural and linguistic backgrounds of their students differ from their own (Zeichner, 1993). And it is most probable that classroom teachers, of every subject matter and at each grade level, will teach LEP students.

There is a nationwide call to better provide schools with a teaching force equipped with knowledge, skills, and abilities to effectively teach this diversifying U.S. student population, and to foster the academic achievement of all students, including the achievement of English language learners (ELLs).

This series aims to contribute to the field's responses to this nationwide call. This series is designed for both classroom teachers and ESL teachers, for both subject matter specialists and language education specialists—for all educators who are responsible for the academic achievement of all our students.

Traditionally, teacher preparation for ELLs has taken the approach of talking about mainstreaming—conversations directed towards classroom teachers about how they might integrate ESL students into the mainstream classroom. However effective these mainstreaming approaches have been, there is a gap in the professional development literature. There is a paucity of information or literature that offers specific, detailed direction about how and why ESL, subject matter, and grade-level educators can work together. This series recognizes that each educator is a specialist in his or her own field and that, in order to promote academic achievement for ELLs, educators must know elements of one another's disciplines and develop techniques for working together, building on the particular strengths, knowledge, abilities, and dispositions that each partner brings to the collaborative effort.

This volume of Collaborative Partnerships between ESL and Classroom Teachers gives emphasis to collaborative partnerships for middle and high school students. Editors Faridah Pawan and Ginger Sietman present us with classroom-based examples of collaborations that move us beyond notions of mainstreaming. They have gathered expert authors who provide examples of ideal collaborations that require "systematic, planned language development, not just the inclusion of ESL students in the ongoing activities of the mainstream classroom" (Davison, 2006, p. 457).

Each chapter is directed to both ESL specialists and subject matter or grade-level specialists. The volume is organized around knowledge that is required of all educators, such as knowledge of curriculum, standards, assessment, and community. This volume is further organized around knowledge that is required of all educators if they are to be effective in teaching ELLs, such as knowledge of language, culture, advocacy, and issues about ELL students with disabilities. Each chapter discusses pedagogical dilemmas and challenges from the perspective of the teachers and administrators.

After a focused literature review, each chapter offers examples of classroom-based and school-based collaborative partnerships from middle and high schools across seven states: Alabama, California, Indiana, Oregon, Texas, Vermont, and Washington. Each chapter includes a case study that readers may analyze and apply to their own settings. By so doing, this volume builds a knowledge base for teachers and educators. In this volume, the editors provide state-of-the-art, research-based strategies that illustrate the processes and ways of thinking and planning that are fundamental to productive collaborative work. They present us with a collection of collaborative practices that meaningfully bring together the best of subject matter pedagogy with the core underlying principles of second language learning and teaching. This volume will serve as a guide and an inspiration to teachers as they plan for collaborative partnerships in which knowledge and expertise are shared, and in middle and high schools where English language learners succeed.

References

Banks, J. A. (2001). Citizenship education and diversity: Implications for teacher education. *Journal of Teacher Education, 52*(1), 5–16.

Davison, C. (2006). Collaboration between ESL and content teachers: How do we know when we are doing it right? *The International Journal of Bilingual Education and Bilingualism, 9*(4), 454–475.

Macías, R. F. (2000). The flowering of America: Linguistic diversity in the United States. In S. L. McKay & S. C. Wong (Eds.), *New immigrants in the United States* (pp. 11–57). Cambridge: Cambridge University Press.

National Clearinghouse for Bilingual Education (NCBE). (2000). *Summary report of the survey of the state's limited English proficient students and available educational programs and services, 1997–1998.* Washington, DC: George Washington University.

National Clearinghouse for English Language Acquisition and Language Instruction Educational Programs (NCELA). (2006a). NCELA FAQs: How has the limited English proficient student population changed in recent years? Washington, DC: George Washington University. Retrieved October 1, 2007, from http://www.ncela.gwu.edu/expert/faq/08leps.html

National Clearinghouse for English Language Acquisition and Language Instruction Educational Programs (NCELA). (2006b). NCELA FAQs: How many school-aged English language learners (ELLs) are there in the U.S? Washington, DC: George Washington University. Retrieved October 1, 2007, from http://www.ncela.gwu.edu/expert/faq/01leps.html

National Council for Accreditation of Teacher Education (NCATE). (2002). *Professional standards for the accreditation of schools, colleges and departments of education.* Washington, DC: Author.

Sleeter, C. E. (2001). Preparing teachers for culturally diverse schools: Research and the overwhelming presence of whiteness. *Journal of Teacher Education, 52*(2), 94–106.

Taylor, S. V., & Sobel, D. M. (2001). Addressing the discontinuity of students' and teachers' diversity: a preliminary study of preservice teachers' beliefs and perceived skills. *Teaching and Teacher Education, 17*, 487–503.

Zeichner, K. M. (1993). *Educating teachers for cultural diversity.* NCRTL Special Report. East Lansing, MI: National Center for Research on Teacher Learning, Michigan State University.

Dedication

Thank you to all collaborators near and far; to my coeditor, Ginger; to Debra; to Tomiko at TESOL; and to Charles, Joshua, and Samuel, who have made this project and all other equally wonderful endeavors possible.

Faridah Pawan

Thank you to Faridah, my coeditor; the chapter authors; Debra; and Tomiko for a truly collaborative experience. And to my husband Tim: Thank you for sacrificially commuting so that I could pursue my dreams and for never giving up on showing me the beauty of Greek grammar.

Ginger B. Sietman

Thank you to the teachers who shared their stories, to the authors for sharing their knowledge, to the coeditors Faridah and Ginger for sharing their expertise. And, as always, thanks to Tomiko Chapman for her dedication and patience throughout the process. A special heartfelt thanks to my husband and best friend, Michael Cummins.

Debra Suarez

Acknowledgments

Though the names used in this chapter are pseudonyms, we thank all the teachers included in the chapter, whose dedication and camaraderie have been inspirational. We are especially grateful for the initial and continued support of the sheltered program by the high school administrator at Frankfort High School. A special thank you also goes to ICP's teacher cohort that has truly supported the ESL world in Frankfort.

Faridah Pawan and Brenda Ward
Chapter 2

We extend our thanks and admiration to all the Burlington School District content teachers who participated in the QUEST program and to Pat Chira for opening his classroom to us for this study.

Susan Jenkins, Mark Nigolian, Mary Kay O'Brien,
Elizabeth O'Dowd, and Linda Walsleben
Chapter 3

I wish to express my gratitude to the teacher-collaborators who generously shared their classroom experiences with me. Their patience and willingness to discuss their innovative instructional approaches made this study possible.

Heidi Goertzen
Chapter 4

A warm acclamation of gratitude is offered to the literacy coaches and ESL teachers in our school district who all contributed to the support and success of this continuing journey. Their legacy is embedded in their daily work with raising teacher awareness and efficacy as they partner to meet the needs of our ESL community. I offer them thanks in the 54 languages of our students who now feel the impact of their pioneering work.

Trish Morita-Mullaney
Chapter 5

We would like to thank the teachers included in this project for their contributions. Their perspectives in illustrating the complexity of ELLs and their possible LD identification (with the added and new response-to-intervention LD assessment paradigm) provided authentic voices in this discussion.

Michael W. Dunn and Trenia Walker
Chapter 6

The names of all people and places in this chapter are pseudonymous. We are grateful to Jennifer, Diane, James, Sarah, Rebecca, Guy, and Zardos—the educators at B-C Academy who bravely shared their classrooms, their collaboration, and their perspective with the first author during data collection. They have taught us much more than any thanks here can acknowledge.

Thomas H. Levine and George C. Bunch
Chapter 7

A heartfelt thank you is extended to all the teachers of English language learners in City View Independent School District who were open to observation, collaboration, and professional development to embrace students' cultural identities. Names of teachers, researchers, and schools are pseudonyms.

Raquel Oxford
Chapter 8

I would like to thank Robert Davis and Greg Hopper-Moore for the information they provided about MOSAIC. I extend special thanks to the four teachers who created the MOSAIC unit described in this chapter. Without these teachers' patience, creativity, hard work, and perseverance, the MOSAIC project would not have succeeded.

Sally Hood
Chapter 9

CHAPTER 1

Introduction

Collaboration among teachers is essential to both teacher development (Burbank & Kauchak, 2003; Butler, Lauscher, Jarvis-Selinger, & Beckingham, 2004) and the success of English language learners (ELLs) in U.S. schools. In the fields of ESL and EFL, Freeman and Johnson's (1998) reconceptualization of teacher knowledge in the field has given greater prominence to and acknowledgment of the necessity of collaborative models of teacher development. Central to Freeman and Johnson's conception of teacher knowledge is the rejection of *Cartesian dualism*, which says that teachers' knowledge is distinct and separate from the world in which they exist (Feldman, 2002). In this regard, the core of the theoretical perspective is the teaching activity and the prioritization of teachers' insider knowledge of the activity itself. Teacher collaboration hence provides a means for the acknowledgment and inclusion of teacher-generated knowledge as a foundational element of their professional development. Rather than being passive recipients of expert advice in workshops that have limited impact (Kennedy, 1997), the teachers engage actively and meaningfully in understanding their unique classroom circumstances with the support of their colleagues.

In addition to contributing to teacher development, teacher collaboration is also critical in the field of teaching English to speakers of other languages (TESOL). Cohesive and coordinated joint efforts by all educators are needed to address the needs of over 5 million ELLs (U.S. Department of Education, 2004) in the nation's public schools. Traditional pull-out methods in which ELLs are taken out of content classrooms for language instruction have been proven ineffective for several reasons, including limiting and interrupting ELLs' exposure to content knowledge, stigmatizing them for their lack of proficiency in English, and so on. Given the context, content-based instruction (CBI) is gaining prominence in the field as a viable way to address the language needs of ESL students in the classroom (see chapter 1). In CBI, language and content are taught in tandem, and thus the approach brings together professionals from two fields, namely second/foreign language and content area teachers. As the spotlight on CBI grows, attention is being given to the best way to implement CBI in the classroom. One issue in particular is the difficulty in finding teachers who are experts in both language and content. One viable solution to this problem is collaboration between content area and ESL teachers. Consequently, workable models of collaboration are needed in order to facilitate this collaboration and to overcome its challenges.

The purpose of this book is to address the critical issue of collaboration and to provide practical, real-life examples of how schools have worked to develop effective collaboration among teachers. This volume focuses on six important elements that need to be considered as collaboration is undertaken: curriculum, language, standards, assessment, community, culture, and advocacy.

Recurring Themes in the Book

Several themes emerge from the collaborative experiences that are catalogued in this volume. One theme is the administrative support and leadership that is crucial for effective, long-term collaboration. Another theme is the time and organizational resources needed in order to sustain collaboration; supportive leadership that provides for those resources plays an important role in successful teacher collaboration.

In addition, emerging from the authors' contributions is the argument that traditional stand-and-deliver workshop approaches by outside experts are insufficient. To effectively initiate change in the classroom, teachers need to be actively engaged in discussing, reflecting upon, and adapting their teaching to their changing classrooms. Focused collaboration based on immediate teacher needs is an effective method for teacher development. Finally, the combination of informally and formally structured collaboration is also a theme that emerges from the contributions in the book. The combination is most effective in facilitating and sustaining the continuity of teacher collaboration. The informality of the collaboration makes it easy for teachers to participate and engage in it. And when a formal structure is in place, the collaboration is seen as one that has extensive support by administrators who believe and are invested in its success and permanence (Stowitcschek, Lovitt, & Rodriguez, 2001).

Volume Organization

After the introduction, chapters two through eight of the volume present collaboration models between ESL and content area teachers in various settings at the middle and high school levels. The final chapter extends the discussion on teacher collaboration into the area of foreign language education.

In chapter two, Pawan and Ward describe the collaboration between ESL and content area teachers in developing integrated curricula for ELLs in a high school in northern Indiana by using Fogarty's (1991) model of integrated curriculum. The chapter emphasizes the establishment of a strong collaborative foundation between teachers.

In chapter three, Jenkins, Nigolian, O'Brien, O'Dowd, and Walsleben outline specific language-based modifications that an ESL specialist and a high school math teacher developed through teacher-teacher collaboration facilitated by the Quality Utilization of Education, Support, and Training (QUEST) project in Vermont. This chapter highlights how faculty members and ESL specialists collaborate with content area teachers in order to develop their knowledge about language.

In chapter four, Goertzen describes the integrated content and language standards effort in Alabama that uses World-Class Instructional Design and Assessment (WIDA) as a guide. She elaborates on collaboration between an ESL teacher and an English language arts teacher who worked to incorporate ESL and content-based standards in a language arts classroom.

In chapter five, Morita-Mullaney elaborates on the opportunities and challenges of teacher collaboration in ELL assessment in Indiana. She highlights three ways in which collaboration between ESL and content area teachers has affected her district: the alignment of ELP standards with content standards so students can produce assessable products, the use of the first language in assessment, and the reassignment of roles and responsibilities in the assessment of ELLs.

In chapter six, Dunn and Walker continue the discussion on assessment by describing the vital role of collaboration between language, special education, and subject area teachers in diagnosing ELLs with learning disabilities. Collaboration between a special education teacher and a social studies teacher in a Washington school is described to highlight the potential value of teacher collaboration in the appropriate placement of and effective support for ELLs.

In chapter seven, Levine and Bunch approach community outreach via the development and strengthening of community among teachers. They describe how teacher-teacher collaboration at a school in California is used as a springboard for encouraging greater involvement from the wider community.

In chapter eight, Oxford describes a collaborative research and information-gathering process in a rural town in Texas. The collaboration serves as a basis for cultivating culturally responsive teaching and undertaking student advocacy. The importance of culturally responsive teaching and how teachers can empower ELLs through cultivating self-advocacy are also discussed.

In chapter nine, Hood extends collaboration and CBI into a foreign language context in a school in Oregon. She demonstrates how teachers of Spanish collaborate with content specialists to teach geography through Spanish. In the process, Hood demonstrates how geography specialists learn about characteristics of second language teaching through collaboration with language teachers who, in turn, acquire pedagogical content knowledge in geography.

References

Burbank, M. D., & Kauchak, D. (2003). An alternative model for professional development: Investigations into effective collaboration. *Teaching and Teacher Education, 19*, 499–514.

Butler, D. L., Lauscher, H. N., Jarvis-Selinger, S., & Beckingham, B. (2004). Collaboration and self-regulation in teachers' professional development. *Teaching and Teacher Education, 20*, 435–455.

Feldman, S. (2002). Preparing teachers to guide children's language development. In C. T. Adger, C. E. Snow, & D. Christian (Eds.), *What teachers need to know about language* (pp. 113–122). McHenry, IL; Washington, DC: Delta Systems; Center for Applied Linguistics.

Fogarty, R. (1991). *The mindful school: How to integrate the curricula*. Palatine, IL: Skylight.

Freeman, D., & Johnson, K. E. (1998). Reconceptualizing the knowledge-base of language teacher education. *TESOL Quarterly, 32*, 397–417.

Kennedy, M. M. (1997). The connection between research and practice. *Educational Researcher, 26*, 4–12.

Stowitcschek, J. J., Lovitt, T. C., & Rodriguez, J. A. (2001). Patterns of collaboration in secondary education for youth with special needs: Profiles of three schools. *Urban Education, 36*, 93–128.

U.S. Department of Education, National Center for Education Statistics. (2004). English language learner students in U.S. public schools: 1994 and 2000 (NCES 2004–035). Washington, DC: U.S. Government Printing Office.

CHAPTER 2

Integrated Curriculum

Integrated Curriculum Development Through Interdisciplinary Collaboration

Faridah Pawan and Brenda Ward

CASE STUDY

Lilia is a Mexican student in a middle school in Frankfort, Indiana, who has been in the United States for about 2 years. She is doing well in her ESL classes but poorly in academic classes. She is confused because she received a lot of encouragement and assurance of progress in her ESL classes. She wonders whether her ESL teachers (ESLTs) were misleading her regarding her true abilities. Adding to Lilia's confusion is that, although she had taken algebra while in school in her hometown of Oaxaca, Mexico, she was placed in a prealgebra class in the United States. Lilia thinks that perhaps her math teachers are basing their judgment of her ability in algebra on her imperfect proficiency in English.

Sophie, an ESLT with a limited license, and her colleague Isabel, a certified math teacher, work with Lilia and are aware of her frustration and confusion. Nevertheless, they are at a loss as to how to address the situation—one they know is a common experience among many newcomers in their school. Sophie struggles with her role as an ESLT; she feels it requires a constant battle between the balance of her role as a supportive and motivating force and her role as a gatekeeper for providing access to the English language. Isabel's battle, on the other hand, is between being able to ensure that her students successfully meet math standards and addressing, with the limited classroom time she has, the individual needs of students in her class. In addition to English language learners (ELLs), her students include those with special needs as well as mainstream students with a range of abilities. Knowing each other's struggles, Sophie and Isabel sought one another out to jointly pursue a professional development program toward ESL certification. Lilia provided a turning point for them and an impetus to prepare themselves to undertake the challenge head-on.

Throughout the past few years, Frankfort has experienced a growth of 300% in its ELL population, with a projected increase of 20% annually. Already, 30% of students in the Frankfort school system are identified as ELLs, but less than 1% of its teachers are ESL certified or have been trained in any way to work with ELLs. Sophie and Isabel undertake a federally funded ESL certification program, which gives them the opportunity to learn and understand together. Though they are still in the program, Sophie and Isabel have become interdisciplinary collaborators in their own school. Their collaboration is fraught with challenges but also filled with opportunities.

Prereading Questions

- What is an integrated curriculum?
- What is driving the current focus on integrated curricula?
- Why should integrated curricula be included at the middle and high school levels?
- What are barriers to implementing integrated curricula?
- What does a successful collaboration in developing an integrated curriculum look like? And how does the collaboration successfully navigate through various barriers?

but this ∅ enough time for CALP

Setting the Scene in Indiana

The first part of the vignette demonstrates a disconnect between how Lilia perceives and evaluates her progress in her ESL class and in her math class. The second part of the vignette demonstrates a disconnect between how and what Sophie and Isabel perceive as the focus of their jobs as Lilia's teachers. Lilia's plight merely scratches the surface of the problems encountered by immigrant children who are ELLs in school. Lilia is fortunate in that she has had a chance to be successful in her ESL classes and because she has background knowledge in this particular subject area. Many immigrant children in the United States, in addition to studying a new language, are experiencing formal schooling for the first time. And yet, following the mandates of the No Child Left Behind Act (NCLB), within 1–3 years, all of these children must be able to acquire and demonstrate English language proficiency equal to that of a native speaker's in academic subjects. The consequences of the mandate and the expectations derived from it are the subject of much study. In the meantime, the dropout rates among immigrant school children are skyrocketing. From 2002 to 2003, for example, the National Center for Education Statistics (NCES; 2006) reports a 39.4% dropout rate for Hispanic students between the ages of 16 and 24 who were born outside the United States.

Sophie's and Isabel's dilemma highlights the multiple and at times conflicting roles ESLTs and content area teachers (CATs) experience in their daily lives. Pennycook (1999) highlights the *access* and *transformation* models of critical literacy in second and foreign language teaching. The access model refers to the *gatekeeping* aspect of teacher roles whereby teachers help the less privileged to gain access to powerful language and knowledge tools. The transformative model refers to teachers being engaged in reforming and renegotiating the allocation of power so that all constituencies are able to participate with equal voice and presence. Sophie struggles to find a balance between the two, though her struggle may not be evident to students such as Lilia. On the other hand, Isabel, as a CAT, highlights the realities in mainstream content area classrooms, where teachers are overwhelmed by their role as teachers of students with multiple needs and ability levels. The lives of these CATs are encumbered with a multitude of standards to be addressed for each set of students—a stressful situation derived from role overload (Conley & Woosley, 2000).

Indiana is beginning to realize the gravity and urgency of the need to provide a more workable school situation for immigrant children and their teachers. This recognition is due to the fact that the state is experiencing an overall growth rate of 117% and northern counties such as Elkhart experienced a fivefold increase in its Hispanic population in the 1990s (Indiana Business Research Center, 2002). Kindler (2002) reports that since 1998, Indiana has had an 88% increase in the percentage of school-aged children who are ELLs of Hispanic origin, an increase that is amongst the highest in the nation. The immigration trend in Indiana in many ways mirrors trends in other Midwestern U.S. states. According to Johnson-Webb (2001), the region has experienced the "highest rate of increase of Hispanic population during the past decade (80.1%)" (para. 2) of any region in the United States. She adds that most of the immigration is taking place in "small, rural, and previously homogeneous communities" (para. 2). The immigration trend has moved away from urban centers toward rural and nonmetropolitan areas because of labor demands. In Indiana, the labor demands in small communities are emerging from "restaurant and hospitality industries, construction, recreational vehicle and manufactured housing industries, furniture-making and wood processing, agriculture, and meatpacking and poultry processing, as well as other types of manufacturing" (IUIRC, 2001, Current Trends section, para. 1).

Because of the current demographic trends, several efforts are in place to assist teachers of ELLs. For example, consultants from the Office of Language Minority and Migrant Affairs of the Indiana Department of Education travel frequently to schools to provide targeted workshops. They also organize conferences on specific issues for teachers to attend; conference attendance earns credits toward ESL licensure. The Interdisciplinary Collaborative Program (ICP) is one of the efforts to assist teachers of ELLs. The program brings together ESL and content area teachers in a long-term professional development program lasting from 9 months to 2 years. Two thirds of ICP's teacher participants are middle and high school teachers. The program's focus is on providing opportunities, resources, and support to teachers to enable them to develop integrated curricula in language and content. The program's goal is to increase the number of qualified teachers who work with ELLs by training and certifying not only ESLTs, but also CATs. The need is great for language and content area teachers to come together because there are currently less than 500 certified ESL teachers in Indiana for a population of 57,000 language minority students, approximately 36,000 of whom are limited English proficient (LEP).

This chapter highlights the collaboration between Sophie and Isabel, two former teacher participants in the ICP who are now currently teaching in Frankfort. Their collaborative success is the result of concerted engagement at the macro and micro levels that provide a platform for the teachers to work together in developing an integrated curriculum for ELLs in their school district.

Integrated Curriculum

WHAT IS AN INTEGRATED CURRICULUM?

Integrated and interdisciplinary curricula consist of "the careful orchestration" (Hoewisch, 2001, p. 155) among teachers of various subjects so that the content in each is continued, supported, and reiterated across the subjects. In this chapter, the focus is on the collaboration of teachers to bring about the incorporation of language teaching across subject areas and vice versa. At the macro level, the description will highlight the critical stages that need to occur throughout the school year in order for an interdisciplinary collaborative program to be successful. It will also discuss the efforts by school administrators to support teacher collaboration. At the micro level, the chapter will provide a look at how two teachers (Sophie and Isabel) work together to increase the permeability of the boundaries between their subject areas so that common priorities are supported throughout the instruction of both subjects. In this regard, the teachers' efforts can be viewed from several integrated-curricula perspectives. If viewed from Fogarty's (1991) perspective, their efforts toward developing integrated curricula contain elements at the shared and integrated levels. At the shared level, the ESLT and her CAT counterpart jointly identified specific content that needed to be present and sustained across the teaching of their subject areas. At the integrated level, the teachers made sure that they prioritized and that their students experienced sheltered instruction and multimodal assessment. Figure 1 shows Lake's (1994) summary of Fogarty's 10 levels of integrated curriculum.

WHAT IS DRIVING THE CURRENT FOCUS ON INTEGRATED CURRICULA?

The focus on integrated curricula emerged from several sources. As mentioned earlier, the standards movement and NCLB are putting pressure on all educators to speedily yield commendable academic performances from native and nonnative speakers of English. Although the pressure may lead some to act rashly, others quickly realize that delaying content instruction to ELLs until the learners demonstrate acceptable levels of English language proficiency does them a disservice (Kaufman, 2005). To meet NCLB guidelines, ELLs need immediate and early exposure to content to give them the time necessary to achieve academic proficiency in the subject areas. As evidence that this is not happening, Kaufman and Brooks (1996) point to the high number of language minority students who score below the national average in math and science; they emphasize the detrimental effects that result from the lack of coordination and collaboration between language and content area teachers.

Support for integrated and interdisciplinary curricula also emerges from the field of language teaching, where there is widespread recognition that teaching language in context is more meaningful, purposeful, and motivating than is learning a language in

Name	Description	Advantages	Disadvantages
Fragmented	Separate and distinct disciplines	Clear and discrete view of a discipline	Connections are not made clear for students; less transfer of learning
Connected	Topics within a discipline are connected	Key concepts are connected, leading to the review, reconceptualization, and assimilation of ideas within a discipline	Disciplines are not related; content focus remains within the discipline
Nested	Social, thinking, and content skills are targeted within a subject area	Gives attention to several areas at once, leading to enriched and enhanced learning	Students may be confused and lose sight of the main concepts of the activity or lesson
Sequenced	Similar ideas are taught in concert, although subjects are separate	Facilitates transfer of learning across content areas	Requires ongoing collaboration and flexibility, as teachers have less autonomy in sequencing curricula
Shared	Team planning and/or teaching that involves two disciplines focuses on shared concepts, skills, or attitudes	Shared instructional experiences; with two teachers on a team it is less difficult to collaborate	Requires time, flexibility, commitment, and compromise
Webbed	Thematic teaching, using a theme as a base for instruction in many disciplines	Motivating for students, helps students see connections between ideas	Theme must be carefully and thoughtfully selected to be meaningful, with relevant and rigorous content
Threaded	Thinking skills, social skills, multiple intelligences, and study skills are "threaded" throughout the disciplines	Students learn how they are learning, facilitating future transfer of learning	Disciplines remain separate
Integrated	Priorities that overlap multiple disciplines are examined for common skills, concepts, and attitudes	Encourages students to see interconnectedness and interrelationships among disciplines, students are motivated as they see these connections	Requires interdepartmental teams with common planning and teaching time
Immersed	Learner integrates by viewing all learning through the perspective of one area of interest	Integration takes place within the learner	May narrow the focus of the learner
Networked	Learner directs the integration process through selection of a network of experts and resources	Pro-active, with learner stimulated by new information, skills, or concepts	Learner can be spread too thin, efforts become ineffective

Figure 1. Ten levels of curricula integration

Source: Lake, 1994

abstraction and isolation (Dong, 2002). Also, the superiority of the a priori approach over the pull-out approach for ELLs is gaining acceptance. Pull-out programs deprive ELLs of continued exposure to the content area instruction, stigmatize ELLs, and are implemented only when problems occur. In the a priori approach, in which ESL and content teachers collaborate, the problems are preempted via the ESLTs and CATs collaborating with a joint focus on areas of emphasis in ESL and content area classes (Petrie & Sukanen, 2001). Among educators, there is also increasing acceptance of the need to fruitfully "harvest" the time ELLs spend with their CATs. This requires these teachers to be more adept at scaffolding content-laden instruction. Yu (2002) reports that "in the middle and high schools, many students spend two or three periods with English as a second language (ESL) teachers and the rest of their school day with subject matter area teachers" (p. 40). Curricular collaboration between the content area and ESL teachers thus becomes essential.

WHY SHOULD INTEGRATED CURRICULA BE INCLUDED AT THE MIDDLE AND HIGH SCHOOL LEVELS?

The current movement toward an integrated curriculum has roots in the constructivist views of learning theorists. This view promotes Dewey's concept of the learner as an explorer and a curious person who seeks to answer personal questions. Hence, at the middle and high school levels, the integrated and interdisciplinary curriculum is ideal because it takes advantage of a period of curiosity and exploration in the lives of young people. Furthermore, Schurr (1989) points out that adolescents at this stage are highly motivated and interested in delving into specific areas in exhaustive detail and are intensely curious and imaginative. This is particularly the case if those areas converge with students' affective needs (Egan, 1992) and individual curiosity about the world. These adolescents are in an exploratory mode: They wish to discover the world in an attempt to gain control and identity (Cristelli, 1994). An integrated curriculum, if based on the constructivist approach to learning, is ideal because it is learner-centered and predicated on students' inquiries that are sustained and supported across subject areas and disciplines. For ELLs, an integrated approach that is constructivist in nature gives them room to meaningfully engage according to their individual experiences, background, and abilities (Olivares & Lemberger, 2002) in their first and second languages. The constructivist approach allows students to utilize all the tools at their disposal. More important, meaningfulness of activities within the approach is boosted by the fact that they are driven by students' interests and queries that are derived from the students' individual circumstances.

At the practical level, this approach at the middle and high school levels is critical because a young student's interest can be easily lost in today's classroom environment, where students encounter an ever-increasing body of knowledge, large classes, and many mandates to which their teachers must simultaneously attend. For that matter, an integrated curriculum is a means to make larger classrooms feel smaller and to acknowledge that a sense of community combined with a sense of caring and concern bring together an increasingly diverse student population. The importance of a sense of community in schools cannot be underestimated given the increasingly high incidence of serious discipline problems. NCES (2006) reports that 37% of high school principals reported at least one serious discipline problem in their schools, while only 18% of middle school principals and 8% of elementary school principals reported such incidents. The collaboration between language and content area teachers in an integrated curriculum helps sustain the continuity of care concept whereby students feel that they are among a community of teachers who are working together for the students' benefit. In terms of ELLs, the collaboration between the two sets of teachers contributes to the overall feeling of acceptance that ELLs are part of the larger school community and that they are not separate and external inconveniences.

Beane (1993, 2002), a proponent of integrated curricula, has argued that middle schools' curricula should focus on widely shared concerns about early adolescents and the larger world rather than continue to increase in specialization and differentiation among separate subjects. The compartmentalization of subject area instruction is artificial, leads to a fragmentation of knowledge (Cristelli, 1994), and more important, stands in the way of the preparation students need to face real-world challenges.

In addition to cohesive instruction, integrated curricula also contribute to the maintenance of curriculum pressure (Sprague, Pennell, & Sulzberger, 1998) across subject areas, whereby key knowledge is sustained and reemphasized across disciplines. The positive outcome of the pressure is evident in research such as that conducted by Lawton (1994). His study of 15,000 eighth graders showed that students from schools using an interdisciplinary approach scored higher on standardized tests than students who were enrolled in single-discipline subjects. His research results are supported by other studies such as those undertaken by the National Association for Core Curriculum (2000), Vars and Beane (2000), and Arhar (1997). These research studies point to the same general conclusion: Almost without exception, students in any type of interdisciplinary or integrative curriculum do as well as, and often better than, students in a conventional departmentalized program. The seminal research by Thomas and Collier (2002) brings the issue home for ELLs. Their longitudinal study, involving 210,000 student records over a period of 5 years (1996–2001), demonstrated that students who experienced unsegregated language and content instruction began to close the achievement gap with mainstreamed students in the middle school years and began outperforming the latter in high school. Integrated curricula for ELLs, in other words, provide instruction that leads to success in the long term. Once teachers and administrators are cognizant of integrated curricula's potential, they may be more willing to confront barriers that may stand in the way, and work toward achievable solutions.

WHAT ARE BARRIERS TO IMPLEMENTING INTEGRATED CURRICULUM?

Schools are "arenas of struggle" (Ball, 1987, p. 19) as they consist of members in communities who coexist and work together amidst differences that can range from ideological to professional. Communities are born out of conflict (Achinstein, 2002) because working and living together require members to make substantial changes and adjustments to the status quo. In the case of teacher communities in schools, the communities "demand substantial change in school norms of practices, challenging existing norms of privacy, independence, and professional autonomy, and may question existing boundaries between cultures and power groups at school sites" (Achinstein, 2002, p. 425). When collaborating within their school community, teachers' expectations of conflict and their ability to identify and understand conflict are essential to the process.

Given the context described above, the collaborative planning for and implementation of integrated curricula is an undertaking prone to failure and frustration unless orchestrated well. A major barrier to developing an integrated school-to-work curriculum is *turfism*, or territorial conflict (Roegge, Galloway, & Welge, 1991) between language and content area teachers. Turfism is a problem when teachers have inflexible boundaries regarding the extent of their responsibilities to students (mainstream and ELL) and knowledge area expertise. In terms of the former, turfism can be manifested, for example, in the reluctance and confusion that arise with the question of whether content or ESL teachers should assume primary responsibility in teaching and nurturing ELLs (see Walker, Shafer, & Liam, 2004). Turfism in the latter case can result from the difficulty some content area teachers may find in working with ESL colleagues when the CATs question the content area expertise of the ESLT. Turfism is also evident when the reverse is the case (Crandall & Kaufman, 2002; Tang, 1994). Consequently, in many schools, the two sets of teachers may exist in two separate worlds.

ESL and content area teachers who take the plunge and go beyond turfism issues to try to work together face challenges at the macro level. Among these difficulties are the systemic nature of schools that do not always allow time for joint planning and the lack of training and financial resources to develop and sustain integrated programs (Hicks, 1997; Rojewski, 1990). As Paris (1998) explains, "teachers too frequently are expected to create a more applied and integrated curriculum without adequate skills, training, or time" (Implementation Pitfalls, para. 6).

Finally, the separate and isolated competencies developed for standards across subject areas are a monumental hurdle beyond the immediate control of ESLTs and CATs who are attempting to work together toward an integrated curriculum. Vars and Beane (2000) argue that the sheer number of competencies specified in the standards for each subject has led "one research team to estimate that it would take even a very competent student 9 additional years in school to reach acceptable performance in all of the standards recommended by national organizations" (Standards-Based Integration Curriculum, para. 1). Therefore, greater links must be made across subject areas in order to begin to address the situation. For example, the Indiana Department of Education spearheaded the effort to link English language proficiency standards with academic content standards in English/language arts and mathematics beginning in 2002; in the 2005–2006 academic year, the linkage was extended to science. Nevertheless, because of the prevalence of a wide range of competencies to be addressed by both and ESLTs and CATs in their attempts to meet standards, there remains an unfounded fear that integrated curricula will lead to curriculum regression or the watering down of the subject content to be taught (Crandall & Kaufman, 2002, p. 3). However, the following description of a thoughtful and deliberate collaboration effort at a high school in Indiana illustrates the potential that exists for the enhancement and enrichment of curricula when teachers work together and merge their expertise.

WHAT DOES A SUCCESSFUL COLLABORATION IN DEVELOPING AN INTEGRATED CURRICULUM LOOK LIKE? AND HOW DOES THE COLLABORATION SUCCESSFULLY NAVIGATE THROUGH VARIOUS BARRIERS?

When the collaboration process began at Frankfort High School, the ESL program was experiencing the dilemma of how best to assist ELLs and their teachers. The number of ELLs was increasing dramatically—from 192 to 856 in just 5 years—and ELL dropout rates were on the rise, with 90% of ELLs not finishing school. The situation left both students and teachers feeling defeated in their efforts. The high school principal and the ESL program director decided to ask for volunteers in the content areas to collaborate in developing and teaching sheltered content classes and content-based ESL classes. In the case of the former, content area teachers had to know how to scaffold their instruction in English so that it was accessible to diverse learners. In the case of the latter, the ESLTs would need to be proactive in not only incorporating content area material into their classes but also being able to identify subject matter in content areas that required specific language assistance. To achieve these goals, the content area and ESL teachers would have to collaborate in developing curricula that integrate, target, and manifest content as well as language objectives.

When the effort began, in the 2003–2004 school year, Frankfort High School's principal and the ESL program director further explained that for the content area teachers, the collaboration would mean that only one of their scheduled classes would be a sheltered class and the students in those classes would not be over an LEP level of four. (There are five proficiency levels altogether.) For ESL teachers, including the ESL director, curricula were to take shape as content-based ESL classes. Teachers typically conduct five 70-minute classes each day. Additionally, teachers have a 30-minute "bonus period" at the end of each day to spend reteaching, revising, or simply communicating with students. Students are allowed to revisit any class period to receive extra help in that subject matter. This system allows for students to receive the help they need and for teachers to know which students are experiencing difficulty with their subject matter. The school is set up on a trimester schedule, so students are able to take more classes each year. This has allowed Frankfort High School to extend some of the sheltered classes (Algebra and English 9 and 10) to be three-trimester classes instead of just two, enabling the teacher to moderate the pacing of content instruction.

The content area teachers who were teaching the sheltered classes were, as a whole, open-minded and accepting individuals. They didn't mind having students in their classes who did not speak English. They did, however, worry about appropriately meeting their students' needs. None of the content area teachers who volunteered had any training in ESL or Sheltered Instruction Observation Protocol (Echevarria, Vogt, & Short, 2000). Sophie, the ESL teacher at the time the collaboration started, was on an emergency license to teach ESL and was nearing completion of all requirements toward ESL certification through Indiana University. She was not only eager and dedicated to find ways to strengthen her knowledge and thus her credibility as a professional in the field, but she was also working very hard to increase the support network for ELLs and to be a stronger voice in their advocacy. Table 1 shows the composition of teachers who, over the past few years, volunteered to engage in the collaboration toward integrated curricula.

The following sections describe the collaboration at the macro and micro levels in Frankfort. They demonstrate the intense, multi-level engagement necessary to bring about a successful collaboration between ESLTs and CATs.

The Macrodynamics of the Collaboration

The collaboration began in 2003 with the administration organizing training sessions for the collaborating teachers to learn how to successfully meet the needs of second language learners. Finally, after one year of trying to get a collaborative program off to a good start with limited success, the ESL program director for Frankfort schools sought assistance from the Interdisciplinary Collaborative Program (ICP). The program provides embedded (online combined with on-site professional development), sustained (9–24 months), and joint professional development programs in ELL pedagogy for ESL and content area teachers. The ICP is fully funded by a U.S. Department of Education grant through Indiana University. Although only five teachers were successful recipients of the ICP scholarship, the program helped to create a cadre of teachers trained in ESL pedagogy. These teachers also became teacher leaders in the collaborative efforts to jump-start the content area and ESL teacher collaboration.

For an interdisciplinary collaborative program to be successful, the following key stages need to occur throughout the school year:

1. Meetings early in the year as a precursor to collaboration
2. Short meetings throughout the year to sustain collaboration
3. Targeted joint in-service professional development
4. All-faculty share fair

These critical stages of the program are discussed below, with the participating ICP teachers' own words and experiences.

1. Meetings early in the year as a precursor to collaboration

Before the school year starts, it is critical that the ESL and content area teachers take time to meet, get to know each other, and discuss the enrolling students. For example, in the Frankfort High School sheltered classes program, the eight collaborating teachers of different subject areas met to discuss students who were entering high school that year. Patrick, a sheltered World Geography teacher, commented on the importance of the meetings: "We want to keep current on their [students'] lives, where they came from and the problematic areas that we may see in school." Jenna, who taught sheltered Algebra, added that the time spent at the meeting "always benefits the students because I get to know them better through their ESL teachers." Sophie, the ESL

Table 1. Frankfort High School teacher collaborator data

Name, Subject	Gender	Total Years of Teaching Experience	Years of Teaching Sheltered Classes	Potential Partners in Integrated Curriculum
Isabel: Algebra and Sheltered Math Lab	F	7	4	ESL World Geography
Lee: English 9, 10	F	7	3	ESL Math Lab U.S. History
Amanda: English 9, 10	F	17	2	ESL Math Lab U.S. History
Grace: Biology	F	6	4	ESL World Geography
Lou: U.S. History	F	5	3	English 9, 10 ESL Math Lab
Patrick: World Geography	M	4	4	Algebra Biology ESL Math Lab
Robert: Health	M	2	1	ESL Math Lab Nutrition and Wellness
Sophie: ESL	F	5	3	Algebra Beginning Chorus Biology English Functional Economics Health Math Lab Nutrition and Wellness U.S. History World Geography
New Class Offered: Nutrition and Wellness	TBA	TBA	TBA	ESL Health Math Lab
New Class Offered: Functional Economics	TBA	TBA	TBA	Algebra ESL Math Lab
New Class Offered: Beginning Chorus	TBA	TBA	TBA	ESL

teacher, whole-heartedly resolved that "it [the meeting] is time well spent" because she and her content area colleagues collaborate on helping each other understand each student's strengths, weaknesses, interests, disciplinary issues, and so on.

Teachers at these collaborative early-year meetings were excited about the coming school year and were creative and far-reaching in their plans; the meetings gave rise to teachers' requests for time to have frequent but short informal meetings among themselves, formal training opportunities to support what they learned informally, and opportunities to showcase their knowledge and leadership within the school setting.

2. Short meetings throughout the year to sustain collaboration

Once plans for teacher collaboration get underway, it is critical that there are support systems in place to help sustain that collaboration throughout the school year. The teachers found that informal, short but frequent meetings are most effective. It was these monthly meetings of about 30 minutes (during bonus-period or lunch sessions) that sustained the collaboration process and led to the development of a joint content and language curricula. Although informal in nature, the meetings inspired teachers to take deliberate action to plan ahead and decide upon a focus for each future meeting; they found that it was beneficial to focus on one topic during these meetings. Teachers collected and brought examples, assignments, or stories related to that month's focus. Some examples of focus topics are listed in Table 2.

Speaking of this informal collaboration time, one teacher had this to say:

> We are all helpful towards one another and can give each other some outstanding advice. I like to know what works well in other classes that I can use in my class. I like to know what works well with particular students to maximize their learning potential. Our ultimate goal is for all students to learn, no matter what challenges they might have. We all agree with this statement and will do what it takes to help everyone out!

Table 2. Sample focus topics

Sample Focus Topics for Bonus Period Meetings
Integrating a Measurement Unit
Integrated Units
Discipline
Procedural Issues (Homework)
Building Background
Comprehensible Input
Gangs
Scheduling
Problem Solving

The informal nature suggested by this type of meeting is also maintained in e-mails, lunch meetings, and one-on-one conversations. The simplicity of these meetings is paramount in creating the ease and flow from which the teachers can collaborate.

The following example from Grace, the Biology teacher, provides insight into the way things flowed during a typical meeting. Referring to Krashen's (1982) comprehensible input, she asked for help in making her content comprehensible. She was teaching acids and bases in her content area classes, but she first had to teach her colleagues about acids and bases and define what it was that she wanted the students to understand:

> Okay, you have a scale that goes from 0 to 14, and you know if something is a base or an acid depending on the ratio and makeup of ions in the solution being tested. It depends on what kinds of ions are creating the solution. . . . How can I preteach that? How can I build background, make the content comprehensible when the content is so heavy . . . and we may have nothing to build on.

The other teachers quickly came to her rescue by giving her some ideas that were quite helpful and some that were supportive, but not useful in this situation. After much struggle, Heather, a social studies teacher and volleyball coach, quipped, "I don't know anything about ions, but it sounds like a tug of war to me." That was the beginning of a great collaborative discussion about building background and comprehensible input in an informal setting. Grace decided to initiate her lesson on acids and bases by having a tug-of-war contest. She came up with many other correlations to explore with the students regarding tug of war and acids and bases. As the ideas flowed from teacher to teacher, trust and a sense of camaraderie began to develop and confidence levels rose in terms of the utility of the collaborative efforts.

3. Targeted joint in-service professional development

Meetings early in the year, followed by short, informal but focused monthly meetings create the foundation for teacher collaboration. These types of meetings are necessary but not sufficient. To give teachers the skills they need to follow through on the work they accomplished during the informal meetings, formal professional development sessions are essential. Before ICP's involvement in the 2004–2005 school year, the high school principal and the ESL program director organized professional development sessions. However, after that academic year, the two were joined by the ICP-trained teachers in their efforts, and the sessions took place once a trimester. This only helped to strengthen notions of collaboration. A principal benefit of the professional development sessions is that they were a combination of both theory and practice. Research and its relevancy to pedagogy was discussed, thoughtfully considered, and questioned. The particular power of these sessions was that the topics that were addressed, such as sheltered instruction, comprehensible input, and thematic instruction, came directly from those that emerged from the informal meetings.

4. All-faculty share fair

Faculty meetings can become a means for staff development and an avenue for highlighting teacher achievement. They can provide information about integrating curricula as well as a celebratory step in the collaborative process. In the Frankfort High School program, all of the school's 70 teachers assembled for the general faculty meeting at the end of each trimester. The ESL program director was charged with engaging all of the teachers with concerns and theoretical and practical ideas relevant to ELL instruction. Because higher level ELLs are placed in regular education classes, all teachers must know the basics of modifying lessons for these students. The ESL program director took the opportunity presented by these all-faculty meetings to report on the learning and achievement of the ESL and content area teachers who were engaged in collaboration. She featured these teachers as experts in ELL instruction and as trustworthy collaborators who could be counted upon for assistance. She also structured activities so that teachers could experience what it means to collaborate on lesson planning. The ESL and content area teachers who were already engaged in collaboration assumed the roles of group leaders and facilitators for the rest of the faculty.

Outcomes from the meetings were wide ranging and included strategies, modifications, and best practices. The most commonly shared strategies are reflective of the SIOP model by Echevarria et al. (2000). In terms of incorporating content into ESL classes, some of the more commonly shared strategies are similar to those in the cognitive academic language learning approach (Chamot & O'Malley, 1994). These activities during all-faculty meetings ensured that modeling and training for all teachers in the school were undertaken systematically. The activities also consistently bolstered the confidence and increased the visibility of those championing the cause. In addition to showcasing teachers' collaborative efforts, the share fair also served to reassert the support of school administrators. As mentioned earlier, this macro-level support is essential to sustain teacher collaboration.

The Microdynamics of the Collaboration: An Example of a Teacher-Teacher Collaboration in Developing Integrated Curricula

In this section, the micro-level dynamics of collaboration are described, focusing on teacher collaboration in instruction. The description shows how an ESL and a math teacher worked together to ensure that their common goals and objectives were sustained and supported throughout the instruction of both subjects. Specific examples of two elements of planning for instruction are given:

1. Lesson/thematic unit planning
2. Year-long plan development

1. Lesson/thematic unit planning

Sophie, the ESL teacher, and Isabel, the Algebra teacher, were the initial leaders of the collaborative process. They were coparticipants in the ICP, and their experience

Table 3. Scaffolding and content strategies

Scaffolding Strategies for Content Classes	Content Incorporation Strategies for ESL Classes

• Drawing pictures
• Using gestures
• Using Spanish as support
• Speaking clearly
• Writing everything down—and saying it, too
• Acting things out when possible
• Connecting to prior knowledge
• Grouping bilingual students with level 1 students
• Using daily manipulatives
• Utilizing demonstration
• Doing anything kinesthetic
• Frontloading
• Doing lower level readings
• Utilizing word banks for tests
• Connecting whole to part
• Building background
• Doing constructivist and problem-based activities
• Teaching backwards—
  1. Extension activities
  2. Discuss
  3. Answer questions
  4. Read the text
	• Comparing academic and informal discourse
	• Introducing content themes, a priori
	• Using content textbooks
	• Using content-specific vocabulary
	• Identifying and linking concepts that are similar across content
	• Mapping difficult ideas conceptually
	• Discussing background or personal knowledge related to academic topics
	• Identifying and practicing content area study skills
	• Identifying and practicing personal study skills that would be useful in learning content
	• Identifying and practicing common study skills across content areas
	• Working in groups with native speakers of English
	• Identifying content resources in students' first language

working together in the program for almost a year provided an impetus for them to continue to collaborate at Frankfort High School. During a faculty meeting at the beginning of the 2004–2005 school year, they decided that they could begin their collaboration with a lesson on compounds. Sophie was teaching compound sentences and Isabel compound equations. Sophie and Isabel exchanged *manipulatives*, or teaching materials and objects, for their subjects. After the success of the initial collaboration, the compound lesson quickly became the start of an integrated series in ESL and Algebra on measurement units. The joint focus of the measurement units was critical. Many ELLs struggle with moving from the metric system to the U.S. system of measurement. Also, working knowledge of measurement, a competence prevalent in multiple Indiana state educational standards and English language proficiency standards, is an essential and authentic life skills component. Table 4 shows a thematic unit that was created by Sophie and Isabel. The two also consulted with the Building Trades teacher, and together they identified that students were having difficulty with fractions in reading measuring tape, reading floor plans, and calculating the area of irregularly shaped rooms.

Sophie and Isabel jointly developed their plans using components from the SIOP

Table 4. Integrated lesson plans

Sophie: ESL Level 2	Isabel: Sheltered Math Lab 9
Overall Goals: Aggressively teach the "language" of measurement. Emphasis will be on content through vocabulary building. Higher order thinking and standards will be met via reading comprehension and discussions.	Overall Goals: Aggressively teach the "actions" of measurement. Students will be able to take measurements and calculate areas, material needs, and costs.
Preparation 1. Write content and language objectives clearly on the chalkboard and state them orally	**Preparation** 1. Write content and language objectives clearly on the chalkboard and state them orally

Supplementary Materials: Sources
1. Tangibles:
  a. Have actual hands-on measuring tools available for the students
  b. Demonstrate – step-by-step use of the tangibles
2. Crossword Puzzle:
  a. Present target vocabulary in both text and picture support (visual vocabulary)
3. Graphic Organizers: "Vocabulary Web"
  b. Give the students three sample webs to do in class
  c. Give the students 10 measurement vocabulary words; they complete the web based upon free association/brainstorming
	Building Background
	1. Elaborate on students' prior knowledge of measuring distances, finding areas, and calculating expenses
	2. Frontload key vocabulary for the formulas utilized in calculating areas and expenses

Building Background 1. Elaborate on students' prior knowledge of the metric system and the American system of measurement 2. Elaborate on the students' prior knowledge of fantasy storytelling containing measurements (wizards' potions, magic doses, creatures of different sizes) 3. Frontload all key vocabulary from the storybook	**Comprehensible Input** 1. Clarify key concepts in the students' first language 2. Employ visuals for understanding floor plans 3. Use realia for students to have an authentic experience with carpet, tile, paint samples, and pricing 4. Use multimedia to support multi-level comprehension and understanding 5. Identify and use academic strategies
Comprehensible Input 1. Provide the vocabulary in both English and Spanish 2. Provide time/seasons flashcards in both English and Spanish 3. Use multimedia to support multi-level comprehension and understanding	**Interaction** 1. Use cooperative groups of three to four students for problem-based learning in home improvements
Interaction 1. Have the students create a structured outline/worksheet in groups of three; the product is a blueprint for a building in the story that they create jointly 2. Identify and use academic strategies	**Review:** Students self-assess and teachers monitor student progress
Review: Students self-assess and teachers monitor student progress	*(Continued on p. 21)*

Table 4 (continued). Integrated lesson plans

Evaluation/Assessment Procedures

• Self-Assessment
  — students evaluate their comprehension and effort using a self-assessment form
• Quizzes
  — frequent quizzes check daily comprehension
• Authentic Assessment
  — culminating project integrates multiple skills in real-life situations (home improvement project)
• Performance Assessment
  — aural and oral assessments measure key vocabulary comprehension and acquisition

model (preparation, building background, comprehensible input, review and assessment). Using Fogarty's (1991) shared level of integration, Sophie and Isabel identified measurement units, as well as academic learning strategies, to be included in both of their lessons. For Sophie, the measurement units were introduced within the context of a story. For Isabel, they were contextualized in home improvement projects. Similarly, Sophie wove in academic learning strategies and explicitly taught them ways to interact in group work, and Isabel emphasized strategies that would help students understand concepts through multimodal means. At the integrated level, both prioritized sheltered instruction and alternatives in assessment. Consequently, they drew their lesson plans from SIOP and different types of assessment that addressed ELLs' multiple skills and diverse backgrounds.

In addition to the lesson planning, Sophie and Isabel also collaborated on developing an inventory of learning strategies (See Table 5) to be used by students for every unit that Sophie and Isabel jointly created. They believed that the utility of these strategies went beyond their own classrooms.

2. Year-long plan development

As Sophie and Isabel completed the measurement unit, they also created a projected year-long plan together (See Table 6). This plan included many functional mathematic and language opportunities. The application, evaluation, and skills are all authentic.

The yearlong plan became the basis upon which Sophie and Isabel developed and implemented their integrated curriculum. They identified units to be jointly included in each class and incorporated the SIOP model for the implementation of the plan. In that regard, they frequently met to decide on shared teaching strategies, curricula, and finally, planned evaluation methods for each unit.

Lessons Learned and Next Steps

The collaboration process involved in developing integrated curricula is complicated and extensive. Nevertheless, Frankfort High School has been successful in that there are now eight content area teachers undertaking sheltered instruction in the following subjects: English 9, English 10, Algebra, Biology, Geography, U.S. History, Health, and

Table 5. Learning strategy inventory

- Note taking
  — using writing formulas and sample problems
  — incorporating skeleton worksheets using key vocabulary in context
- Cooperation
  — learning to work together to accomplish tasks
- Elaboration of prior knowledge
  — using prior knowledge to tackle complex projects (multistep measurement problems)
- Monitoring comprehension
  — using "think aloud" strategies in all lessons
- Questioning for clarification
  — learning to ask questions as necessary
- Resourcing
  — bringing their electronic Spanish-English dictionaries to class each day
- Self-assessment/self-monitoring
  — using this skill in all activities
- Advance organization
  — creating plans/outlines for accomplishing tasks
- Monitoring production
  — making sure that procedures are correct while working through assignments

Keyboarding. These teachers are a collaborative cohort who work with one another as well as with the ESL teacher and program director. Their experience yields the following insights:

- **Administrative support:** The support of the school principal in prioritizing ELL instruction is no doubt a key element in the success of any collaborative effort. The Frankfort principal created space and time for the collaboration, gave strong backing to the ESL program director to assume leadership in training all teachers in the school, and contributed to the prioritization of ELL instruction and teacher collaboration.

- **Collaborative foundation:** Teachers have to be given opportunities to become familiar and experience working with colleagues in a helpful and purposeful fashion. The bonus meetings, faculty meetings, and professional development opportunities all contributed to the sense of camaraderie, identification, and dedication to a joint mission, and they helped teachers feel comfortable asking questions and sharing vulnerabilities. Without a collaborative foundation, efforts to encourage teachers to develop an interdisciplinary curriculum could have been taken as threats to teacher autonomy and professional knowledge.

- **Informal communities of practice:** The informal, bonus teachers' meetings and even the informal e-mailing practices between teachers were critical to sustaining their collaboration. Top-down measures admittedly would get the process started, but by nature they are usually expensive, cumbersome, slow, and generalized in their focus. The willingness of teachers to continue to work together in an effective manner depends on how comfortable they feel with each other. The informal nature of groups working collaboratively is one of the central precepts

Table 6. Sophie's and Isabel's integrated curricula

Unit	CAT (Math Lab)	ESL	Evaluation
What's For Dinner? Restaurant Theme	• Compute food prices • Compute sales tax • Compute tips • Compute percents • Given X amount of money, what could you buy? How much will sales tax be? How much tip will you need to include? How much money will you have remaining?	• Take food orders • Order food • Name different foods • Decide what is at various restaurants • Use real menus to act out restaurant scenes	• Simulate a restaurant interaction/ experience in both skill areas: Math and ESL.
Exploring Your City	• Calculate time passage • Decide on movie times • Read schedules for various leisure activities: movies, shows, museums, malls, etc. • Calculate admission prices for the various places they will visit • Calculate elapsed time • Calculate how much money they would make if they worked at the city museum	• Read schedules • Learn vocabulary for navigating through the various leisure activities they've chosen • Read work schedules • Learn how to "clock in" and "clock out" • Emphasize timeliness and work ethic • Emphasize leisure time • Learn time management	• Plan a 3-event day with appropriate rest time and travel time built in and costs figured for two people. • Plan a typical day working an 8-hour shift. How much money would you make? How much money in taxes would be withheld?
Buying a Home	• Calculate how much a home will actually cost given different percentage rates, down-payment amounts, and house prices • Utilize amortization charts to decide how much a house will end up costing them if they pay it off in 10, 20, or 30 years	• Expand vocabulary by studying the rooms in a house • Role-play how to talk to a realtor and a loan officer • Use the phonebook to shop for a realtor • Use the newspaper to shop for houses with specific qualities • Learn how to read the house listing advertisements	• In a group, simulate the process of being a prospective home buyer by utilizing the newspaper, phonebook, a realtor, and a loan officer. The project will conclude with a field trip to the class's house of choice.

(Continued on p. 24)

Table 6 (continued). Sophie's and Isabel's integrated curricula

Unit	CAT (Math Lab)	ESL	Evaluation
Frankfort Home Makeover	• Calculate square feet in a house • Calculate how much paint is needed to paint the rooms in the house • Calculate how much wallpaper is needed to paper one room in the house • Calculate how much carpet is needed to cover specific rooms in the house • Calculate how much tile is needed for the kitchen and the bathroom	• Expand vocabulary by learning the names of furniture • Learn how to compare prices at different furniture stores • Comparison shop for paint, carpet, tile, etc. • Make phone calls to the gas and electric company to inquire about billing history	• Create a design mat showing a layout of furniture, pictures of furniture, carpet samples, fabric samples, paint samples, and wallpaper samples. Calculate how much is needed of each, if the size of the furniture is appropriate, and where it will be located.
You Are What You Eat!	• Visit the grocery store • Price food for specific recipes • Enlarge recipes • Halve recipes • Make the recipe for the group	• Expand vocabulary by naming foods and food groups • Make healthy food choices • Comparison shop using advertisements from the newspaper	• Plan a healthy, well-balanced menu for a week for different-sized groups.
Sequencing	• Determine order of operations • Determine order of solving an equation	• Learn cause and effect • Create plot lines • Learn the writing process	• Plan an appropriate schedule for the Latino fair. Plan the proper layout of booths (with reasons). Plan the sequence of the program: who, what, and when will happen first, next, and last.
All Around the World . . . Travel	• Calculate gas mileage • Calculate miles (distance) • Estimate cost of travel • Decide to take the train, a plane, or an automobile • Exchange cost into pesos or yen	• Discover main attractions of a specific city • Decide on mode of travel • Use the map to create driving directions • Use the Internet to find out prices for renting a car, travel, and activities while there.	• Give students "money" to plan a trip. How will they travel? Where will they stay? What will they do? What is their timeline for their trip?

of communities of practice (Lave & Wenger, 1991). The informality of interactions between individuals can lead to a genuine sense of engagement and can overcome the challenges that are derived from "contrived collegiality" (Rhodes & Beneicke, 2002, p. 301).

- **Teacher-generated strategies:** The Frankfort teachers who went through the ICP were introduced to many integrated-curricula principles and strategies. However, the strategies that emerged from discussions during the monthly faculty meetings are the ones that are grounded in the teachers' lived experiences. Although connections can be made to published literature on many of those strategies, the teachers gave immediate validation to strategies that emerged organically from among their fellow practitioners. Teachers expressed appreciation for the useful strategies. One teacher commented, "What has changed in my teaching is the strategies I use in the REST of my classes! I do more demonstration, acting things out, kinesthetic components in lessons—oh, and frontloading!!! These are things that work not only with my ELLs, but with my honors classes, too!"

- **Teacher leaders:** The careful and deliberate selection of a set of teachers to lead the collaborative process in developing integrated curricula contributed significantly to its success. In the beginning of the process at Frankfort, teacher leaders were selected among a cadre of relatively new teachers who were in the process of developing and learning. In that mode, turfism that could usually forestall any collaborative efforts is usually overshadowed by the teachers' continuous efforts to search for answers and to connect with other professionals. The acknowledgment of their leadership and expertise is also a critical factor. It provides the teachers with a sense of pride and responsibility.

Despite these successes, challenges remain. There are only two ESL teachers (including the ESL program director) on the staff at Frankfort High School, and they must collaborate with all the teachers. Although at this point there is a cohort of informed content area teachers who can mentor colleagues, there is extra and continuous pressure on the two ESLTs to remain central players in the extensive collaboration. In addition, their supportive role may be mistakenly perceived at times as a service role to content area teachers, and such a perception can compromise their status as professionals with their own established areas of expertise. Finally, despite the intense focus on collaboration as a precursor to development of integrated curricula, several teachers continue to report feeling separate, isolated, and inconsistent in their teaching of ELLs.

Nevertheless, despite the challenges, the success at Frankfort High School is repeated in various ways by teachers throughout Indiana. Although having integrated curricula is the end goal that has yet to be fully achieved, the collaborative processes toward that goal are underway and can be seen in the following efforts:

> Miriam, an award-winning language arts teacher in northern Indiana, successfully advocated for the hiring of Dina, an ESL specialist, as a member of the English

language faculty. Dina assists in the development of curricula and modifications, and provides the English faculty with personal and educational insight into the process of language acquisition. Miriam and Dina conduct in-services for the school staff, and this year, they focused on vocabulary as an essential element of language acquisition. They implemented and reinforced a reading program for all students. To help language learners overcome the anxiety of reading, they motivated students to read bilingual books at the students' reading level. The students completed the same tasks as the target language population, but with modifications.

Jane was a social studies teacher in Indianapolis, but is now an ESL literacy coach. She works with teams of three teachers who have requested to have ESL students in their classrooms. She meets with them bimonthly to modify and adapt curricula to meet the needs of diverse learners. Jane works on what she calls the closing of the "knowing and doing gap." She oversees the teachers' writing of lesson plans to ensure that second language pedagogy is incorporated. Because of her own content area teaching in social studies, she says that she has gained credibility with the content area teachers.

Cyn is a math teacher in the northwestern tip of Indiana. She was invited to collaborate over distance via interactive video with math teachers in a small school in central Indiana, to share with them her sheltered math curriculum. Cyn has been a distance coach to these math teachers who otherwise would not have had access to someone with knowledge of both math and second language pedagogy.

Questions for Discussion

Review the case study at the beginning of the chapter. Discuss the following questions that aim to extend the discussions included in the chapter.

1. In your opinion, how would Sophie's and Isabel's perceptions of Lilia's dilemma change as a consequence of their collaboration? How would Lilia's struggles with language and math be repositioned?

2. As an ESL teacher, Sophie's role can at times be that of an ELL advocate. Would working with Isabel compromise Sophie's advocacy role?

3. Are there other people in the school who could collaborate with Sophie and Isabel to ensure that proper placement for Lilia is identified from the beginning? Who could those people be in your school?

4. What information could Lilia give that could help her teachers when planning, implementing, and evaluating integrated curricula? What information could other students provide? Do you have suggestions for how Sophie and Isabel could collect that information?

Summary of Main Ideas
1. Definition of integrated curricula: Integrated and interdisciplinary curricula consist of "the careful orchestration" (Hoewisch, 2001, p. 155) of the teaching of subjects so that the content in each is continued, supported, and reiterated across the subjects.

2. The driving forces behind integrated curricula consist of the following:
   a) NCLB guidelines that require ELLs to experience early exposure to content to give them the time needed to achieve academic proficiency in the subject areas
   b) widespread recognition that teaching language in context is more meaningful and purposeful
   c) superiority of the a priori approach over the pull-out approach

3. Reasons to include an integrated curriculum at the middle school and high school levels include the fact that an integrated curriculum
   a) takes advantage of an age and a period of curiosity and exploration
   b) makes larger classrooms feel "smaller" and contributes to a sense of community
   c) helps maintain curriculum pressure across subject areas
   d) can help students experience unsegregated language and content instruction, which has been shown to close the achievement gap with mainstream students in the middle school years

4. Barriers to the implementation of an integrated curriculum include the following:
   a) teacher turfism or territorial conflict
   b) teaching time conflict and lack of joint planning time
   c) lack of training and financial resources for teachers
   d) sheer numbers of separate and isolated competencies developed for standards across subject areas
   e) fear that integrated curricula will lead to curriculum regression

5. Successful teacher collaboration in integrated curriculum is premised on the following factors:
   a) assertive and continued administrative support
   b) strong collaborative foundation
   c) establishment of informal communities of practice
   d) utilization of successful strategies that are teacher generated
   e) informed selection of teacher leaders

6. Challenges to successful collaboration in developing integrated curricula:
   a) overreliance on ESL teachers who are limited in number
   b) isolated and inconsistent practice

References

Achinstein, B. (2002). Conflict amid community: The micropolitics of teacher collaboration. *Teachers College Record, 104,* 421–455.

Arhar, J. M. (1997). The effects of interdisciplinary teaming on students and teachers. In J. L. Irvin (Ed.), *What current research says to the middle level practitioner* (pp. 49–56). Columbus, OH: National Middle School Association.

Ball, S. J. (1987). *The micro-politics of the school: Towards a theory of school organization.* New York: Methuen.

Beane, J. A. (1993). *A middle school curriculum: From rhetoric to reality* (2nd ed.). Columbus, OH: National Middle School Association.

Beane, J. A. (2002). Beyond self-interest: A democratic core curriculum. *Educational Leadership, (59)*7, 25–28.

Chamot, A. U., & O'Malley, J. M. (1994). *The CALLA handbook: Implementing the cognitive academic language learning approach.* White Plains, NY: Addison-Wesley Longman.

Conley, S., & Woosley, S. A. (2000). Teacher role stress, higher order needs, and work outcomes [Electronic version]. *Journal of Educational Administration, 38*(2), 179–201. Retrieved September 4, 2007, from http://www.emeraldinsight.com

Crandall, J., & Kaufman, D. (Eds.). (2002). *Content-based instruction in higher education settings.* Alexandria, VA: TESOL.

Cristelli, G. J. (1994). *An integrated, content-based curriculum for beginning level English as a second language learners of middle school age: Four pilot units.* Unpublished master's thesis, School for International Training, Brattleboro, Vermont.

Dong, Y. R. (2002). Integrating language and content: How three biology teachers work with non-English-speaking students. *International Journal of Bilingual Education and Bilingualism, 5*(1), 40–57.

Echevarria, J., Vogt, M., & Short, D. (2000). *Making content comprehensible for English language learners: The SIOP model.* Boston: Allyn & Bacon.

Egan, K. (1992). *Imagination in teaching and learning: Ages 8 to 15.* London: Routledge.

Fogarty, R. (1991). *The mindful school: How to integrate the curricula.* Palatine, IL: Skylight.

Hicks, B. G. (1997). Meeting national science standards in an integrative curriculum: Classroom examples from a rural middle level program. *Journal of Research in Rural Education, 13*(1), 57–63.

Hoewisch, A. (2001). Creating well-rounded curricula with Flat Stanley: A school-university project. *Reading Teacher, 55*(2), 154–169.

Indiana Business Research Center. (2002). How do you say "Hoosier" in Spanish. *INContext, 3*(4). Retrieved November, 29, 2006, from http://www.ibrc.indiana.edu/incontext/2002/july-aug02/news.html

Indiana University International Resource Center (IUIRC). (2001). *Immigration in Indiana.* Retrieved November 29, 2006, from http://jinkims.com/iuirc/other_intl_res2.html

Johnson-Webb, K. D. (2001). Midwest rural communities in transition: Hispanic immigration. *Rural Development News, 25*(1). Retrieved November 29, 2006, from http://www.ag.iastate.edu/centers/rdev/newsletter/Vol25No1-2001/hispanic.html

Kaufman, D. (2005). *Content-based instruction in primary and secondary school settings*. Alexandria, VA: TESOL.

Kaufman, D., & Brooks, J. G. (1996). Interdisciplinary collaboration in teacher education: A constructivist approach. *TESOL Quarterly, 30*, 231–251.

Kindler, A. (2002). *Survey of the states' limited English proficient students and available educational programs and services: 1999–2000 summary report*. Washington, DC: National Clearinghouse for English Language Acquisition and Language Instruction Educational Programs.

Krashen, S. D. (1982). *Principles and practice in second language acquisition*. New York: Pergamon.

Lake, K. (1994, May). *Integrated curriculum*. Retrieved November 29, 2006, from http://www.nwrel.org/scpd/sirs/8/c016.html

Lave, J., and Wenger, E. (1991). *Situated learning: Legitimate peripheral participation*. Cambridge: Cambridge University Press.

Lawton, E. (1994). Integrating curriculum: A slow but positive process. *Schools in the middle, (4)*2, 27–30.

National Association for Core Curriculum. (2000). *A bibliography of research on the effectiveness of block-time, core, and interdisciplinary team teaching programs*. Kent, OH: Author.

National Council on Education Statistics. (2006). *Dropout rates in the United States: 2002 and 2003*. Retrieved November, 29, 2006 from http://nces.ed.gov/pubs2006/dropout/tables/table_6A.asp?referrer=report

Olivares, R. A., & Lemberger, N. (2002). Identifying and applying the communicative and the constructivist approaches to facilitate transfer of knowledge in the bilingual classroom. *International Journal of Bilingual Education and Bilingualism, 5*(1), 72–83.

Paris, K. (1998). Critical issue: Developing an applied and integrated curriculum. Retrieved November 29, 2006, from http://www.ncrel.org/sdrs/areas/issues/envrnmnt/stw/sw100.htm

Pennycook, A. (1999). Introduction: Critical approaches to TESOL. *TESOL Quarterly, 33*, 329–348.

Petrie, L., & Sukanen, R. (2001). Combining forces: Collaboration between bilingual/ESL teachers and the regular classroom using an a priori approach. *Midwestern Educational Researcher, 14*(4), 32–36.

Rhodes, C., & Beneicke, S. (2002). Coaching, mentoring and peer-networking: Challenges for the management of teacher professional development in schools. *Journal of In-service Education, 28*(7), 297–310.

Roegge, C. A., Galloway, J. R., & Welge, J. A. (1991). *Setting the stage: A practitioner's guide to integrating vocational and academic education.* Springfield: Illinois State Board of Education.

Rojewski, J. W. (1990, October). *Issues in vocational education for special populations in rural areas.* TASPP Brief, (2)2. Champaign, IL: Technical Assistance for Special Populations Program. (ERIC Document Reproduction Service No. ED326630)

Schurr, S. L. (1989). *Dynamite in the classroom.* Columbus, OH: National Middle School Association.

Sprague, M. M., Pennell, D., & Sulzberger, L. A. (1998). Engaging all middle level learners in multi-disciplinary curricula. *NASSP Bulletin, 82*(602), 60–66.

Tang, G. M. (1994). Teacher collaboration in integrating language and content. *TESL Canada Journal*, 11(2), 100–116.

Thomas, W., & Collier, V. (2002). *A national study of school effectiveness for language minority students' long-term academic achievement* (research findings). Santa Cruz, CA and Washington, DC: Center for Research on Education, Diversity & Excellence. Retrieved November 28, 2005, from http://www.crede.ucsc.edu/research/llaa/1.1_final.html

Vars, G. F., & Beane, J. A. (2000). *Integrative curriculum in a standards-based world. ERIC Digest.* Champaign, IL: ERIC Clearinghouse on Elementary and Early Childhood Education. (ERIC Document Reproduction Service No. ED441618)

Walker, A., Shafer, J., & Liam, M. (2004). "Not in my classroom": Teacher attitudes towards English language learners in the mainstream classroom. *NABE Journal of Research and Practice, 2*(1), 130–160.

Yu, R. D. (2002). Integrating language and content: How three biology teachers work with non-English-speaking students. *International Journal of Bilingual Education and Bilingualism, 5*(1), 40–57.

CHAPTER 3

Language

Collaborating for Content-Based Academic Language Instruction

Susan Jenkins, Mark Nigolian, Mary Kay O'Brien, Elizabeth O'Dowd, and Linda Walsleben

---
(CASE STUDY)

The English language learner (ELL) population of Burlington School District, in rural Vermont's largest city, has increased by 400% in the past decade. Over the years, immigrants and refugees from Cambodia, Vietnam, Tibet, Bosnia, Croatia, Sudan, the Democratic Republic of the Congo, and most recently Somali Bantu have made Burlington their home, bringing more than 27 new languages into the school district. However, a district survey conducted in 2000 revealed that two-thirds of the teachers believed their knowledge base was insufficient for teaching ELLs in their content classrooms.

Pat, a seventh- and eighth-grade math teacher with 5 years of teaching experience, was, until recently, one of those teachers. Then, in 2004, he participated in a weeklong summer institute on teaching ELLs and received yearlong follow-up support from Mark, an ESL specialist.

After the summer institute, Pat tells Mark how disappointed he is that his low-intermediate-level ELLs performed poorly on the standardized math assessments. Pat is feeling particularly discouraged because he believed that the changes he had made in his classroom to include group work and instructional scaffolding had shown that ELLs could do math computations successfully. Why, then, could they not demonstrate this performance on the tests? Mark looks at the math tests and draws Pat's attention to the complex sentence structures; vocabulary; and unfamiliar, culturally laden information in the word problems, which make the math inaccessible.

Pat and Mark begin to collaborate on modifying the academic language on the assessments. Pat is able to show Mark exactly what specific math vocabulary and conceptual knowledge the students need to master in the seventh and eighth grades. By pooling their expertise, Pat and Mark create a pilot assessment using simplified sentences, familiar topics, pictures, charts, and tables. Pat's ELL students are successful on the modified assessments, and Pat and Mark continue to meet regularly to adapt the language of the text and assessments, while gradually increasing the linguistic complexity to prepare students for the demands of standardized and high school math assessments.

Prereading Questions

- What kind of collaborative relationship between ESL specialists and content area teachers is most effective in helping ELLs successfully access academic language?

- What are some of the challenges faced by ESL specialists and content area teachers in collaboratively addressing language issues?

- How can university/college faculty best contribute to teacher professional development and share knowledge about language?

- How much knowledge about language do content teachers need in order to collaborate in sheltered instruction?

WHAT KIND OF COLLABORATIVE RELATIONSHIP BETWEEN ESL SPECIALISTS AND CONTENT AREA TEACHERS IS MOST EFFECTIVE IN HELPING ELLS SUCCESSFULLY ACCESS ACADEMIC LANGUAGE?

The recent emphasis in public schools on standards and accountability for all learners brings ESL and content teachers together with a common responsibility for the education of ELLs. The priority is no longer seen as one of teaching English so that learners can progress eventually into the regular classroom, but rather of integrating language and content simultaneously in such a way that newcomers can learn English *through* content as they work toward grade-level expectations (Irujo, 2000).

With the pressure on for ELLs to achieve academically, most of the recent pedagogical literature for ESL teachers has focused on how to scaffold content instruction while building language, literacy, and learning strategies so that learners can close the gap between themselves and their more proficient peers (Chamot, 1999; Garcia, 2003; Gibbons, 2002). The message to ESL teachers is that language is best learned through content in the "regular classroom" (Gibbons, 2002, p. 119). Most notably, the Sheltered Instruction Observation Protocol (SIOP) has bridged the gap between TESOL and general education as a methodology for involving not only ESL teachers, but all teachers in the education of ELLs (Echevarria & Graves, 2006; Echevarria, Vogt, & Short, 2004).

However, most of the pedagogical literature still tends to speak either to ESL teachers or to content teachers as separate audiences, addressing what each party can do to shelter academic instruction, rather than what they can do together. A striking example of this separation of labor is an issue of *Educational Leadership* (December 2004/January 2005) devoted to the education of ELLs, which addresses the "pressing needs of content teachers" (Azzam, 2004, p. 7). The articles offer practical strategies on how to help struggling language learners, including an introduction to SIOP (Short

& Echevarria, 2004). Although this introduction acknowledges that SIOP derives from 20 years of effective TESOL methods, neither this nor most of the contributions discuss specifically enlisting the expertise of ESL teachers. The exception is Abrams and Ferguson's (2004) description of the curriculum at New York's United Nations' International School, which stresses the importance of an "eclectic, collaborative approach" (p. 66) involving both second language specialists and mainstream teachers.

This issue of *Educational Leadership* attests to a traditional divide that is no longer feasible in light of the No Child Left Behind Act (NCLB). As linguistic diversity becomes the norm in U.S. schools, but fewer than 15% of classroom teachers are prepared to respond to it (Azzam, 2004), close and sustained collaboration between TESOL and content teachers becomes imperative. In an English-only instructional environment, it takes several years for language learners to reach grade-level language proficiency, and they need continued instructional intervention long after they have acquired basic fluency; the traditional pull-out ESL program is less effective than classroom-based sheltered instruction in providing this support (Thomas & Collier, 2002). ELLs in content classrooms face the risk of marginalization if teachers lack the time and skills to facilitate these students' academic language development. (Harklau, 1994; Platt & Troudi, 1997). Thus, the specialized skills of ESL teachers can no longer be relegated only to the ESL classroom, but must be shared with all teachers so that struggling students can obtain the language support they need in the classrooms where they need it, without segregation from their classmates.

This kind of sharing adjusts the ESL teacher's role from support teacher to coinstructor. It also adjusts the content teacher's role and dispels the mystique of ESL by giving all educators a role in teaching ELLs. Both sides bring crucial knowledge and skills to the collaboration. ESL teachers contribute insights about the processes of social and academic second language acquisition and about the relevance of home culture to language learning, as well as appropriate ways of reaching out to culturally diverse families. Correspondingly, content teachers can inform TESOL practitioners about the academic discourse of their disciplines and about content standards and grade-level expectations. Their classrooms are a venue for "plentiful, authentic input" (Harklau, 1994, p. 266) and purposeful academic interactions with native-English-speaking peers. Content teachers can judge the cognitive challenge of their lessons, while ESL teachers can judge the linguistic challenge from a nonnative speaker's perspective. Working together, they can plan instruction to be both academically rigorous and linguistically sheltered.

What would a content-ESL teacher partnership look like? Degrees and types of collaboration vary as widely as the contexts in which they operate (Clegg, 1996), but successful models generally involve cross-disciplinary teams planning sheltered instruction with a focus on language development. The instruction may range from integrated units in one subject area (Gibbons, 2002; Laturnau, 2003) to a generalized curriculum with joint lesson-planning and SIOP-oriented workshops. The program may include a limited withdrawal to ESL classes, which may be especially helpful for newcomers, or English language teachers may be "pushed in" to support learners within their regular classes.

Whatever its format, the instructional plan should respond to the needs of its learners. It must be acknowledged that not all ELLs are the same (Clegg, 1996); from newcomers of all ages to second-generation immigrants, their needs will be defined by many factors, including prior education and whether their English is supported at home. They may live in large, urban communities with well-established cultural minorities, in rural states that are home to resettled families from widely diverse cultures and languages (as is the case in Vermont), or as adoptees in isolation from their home culture.

An effective ESL-content collaboration will face this complexity of issues and make a range of decisions shaped by the constraints and possibilities of the institutional setting. Such decisions include the scope and sequence of the curriculum, thematic integration across subject areas, and the balancing of academic and language objectives. Curricular coherence may be achieved by clearly formulated standards for success, both academic and linguistic (Irujo, 2000; Laturnau, 2003; The Board of Regents of the University of Wisconsin System, 2005).

WHAT ARE SOME OF THE CHALLENGES FACED BY ESL SPECIALISTS AND CONTENT AREA TEACHERS IN COLLABORATIVELY ADDRESSING LANGUAGE ISSUES?

Despite its evident common sense, the collaborative approach to ELL instruction often remains an ideal that is unrealized or unsuccessful in practice. The realities of district budgets, constant pressures to comply with state and federal assessment requirements, and teacher overload in general constrain the efforts of even the most dedicated educators in several ways. Many schools and districts lack a network for instructional problem solving and support (Little, 1993). Teachers often find themselves isolated within their own classroom or subject area, and sadly, opportunities to share ideas are often lacking. This is especially true for ESL teachers, who often have no classroom of their own and may even find themselves operating out of the trunk of their car in rural or low-incidence regions as they travel across one or several districts to serve K–12 ELLs.

When newcomer numbers increase dramatically in a certain district, the very urgency of the situation often preempts an adequately planned response. Consider the following example. A working-class school district in Vermont with a predominantly Caucasian, European cultural base has recently seen an influx of African and Turkish refugee families. The school district has highly qualified ESL teachers, some with teacher-training experience, who are well equipped to share essential TESOL knowledge with their mainstream colleagues. Furthermore, the Vermont Department of Education, in compliance with NCLB, participates in the World-Class Instructional Design and Assessment (WIDA) consortium, which includes standards and assessments to include newcomers at the lowest, "entering" level of language proficiency (The Board of Regents of the University of Wisconsin System, 2005). This would seem to provide an ideal setting for a coordinated instructional response by content and language specialists. However, more than a year after the latest wave of refugee resettlement, the ESL teachers report that they are working largely in isolation. Their own time is taken up primarily with teaching survival skills and helping the new families access basic services, as well as trying to maintain support for students who arrived in previous years and still need help. Their ELL caseload spans the whole pre-K–12 age range, with prior education levels varying from preliterate to age-appropriate. Faced with the difficult choice of allocating limited resources, they have divided their caseload into several small pull-out groups, arranged loosely by grade and literacy level. Newcomers receive the most intensive services, but even this is limited to a few hours a week. The rest of their time is spent in the regular classroom.

The content teachers, though welcoming to their new students, are overwhelmed by the new demands of their multilevel, multicultural classrooms. The school district, which struggles every year to pass its budget, is not in a position to afford them the extra planning time they need. The likelihood of common planning opportunities for ESL and content teachers is even more remote. As a result, the ELLs are often relegated to the periphery of content classrooms as nonparticipants for a large part of the school day.

This local illustration is pertinent because as diversity increases in U.S. schools, it is likely that this example will become more representative of the national situation. By 2010, the number of foreign-born students is expected to pass 13% of the total student population. Until 2000, more than two-thirds of foreign-born students were situated in six states with large urban populations, but the fastest-growing populations of newcomers are now dispersed across the country, including in rural states such as Vermont, which has traditionally had very low ELL populations (Capps et al., 2005) and is therefore in some ways far less prepared to serve them.

The long-standing tendency to shift responsibility for the education of linguistic minorities to ESL "experts" is understandable in such settings. It is sometimes intensified by the assumption that minorities do not have the same aspirations as their mainstream peers and are less likely to compete for academic excellence. According to Walqui (2001), this is partly because teachers may "correlate the linguistic limitations of second language learners . . . with academic limitations" and partly because content teachers may simply lack familiarity with the cultures and communities of their students and have no perspective from which to understand the students' "strengths, aspirations, and struggles" (p. 54).

Finally, when second language educators are perceived as playing a less central role and even as holding less status than mainstream teachers, collaboration is further discouraged. This perception is not limited to U.S. schools where, as Harklau (1994) notes, the ESL program may be perceived even by the administration as a "necessary nuisance" (p. 244). Creese's (2002) study of London secondary schools describes unequal power relationships between ESL and subject teachers, and Arkoudis (2003) notes the same in the Australian school setting. Ironically, it seems that the same specialists whose priority it is to help integrate their learners into the school community often find themselves similarly marginalized. According to Clegg (1996), the bizarre reductionism that perceives ELL education as a "purely linguistic" problem (p. 3) may be what motivates this tendency for ESL teachers to be dismissed as unequal academic partners within school culture.

In short, even though research and practice have clearly established the importance of collaboration between ESL and content teachers, with well-developed standards and instructional methodologies for integrating language and academic development, successful partnerships are difficult and still relatively rare. The pressures of meeting increasingly challenging expectations for the majority population, combined with an institutional culture that often marginalizes both ESL teachers and their students, effectively blocks whole-school participation in the education of language learners.

HOW CAN UNIVERSITY/COLLEGE FACULTY BEST CONTRIBUTE TO TEACHER PROFESSIONAL DEVELOPMENT AND SHARE KNOWLEDGE ABOUT LANGUAGE?

The importance of collaboration between ESL and content specialists is recognized by the federal government's Office of English Language Acquisition (OELA), which has committed grant funding resources to the Title VII grant project Training for *All* [italics added] Teachers. Generally, school districts applying for such grants are required to form partnerships with higher education institutions. Any such involvement of higher education in teacher development must take into account the kinds of contextual constraints and challenges that have been described above. The authors view teacher development as a mandate not only to improve the specific skills of teachers, but also to enable the application of those skills by improving conditions in their particular environments. This calls for a systemic type of reform, which builds the capacity of entire institutions to support teacher change. To participate in such reform, higher education faculty must go beyond the walls of their institutions to assist in the formation of school-based or district-based teacher networks that are committed to problem solving and redirecting the course of instruction in their organizations.

Richardson (1990) argues convincingly in her thesis for general teacher development that change happens when (a) teachers are in control; (b) teachers' practical knowledge is the focus of professional development projects; (c) teachers have access to meaningful new input from research; and (d) the context in which change will occur is a supportive collective of teachers, administrators, and other personnel.

First, teachers must be in control of their own change. Schools build their capacity for effective reform when principals delegate broad-based leadership for instructional policy. Richardson and Placier (2001) argue from an extensive literature base that traditional top-down training programs are less effective for long-term teacher change than a normative-reeducative approach, grounded in the teachers' own attitudes and beliefs, where the change is directed by the teachers' community of practice in collaboration with external agencies.

Second, any successful professional development program must take the teachers' practical knowledge as its focus. The credibility gap between higher education and school practice will not be narrowed by having academics simply tell teachers what they have read or observed about best practices in other institutions, even when their observations are broad based and accurate. Universities need to acknowledge school educators as the experts on what works within their own settings (Rintell, 2004). Thus, rather than impart knowledge, universities could help teachers formulate hypotheses about teaching ideas, test those hypotheses, and examine the results in a forum that exposes them to public validation. Hiebert, Gallimore, and Stigler (2002) envision that over time, such action research could become a common way to test and refine innovative practice and accumulate the type of professional knowledge base that is most useful for teachers.

Third, while acknowledging school educators as the agents of their own professional development, higher education can still play a valuable role by making new and relevant research accessible. The very fact that university educators are not immersed in the local school context gives them a unique vantage point from which to observe a broader landscape of successful innovations, lessons learned, and outside inquiries. The trick, of course, is to not take a "one size fits all" approach to research findings, nor even to assume responsibility for deciding which findings are most applicable.

Finally, even the most enlightened professional development partnership needs to be sustained organizationally. Desimone, Porter, and Garet (2002) conclude from their 3-year longitudinal study of 30 schools across five states that great variation exists in the effectiveness of teacher professional development, largely because participation is left up to individual teachers. They note the need for schools and districts to set long-term priorities, provide material support, and build the infrastructure needed for teachers to implement their new instructional ideas. Recognizing that teacher change is difficult, Guskey (2002) insists that professional development experiences must be supported by follow-up encouragement, and even by the "occasional nudging that many practitioners require to persist" (p. 388). The best experiences are not isolated courses or short-term workshops, but rather sustained, intensive projects integrated within a plan for systemic reform.

These constructivist principles for general teacher education have also found expression in the field of TESOL, where several scholars have asserted that reflective pedagogy, rather than language, should be the main focus of teacher education (Freeman, 2002; Freeman & Johnson, 1998; Johnson, 2000; see also Mann, 2005). From this perspective, higher education faculty members become partners in dialogue rather than lecturers. Their role may be to facilitate collaborative teacher conversations across disciplines (Hawkins & Irujo, 2004). The goal would eventually be to form networks of teachers who could observe each other's work as mutual mentors—networks where ESL and content teachers could not only share their respective expertise but also achieve a common discourse for understanding the issues involved (Willet & Miller, 2004).

Within their new role as collaborators, university educators need to rethink the knowledge about language (KAL) that is shared with teachers in public schools. They can no longer transmit KAL as a "codified body of knowledge" (Freeman & Johnson, 1998, p. 402), assuming that it will automatically transfer to better language teaching, and they need to concede that the English language they teach needs to be directly relevant to the learners' contexts. As proponents of reflective teaching, educators need to bring the same self-reflection to their own instructional practice (Johnston, 2000).

In the school–higher education partnership, K–12 ESL teachers are the "critical mediator" (Sharkey, 2004, p. 279). They are far more intimate than most college faculty with the language learning processes and the home cultures of their students. As they work with ELLs every day, they notice the gap between these students' performances and grade-level expectations. As they interact with content teachers, they are best positioned to negotiate ways of closing this gap through sheltered instruction. As KAL practitioners, they have already built a professional relationship between their discipline and the local work setting (Larsen-Freeman, 2004); they know what language is needed for school. Finally, they know the sociopolitical ethos of the school, including key players in educational reform and levels of administrative support.

In summary, universities can no longer adopt a top-down training model for in-service teachers serving ELLs. Nevertheless, through the agency of school-based ESL teachers, higher education faculty can bring a helpful research-based orientation to K–12 practitioners. Such an orientation might include providing examples of successful instructional models in comparable contexts, using course projects to build a resource bank of instructional materials for public sharing, or encouraging teachers to present their work in professional publications and conferences where the common focus is the discourse of sheltered instruction.

HOW MUCH KNOWLEDGE ABOUT LANGUAGE DO CONTENT TEACHERS NEED IN ORDER TO COLLABORATE IN SHELTERED INSTRUCTION?

Even acknowledging the concessions made above about transmitting knowledge, it is clear that the discourse of sheltered instruction is rooted in KAL. Such discourse is premised on certain information:

- the myths and realities of second language acquisition (McLaughlin, 1992)
- indicators of language proficiency at different stages (The Board of Regents of the University of Wisconsin System, 2005)
- the difference between social and academic language, and how long it takes to acquire each (Cummins 1984; Thomas & Collier, 2002)
- the role of the student's first language in language acquisition

Admittedly, much of this information is readily accessible. Content teachers may not need very detailed KAL to engage in sheltered instruction conversations, nor even, more important, to shelter their own instruction through strategies such as the following:

- supporting new concepts and vocabulary contextually with visual aids, graphic organizers, and experiential learning (Herrell & Jordan, 2004)
- adjusting content objectives based on language proficiency levels
- providing opportunities for interaction and cooperative learning

For most subject teachers, such strategies are simply part of good teaching. They conform to the five standards of pedagogy advocated by the Center for Research on Education, Diversity and Excellence (CREDE) as applicable for all struggling or at-risk learners (Dalton, 1998).

Far less accessible to nonlanguage teachers, however, is systematic knowledge about the English language itself and what kind of challenge it presents for non-native speakers. For example, it is usually much easier for teachers to identify new content vocabulary, or the "bricks" of language, than the grammatical relations, or the "mortar" that holds the bricks together, such as prepositions, modal verbs, and complex tenses (Dutro & Moran, 2003). Such relations, which are seemingly obvious to a native speaker but complex for English learners, can render academic text almost meaningless if not mastered. This sort of KAL goes deeper than anecdotal or descriptive-level information, involves thinking about familiar subject matter in a very unfamiliar way for nonspecialists, and includes the following:

- knowing the general sequence of grammatical development and which forms (e.g., tenses) are likely to cause most difficulty

- understanding how English differs from other languages in its rhetorical and discourse structure

- adapting linguistic complexity (functions, structures, and vocabulary) at different stages of development

- identifying the structures needed for specific communicative or academic tasks

Such KAL, and knowing how to use it, is important for those sheltered instruction strategies that go beyond mere accommodation to develop ELLs' academic language skills toward grade-level proficiency and eventual independent learning. Fillmore and Snow (2002) argue that in order to serve all students well in linguistically diverse classrooms, teachers need to know the basic units of the English language as well as its irregularities and variations. They conclude with a recommendation of course components, including linguistics, sociolinguistics, and text analysis, that would help teachers make instructional decisions regarding their students' academic language and literacy development.

Understandably, such recommendations are likely to be met with resistance by in-service content teachers, most of whom have received no preparation in this area and may be intimidated by its complexity. Awareness of English as a nonnative language does not come intuitively to native speakers who see nothing inherently difficult in the structures, idioms, and colloquial vocabulary that they use every day. And teachers' overloaded work schedules allow no time for learning a new discipline.

Content teachers' reluctance to take on what they see as the ESL teachers' job is often reinforced by an assumption that explicit language teaching is not necessary for sheltered instruction, since language can be learned implicitly in the content classroom on the basis of comprehensible input alone. This assumption, however, has been corrected by research, particularly in Canadian immersion programs, showing that some features of language necessary for academic achievement are unlikely to be acquired without explicit instruction (Ellis, Basturkmen, & Loewen, 2001). Examples might include mastery of the modals *would* versus *would have* in distinguishing possible from impossible hypotheses or knowing how to understand and use such subtle meaning differences as *even if* versus *even though*, *in contrast* versus *on the contrary*, or *unless* versus *if not*.

Even within the TESOL field, an ongoing debate centers on how much KAL is needed by ESL teachers (Bartels, 2004; Muchisky & Yates, 2004). Bartels accuses the field of linguistic imperialism in its promotion of applied linguistics as central to language teacher preparation. Bartels may have a point. ESL teacher education is not an apprenticeship in applied linguistics. This is especially true when higher education faculty work with in-service teams of ESL and content teachers, whose priority is not to teach the English language directly but to integrate language with content to help their ELLs succeed academically. Nevertheless, Muchisky and Yates argue the valid point that the deemphasizing of linguistic knowledge that is fundamental for language teaching cannot serve the best interest of ESL teacher education. Specifically, it is possible that in K–12 settings the deemphasis reduces the effectiveness of ESL teachers to advocate for their students' instructional needs, by sending the message that there is nothing special about English language learning that good teaching cannot overcome. As a result of this message, those strategies of sheltered instruction that require any depth or breadth of KAL are less likely to be adopted by nonlanguage teachers.

Furthermore, Dutro and Moran (2003) justifiably contend that even content teachers who work with ELLs need to be aware of how English works. If teachers know which aspects of their languages are most challenging to second language learners, they can modify their own output to accommodate different levels of proficiency and make sure the whole class is included in instruction. And they can ensure—far better than ESL teachers—that they teach the predictable, key language structures that form the academic discourse of their subjects.

In a volume devoted to this issue (Adger, Snow, & Christian, 2002), several authors acknowledge that expecting content teachers to follow Fillmore and Snow's (2002) recommendations for linguistics training may be unrealistic. At the same time, they insist that some depth of KAL is crucial for all educators charged with developing literacy and academic skills for linguistically and culturally diverse students. In the same volume, Richardson's (2002) approach is reassuringly optimistic for encouraging collaboration between ESL and content area teachers in sheltered instruction. Drawing a distinction between formal, foundational knowledge and practical knowledge, Richardson proposes staff development "in which foundational knowledge may be used to question, explain, justify, and develop practical knowledge" (p. 96).

In light of the preceding discussion and the literature reviewed here, it seems a strong possibility that such an approach has a realistic hope of achieving the "plausibility," or coherence with practice, that Prabhu (cited in Mann, 2005) claims is a prerequisite for teacher development. Acknowledging that teachers' practices are dialogical in their evolution (Freeman, 2002), KAL can be brought centrally into the dialogue between ESL and content specialists. ESL teachers understand the linguistic challenges of academic English. They can anticipate where language-based modifications are needed and suggest appropriate strategies. But it is the content teachers who must implement them. As practitioners of sheltered instruction, their internalized KAL is vital for those immediate, spontaneous decisions that good teachers make every day in the course of instructional conversations. Thus, with a common focus on the students they jointly know and the problems those students encounter, ESL and content teachers can bring their foundational knowledge to bear on developing best practices for sheltered instruction.

Description of the Collaboration

Background

The Burlington School District's Quality Utilization of Education, Support and Training program (QUEST, n.d.) is a federal, Title VII grant-supported, in-service professional development approach for content area teachers. The goal is to provide knowledge and ongoing support for content teachers to enable them to improve academic success for ELL students. Within this overarching goal, improvement in reading comprehension was selected as the most salient need for all content areas.

QUEST has two components. First, teachers take a classroom-based course to learn about key concepts that determine the extent to which ELLs will succeed with grade-level learning, using the CLIF framework: *culture, language* (acquisition stages and KAL), *instruction* (strategies for sheltering instruction and promoting language acquisition), and *family* (communication and involvement). Second, following the course (in the form of a summer institute), content teachers receive continuous support from the ESL specialists in their classroom implementations.

The institute is collaboratively taught by the three ESL specialists, Mark, Mary Kay, and Linda, and two faculty members, Susan and Elizabeth, from Saint Michael's College (SMC), the higher education partner. Content teachers may opt to produce a project at the end of the institute to earn three graduate credits. This self-selected project usually originates in response to the teacher's perceived need for change or a sense that something in the classroom was not working for ELLs. Teachers usually seek advice and help from the ESL specialists as they work on the project, which provides an opportunity for the specialists to initiate a collaborative relationship providing access to the teachers' classrooms.

Collaboration Between Mark and Pat

During the summer institute of 2004, Pat, the seventh- and eighth-grade math teacher from the case study at the beginning of the chapter, identified the need to improve his assessment techniques for ELLs as the focus of his course project and his collaboration with Mark during the upcoming school year. Pat was frustrated with the performance of his ELLs on the math assessments from his standards-based textbook, *Mathscape: Seeing and Thinking Mathematically* (Glencoe/McGraw-Hill, 2005). From the students' in-class performances, he believed that most ELLs understood the math concepts better than their assessments demonstrated; consequently, he had begun to suspect that the problem stemmed from his assessment approaches.

Mark began visiting Pat's classroom after the first few weeks of school to get an understanding of the treatment of rates, ratio, proportion, and percentages in the Buyer Beware unit of the textbook, and to determine the proficiency levels of the five

ELLs in Pat's classes. Pat provided Mark with the assessments he used for the math unit during one of his early visits.

Mark's observation of the ELLs told him that they had difficulty understanding their text-based math problems independently. They had little or no idea what the problem was asking them to do, yet they were working productively in collaborative groups, could follow the teacher's presentation in solving the problems, and could do the computations. Clearly, the students were learning the math concepts, but their inability to extract information from word problems on their own was a major barrier.

When Pat and Mark first met in the third week of school, they spent time reestablishing the relationship and vision that had begun two months earlier in the summer institute. Pat reaffirmed his desire to change his assessment approach for ELLs. Mark told Pat how impressed he was with Pat's math instruction, particularly with the fact that ELL students were learning a great deal from his modeling and group work. After discussion, they concluded that the ELLs had intermediate oral proficiency, but four of the five had literacy skills well below grade level. They then reviewed the two assessments that Pat had created for his first unit on buying products. Mark observed that they contained word problems very similar to the typical math text genre. Pat called these his standard assessments, meaning that he gave them to all students regardless of language background, but ELLs had performed poorly on these items the previous year. Pat also used what he called his alternate assessments, which were computationally less demanding and contained fewer word problems. The ELLs did well on these tests, but Mark and Pat agreed that the alternate assessments did not help ELLs develop the language skills needed to solve grade-level word problems; furthermore, grade-level-appropriate computation was not difficult for these students. Mark suggested designing word problems with less complex structures and more contextual support to prevent the students from getting lost among inaccessible vocabulary and syntax. Pat asked Mark to model this approach by adapting the first assessment, but Mark suggested that they meet the following week to work on the adaptation together, and Pat agreed. See Figure 1 for a visual representation of their approach.

During that second meeting they scrutinized each word problem on the standard assessment. Pat explained the math concepts so that Mark understood the assessment aims. Mark pointed out that many of the problems contained complex sentences with passive voice, if-then conditionals, difficult logical connectors, and embedded clauses. He modeled how to write shorter declarative sentences that would be easier for students to understand. Thus, "If the students need to purchase 37 badminton racquets to bring to the annual school cookout, and these racquets are on sale for 30% off the regular price of $10, how much money will the students need to purchase this equipment?" became "The students need to buy 37 badminton racquets. The racquets cost $10 each, but they are on sale today for 30% less. How much money will the students need to buy 37 racquets?"

After this initial modeling Pat and Mark worked together on simplifying the structure in other problems. Mark also drew Pat's attention to other difficult vocabulary and idioms, such as *each*, *on sale*, and *off* as in *30% off*. Next, Mark helped Pat understand that unfamiliar topics and cultural referents may cause confusion in solving

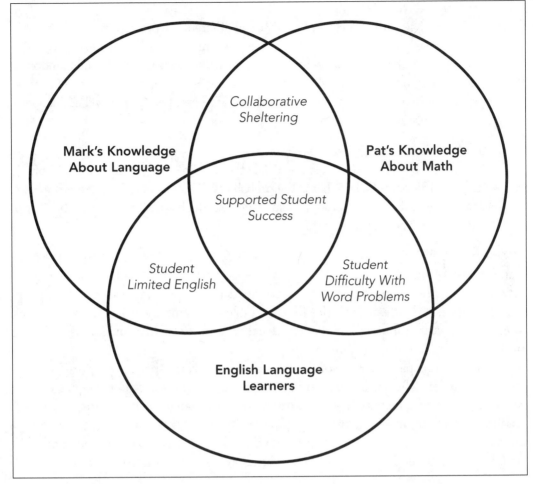

Figure 1. A collaborative approach to sheltering for English language learners

word problems. Some sports (e.g., badminton) may be unfamiliar, making a problem harder than necessary. Mark suggested Pat use visual support or supply more familiar terms. Pat opted to add clip art and to label the badminton racquet. He also supported some of the problems with tables. The ELLs performed well on the modified test, exceeding Pat's expectations. Pat and Mark then adapted the assessment questions about probability, although for that assessment Pat did much more of the modification. Again, the ELLs performed well.

After Pat had completed his course project, Mark continued to visit the class on a weekly basis. Pat now turned his attention to applying the adaptation techniques he had learned to the textbook-based homework and independent class work. Mark helped and supported Pat in these adaptations by reviewing his initial efforts and helping him interpret where students were struggling in their understanding of the language. Soon Pat produced adaptations such as the following example about probability:

Pat's Original Question:
Cyndi has a bag with 50 pieces of candy of all different flavors that she wants to share with her classmates. 15 of the candies are cinnamon, 12 are raspberry, 8 are peppermint, 6 are butterscotch, and 9 of them are apple. If Cyndi's friends randomly select a candy from the bag, what is the probability that the first student will choose a raspberry candy? What is the probability that the first two friends will each choose a peppermint candy?

Pat's Modified Question (see Table 1):
There are 50 balls in a bag. There are 11 red balls, 6 pink balls, 7 black balls, 12 blue balls, and 14 orange balls. What is the probability of picking a red ball from the bag? What is the probability of picking a blue ball from the bag? What is the probability of picking a black ball from the bag?

The intent of Pat's modifications was to simplify the narrative by leaving out extraneous information and to use the simple concept of colored balls rather than candy flavors that might be unfamiliar to the students. He added the table as visual support for students as well as extra practice in using tables. He simplified the questions, using the same structure for each, and made it easier to identify them as questions by listing and numbering them.

As the months passed, some of the textual modifications that Pat produced were still too complex, whereas others were too simple because the modified language structures were well below grade level. As the students' language proficiency expanded and their ability to process text-based problems increased, Pat found it difficult to understand which language structures and vocabulary they could comprehend at any given time, so he tended to simplify text-based problems and questions to the same

Table 1. Probability question

Color	Number of Balls
Red	11
Pink	6
Black	7
Blue	12
Orange	14

Questions:
a. What is the probability of picking a red ball from the bag?
b. What is the probability of picking a blue ball from the bag?
c. What is the probability of picking a black ball from the bag?

degree of simplicity as in his assessment project. Finally, Mark told Pat that his modified language was now too easy for the students and that they needed more complex structures in order to acquire grade-level-appropriate language. Mark also pointed out that the ELLs could understand problems similar to the ball probability example without the additional support of the table. Pat's initial attempt to "raise the language load" was too difficult for students, and he realized that he equated "more complex" with actual grade-level text, rather than with text complexity in the student's zone of proximal development (i.e., somewhere between grade level and extremely simplified). Pat and Mark met monthly throughout the year to continue working on ways to support the students' math development and to gradually raise the language load so that students were successfully able to read and comprehend increasingly complex word problems. By the end of the school year, Pat had confidence in his ability to instruct and assess his ELLs. He willingly shared his knowledge with colleagues, thus assisting in changing the general school approach to working with ELLs.

Successes

In their work together, Mark and Pat established a mutually supportive collaboration in which both were able to contribute their expertise toward the task of improving the math learning of ELLs in Pat's classroom. It was an ideal partnership in that they acted as coteachers in planning and administering language-based modifications, and both gained professionally. Over the year, Pat's adaptations and accommodations showed an expanding awareness of the difficulties and needs of his students: "I saw how hard the math word problems in textbooks and that I create are for ELLs. I learned a great deal about looking at the language I use and supporting students in their interpretation of word problems." Pat was emphatic that without Mark's input he would not have recognized that the students' generally good oral language did not include the ability to express orally their mathematical thinking.

Mark, for his part, sensitively followed Pat's lead in choosing assessment as the focus of the collaboration and the specific math concepts selected for emphasis in this standards-based classroom. Given his choice, Mark would have addressed the immediate barrier of the difficult examples in the textbook by creating alternate word problems for the ELL students to solve in class. However, since Pat was focused on changing his assessments and had made this the topic of his final project, Mark opted to concentrate on this objective, too. He realized that this was Pat's goal for their collaboration, but also recognized that he himself needed to gain confidence in working with Pat in his math content area before offering direct feedback.

The biggest challenge that teachers cite in implementing modifications and accommodations for ELLs is lack of time. Mark and Pat addressed this by setting a schedule for their cooperative work. Mark attended Pat's class regularly, and they continue to meet to work on modifying the language of the assessments. When Pat initially asked Mark to adapt the first assessment for him by way of modeling it, Mark demurred. He reflected later that a year earlier he would certainly have taken the test away for two weeks and returned with an adapted assessment for Pat to use. Mark's initial collaborations with teachers had followed this approach. He had learned, however, that this did not help the content teacher learn how to create such adaptations, nor did it help Mark learn the content area or promote a true collaborative relationship with the teacher. He had found that if teachers relied on the ESL specialist to produce all the modifications, they also tended to assume that he, not the content teacher, would work directly and separately with the ELLs. Because Mark and Pat worked together to modify the language, Mark found that Pat became increasingly receptive to language acquisition issues and open to exploring specific vocabulary and language forms in the word problems. It was not easy for Pat, but he did not shy away from confronting those difficulties, especially because Mark was open about his own uncertainties. It was a continuing challenge for Pat and Mark to support the students' learning of text-based problems in terms of defining what language modifications were appropriate at a given time. The ability to cope with more complex structures varied among the ELLs in Pat's class; like all students, they were progressing at different rates, but all were learning language as well as math concepts and computation.

Considering that Pat's introduction to the role of language in content learning came from the one-week summer institute, his grasp of the essential scaffolding and modifications needed to support his ELLs' math learning was impressive. Susan, who graded his project, commented that it demonstrated "significant changes based on in-depth analysis of the knowledge base needed, including language forms and vocabulary, cultural schemata, essential math concepts and related terms, and the procedural steps in doing math." She also noted that Pat wrote in his postproject reflection that he now realized he might have been more effective had he first modified the language of the word problems from the textbook for use in class, which was Mark's initial response to Pat's project goal. Pat was now able to see the big picture, and this collaborative experience reminded him that a link between teaching content and language assessment was especially important for ELLs.

The project assignment was successful in moving not only Pat but also the other content teachers into a problem-solving stance in their classrooms. The project option was possible because the course was offered for credit, so the faculty were able to implement their commitment to combining "formal and foundational knowledge" with "practical knowledge" (Richardson, 2002, p. 96), enabling the teachers to embark on a self-designed action research project. Initially the SMC faculty were responsible for delivering the KAL information at the institutes and for providing feedback on language-related modifications in the teachers' projects, whereas the ESL specialists were responsible for the practical knowledge geared to instruction that comes from working in the field. Mark and Pat successfully identified and implemented essential language modifications, but regarded their task as a significant challenge, and initially none of the ESL specialists was comfortable in the KAL arena. Similarly, the teachers' willingness to focus closely on the language component of the CLIF framework was mixed and may have resulted from the division of labor that made KAL mainly the domain of the higher education faculty. (This issue is explored in the next section.)

In spite of this caveat, the language-based modifications employed by Mark and Pat were successfully implemented by the majority of teachers working with all three ESL specialists. Some of the KAL information presented in the institute proved to have a profound and lasting effect on the teachers. The two most frequently referenced concepts mentioned by all the teachers are Cummins's (1984) distinction between basic interpersonal communication skills (BICS) and cognitive academic language proficiency (CALP), how long it takes a learner to acquire each style, and the significance of culture and schemata, or background knowledge, in learning. These new concepts alerted Pat to the fact that his ELLs did not have the academic language to talk about math in order to demonstrate their understanding or to respond to the formal schema (word problems) by which math is presented. Pat's successful modifications led him to provide contextualized definitions of key vocabulary and pictures for culturally unknown concepts; to add tables, graphs, and other visuals to text; to simplify structures and functions; to reduce or eliminate irrelevant text; to provide more white space on work sheets so as not to overwhelm with dense text; and to present visual models of the format required for solving the problems.

In addition to their enthusiasm about CALP, all teachers changed their practices with regard to providing accessible reading materials by adapting or creating texts, explicitly teaching vocabulary, and supporting it with visuals and context. They also extended their language modifications to their communications with families. Many have sought translations of weekly newsletters into the student's first language or have changed their formats to include simple sentences supported by visuals. Teachers are now sensitive to idioms and culturally loaded vocabulary and concepts that need to be explained and pretaught, and they have extended this knowledge by monitoring their own instructional language.

The textbook used in the institute was Herrell and Jordan's (2004) *Fifty Strategies for Teaching English Language Learners*. It was very well received by the teachers, and the ESL specialists report that the teachers refer to it frequently when planning lessons and writing unit plans. One clear advantage of the text was that many of the 50 strategies presented were already familiar to the teachers as "just good teaching." As Mark noted, Pat was already supporting his students through group work, interaction, and modeling when Mark first visited his classroom, which was true of most of the QUEST teachers. As was seen with Pat, their classroom practices generally gave them a firm foundation to begin their exploration of the CLIF component they all found the most challenging: language.

Lessons Learned and Next Steps

Among the many lessons learned throughout the QUEST collaboration, none was as significant as the evolution of the approach to developing and incorporating KAL into the institutes, projects, and teachers' classrooms. As mentioned earlier, KAL was initially designated as the domain of the higher education faculty, Susan and Elizabeth, both applied linguists. It was the most difficult aspect to address in the institute and in working collaborations with teachers. The collaborators did not realize it at the outset of the collaboration, but the SMC faculty and ESL specialists held quite different viewpoints about KAL. The ESL specialists felt that language instruction, particularly if associated with grammar, would be too overwhelming for classroom teachers and had little role to play in changing instruction anyway. It also seemed that the ESL specialists had little confidence in their own KAL and thus placed responsibility for its instruction on the shoulders of the SMC faculty. The SMC faculty believed that language awareness, including knowledge about the structure of English itself, was essential for teachers to truly improve their instruction for ELLs. They believed that instruction for ELLs must not be conceived of as permanent sheltering; on the contrary, they saw the goal as helping ELLs attain as full access as possible to grade-level academic language, or CALP. The distance between these beliefs led to a confusing message to teachers about the importance of KAL. The ESL specialists seemed to send the message directly or indirectly that KAL was not essential to changing instruction for ELLs. The detachment of the content specialists from the SMC faculty presentations on language perhaps promoted the concept that higher education instructors do not understand the practical reality of teaching, and thus they were seen as conveying a top-down transmission of information.

In the first institute, the teachers enthusiastically received new information about second language acquisition stages, the role of the first language in promoting second language and content learning, levels of proficiency in oral and literacy modes, and of course, BICS and CALP. Unfortunately, the faculty presentations about KAL, under the title Understanding What Makes Language Difficult, was decontextualized, lecture based, and not understood by many teachers. *Difficult* here covered such aspects as complex tenses, modal verbs, and prepositions (i.e., areas clearly within the grammar domain).

After the first institute, and after the first batch of projects revealed that the teachers' attention to language difficulty was limited to identifying single vocabulary items, it became clear to Susan and Elizabeth that another approach to KAL was needed. It was also obvious to the ESL specialists that some type of direct instruction around language was essential to improving instruction, because very little was addressed in the projects. The team marked that teachers tended to say "Good teaching for ELLs is just good teaching" and "I do that already" in reference to the instructional strategies presented. In other words, they recognized the "good teaching" strategies, but ignored the challenge that language presented for ELLs. To be sure, all teachers identified vocabulary as difficult and proposed preteaching it while developing background knowledge of the topic, supported with context and clip art. But the teachers were missing opportunities to present vocabulary (e.g., north, south) along with collocations (e.g., Chicago is to the north of Cincinnati; Rutland is south of Burlington).

In the institutes in years 2 and 3, the SMC faculty realized that they had to link the teaching of language much more directly to the actual content taught by the teachers. Using teachers' texts to identify troubling language elements for ELLs helped raise the teachers' awareness about the written genre typical of their content area and the potential difficulties for ELLs. For example, a high school physics teacher was amazed to discover that the sentence "Consider a book lying on a table," in a unit on inertia, would almost certainly never appear anywhere other than in a science context. She said that she had never thought there was anything at all odd about it. However, despite the improved emphasis on language instruction and a better understanding of the importance of KAL by the ESL specialists, language-based modifications, other than basic vocabulary instruction, were still minimally acknowledged in the teachers' projects or instruction.

At this point, and after much discussion, the team attributed this continued absence of language-based modifications to the fact that the language dimension of the CLIF framework was presented in isolation from the other dimensions and was poorly linked to other dimensions of the course, particularly to the instruction component. SMC faculty still instructed the KAL section of the course, whereas the ESL specialists taught relevant aspects of language acquisition and proficiency development, and exclusively taught the instruction section. But by this time, everyone had accepted the need for a cohesive strand of language-based instruction throughout the course that could be carried forth in the work with teachers; they all knew that this necessitated a shared instruction of the language elements by all instructors to dissipate the view that KAL was not a necessary aspect of the "practical" work of designing a unit and lesson plans.

Fortuitously, help also arrived from another source. An important catalyst in finally developing a cohesive approach to teaching and promoting KAL, leading to language-based modifications, was Vermont's adoption of the WIDA standards in 2004. The team created a unified approach to teaching language elements by focusing on the academic language promoted in these new content-based ELL standards. Now, five WIDA standards link descriptors of language proficiency levels with performance indicators as functions (e.g., point to, define, match, analyze) for each language domain (speaking, reading, writing, listening) at each grade cluster. Thus the team had the means and the externally mandated motivation to bring teachers into a dialogue about the language functions, forms, structures, and vocabulary at different proficiency levels. Starting with the use of academic language functions in different content areas, teachers learned how to identify and teach the structures and vocabulary necessary to use these functions at different proficiency levels.

At the same time, this identification and differentiation of language modifications, based on the use of academic language functions in different content areas and different domains, was directly tied to a more focused effort to promote differentiated instructional practices and levels of support for ELLs at different proficiency levels. Now, not only is there a streamlined and seamless approach to training around KAL, there is also a greater shared responsibility in teaching "the language piece." The ESL specialists actively participate in teaching about academic language in the WIDA standards, and likewise, the SMC team members participate in teaching how to differentiate instructional practices. Materials used now focus on the language that students need to use and interact with to accomplish content objectives. This approach is illustrated in the following Table 2, which incorporates WIDA language proficiency levels and elaborates Dutro and Moran's (2003) recommendations for a sequence of progressively complex language forms.

Another example, a content unit adapted from Tuchman (2005), models how to present material and assess students while keeping in mind different proficiency levels (see Table 3).

Table 2. Acquisition of language forms: Scope and sequence

1 Entering (Preproduction)	2 Beginning (Early Production)	3 Developing (Emergent)	4 Expanding (Intermediate)	5 Bridging (Fluent)
Responses to instructions and questions	**Phrases or very short sentences.**	**Predictable sentence frames (subject + predicate)**	**Extended sentences**	**Complex sentences**
Basic action words, high-frequency vocabulary, basic prepositions/ adjectives	*(be)*, *have*, *can*, *like*, *want*, and other high-frequency verbs; basic present tense; Basic place prepositions *(in, on, under, around)*; *who, what, where*	Basic past tense (regular and irregular verbs; *was _____ing)*; basic future *(be going to _____)*; more place prepositions *(next to, behind, through, beside)*; *when, how many, how much*; simple modifiers *(some, any, a few, not very)*; simple comparisons	Varied tenses and verb forms *(has _____en; will _____; might, should, would, could)*; passives *(be _____en)*; connectors *and, but, so*, etc. *Why, whose*, extended sentences with natural sequence	Complex tenses and verb forms *(might have _____, couldn't have _____, had_____en, will be _____ing)*; less-frequent connectors and transition words *(in case, unless, even though, whether, however, in fact)*; embedded sentences, nontemporal sequences, reported speech
Show me the blue _____. *Put _____ in the _____.*	*I like/don't like _____.* *The _____ is _____ing.* *Can you _____?*	*_____ lived in _____.* *They ate _____.* *_____ are bigger than _____.*	*Napoleon was sent to an island.* *If I see Mom, I'll ask her.* *I'd like to be either a teacher or a truck driver.* *I saw the rat that ate the cat.*	*Before I ate, I took a shower.* *The rat that ate the cat showed up yesterday.* *Kennedy wouldn't have died if he hadn't gone to Dallas.* *She told the wolf her grandmother was home.*

Proficiency level labels from The Board of Regents of the University of Wisconsin System, 2005.

It is yet to be seen how much this unified approach will ultimately impact instruction and how it will frame the collaboration between ESL specialists and teachers. There are still improvements to be made in teaching language and tying it to instruction, but the common ground that the ESL specialists and college faculty now have makes such improvements possible.

In addition to the continued development of the language component, several other areas needing modification or more attention have been identified. First, the week long summer institute has become institutionalized as a semester-long course, offered partially online to accommodate teachers' busy schedules. It has been incorporated into the SMC ESL teaching licensure program as a TESOL methods course for

Table 3. Content question: Why, when, and how did Spain conquer and settle in America?

Main Concepts	Mainstream Students	Level 4/5 Students	Level 2/3 Students
Where is Spain? Where is the American continent?	**Label** a map of the world with Spain, North America, and South America.	**Label** a map of the world with Spain, North America, and South America.	**Label** a map of the world with Spain, North America, and South America.
The Spanish settled in America for three reasons: 1. To find gold 2. To teach the Catholic religion 3. To make Spain a more powerful nation	**Write a composition** about the three main reasons that Spain settled in America. Explain whether you think this exploration was productive and/or just.	**Complete a cloze exercise** with a word bank that explains the reasons why Spain conquered America. Vocabulary included are *conquistador, settlement, plantations, missions,* etc.	**Create a poster** that shows the map of Spain and America, a Spanish ship, and drawings or sketches that show the reasons why Spain explored America.
Cortes and Pizarro were two of the most famous Spanish conquistadors.	Write a **brief summary** of how Spain conquered Mexico and the Aztecs and how Pizarro conquered the Incas on the coast of South America. **Give your opinion** about whether or not these conquistadors had a right to conquer these people. To **persuade** your teacher, state two or three reasons why you think the way you do.	Write a **brief summary** of how Spain conquered Mexico and the Aztecs and how Pizarro conquered the Incas on the coast of South America. Include terms such as *Incas, Aztecs, Moctezuma, horses, guns, silver mines, gold mines, slaves,* etc.	**Draw and label** a map with Mexico and South America, and use a dotted line to show where Cortes and Pizarro landed in the Americas. On the map, make a sketch and label a picture of an Aztec and an Incan in the correct country.

(Continued on p. 52)

Table 3 (continued). Content question: Why, when, and how did Spain conquer and settle?

Main Concepts	Mainstream Students	Level 4/5 Students	Level 2/3 Students
The Spanish and the Indians exchanged things between their cultures.	**Summarize and list** what the Indians and Spanish exchanged between their cultures.	**Using a graphic organizer**, write as many items exchanged between the two cultures of the Indians and Spanish as you can. Include food items, clothing, tools, animals, weapons, and machinery.	**Sort** cards with the terms *potatoes, tomatoes, corn, turkeys, tobacco, squash, cocoa, peanuts, sweet potatoes, pumpkins, ponchos, horses, cows, goats, chickens, sheep, metal tools, guns, bananas, wheat, oranges, and printing presses* into two groups: (a) what the Indians gave to the Spanish and (b) what the Spanish gave to the Indians.
Ponce de Leon, de Soto, and Coronado were other Spanish conquistadors.	**Write** a short paragraph and **explain** what Ponce de Leon, de Soto, and Coronado were searching for in their quest to settle America. Were they successful? Why or why not?	**Fill in a table** with the names Ponce de Leon, de Soto, and Coronado, and **describe** in a short sentence what each conquistador did.	N/A

Source: adapted from Tuchman, 2005

content teachers on sheltered instruction, thus making it widely available to teachers beyond Burlington School District.

In addition, the school district is now facing its most challenging new population in the form of students from war-torn regions of Africa who come with serious adjustment issues and no literacy skills. The ESL specialists are in great demand to make presentations about the cultures of these students. This need will probably shift much attention to the family component of the CLIF model, as teachers have to deal with family and cultural patterns that are very different from not only their own but also others that they are accustomed to. The influx of these groups has made urgent the need for all teachers to be knowledgeable about ELLs, so it will be important to plan in such a way that the specialists are not spread too thinly. It will be important to bring other ESL teachers into QUEST so that they can join curriculum team meetings and work directly with teachers to encourage ELL-friendly classrooms based on the QUEST model. Busy teachers usually respond to a "just in time" need, so it is anticipated that teachers who limited their QUEST participation to attending the institute and completing the project will now begin seeking out the ESL specialists for ongoing classroom support. There are already signs that this has begun. Linda is now a team member of a Language Arts Curriculum Committee, and Mary Kay reported that a teacher who had never shown interest in collaboration recently approached her and asked "When are you going to do something for me? I've got these new ELL students and I really need help." Thus began a new and fruitful collaboration. Without a doubt, as Vermont becomes rapidly more diverse, many new challenges will appear.

Questions for Discussions

Review the case study at the beginning of the chapter. Discuss the following questions that aim to extend the discussions included in the chapter.

1. If you were in Mark's place as an ESL teacher, how would you structure and sustain the yearlong support for a colleague such as Pat?

2. If you were considering a collaboration similar to the one described in the case study, what specific issues and challenges would you have to consider in your setting? What are the sources of support and opportunities that may arise?

3. If you were a content-area teacher such as Pat, seeking collaboration with an ESL teacher or other teachers who have ELLs, what would be the language-related issues specific to your content area that you would like to address in the collaboration?

4. Why is it often difficult for ESL specialists to help content teachers build KAL to help their ELLs? Can you think of any strategies to overcome these difficulties?

Summary of Main Ideas

1. Recent emphasis on standards-based education and accountability mean that content teachers and ESL specialists need to take joint responsibility for teaching language through content, rather than maintaining the traditional divide.
  a) Pull-out ESL models are less effective than classroom-based sheltered instruction.
  b) Effective ESL–content teacher collaboration for instruction is a preferred model to ensure cognitively challenging content within linguistically supported contexts.

2. Differences in status and unequal power relationships between ESL specialists and mainstream teachers can present barriers to collaboration.
  a) Successful collaboration requires institutional support and time to build cooperative partnerships based on trust and respect for each other's expertise in academic content and language acquisition; ESL specialists and content teachers function as coteachers.
  b) ESL specialists and content teachers learn from each other; content teachers accept responsibility for ELLs' language acquisition through appropriate scaffolding, sheltering, and adaptations, and ESL specialists learn the content concepts.

3. ESL specialists and content teachers need to explore and agree on a plan of action based on the goal of achieving grade-level knowledge.

   a) Higher education faculty can best collaborate by recognizing that teachers control their own change in practice within a supportive community.

   b) Higher education faculty are most effective as facilitators for networking and dialogue about KAL within the context of the teachers' classroom texts and learning materials, rather than through traditional lecture.

   c) ESL specialists' KAL ideally places them as critical mediators between higher education faculty and content teachers; they are familiar with specific ELL needs, gaps between performance and expectations, and the sociopolitical ethos of the school regarding change.

   d) Joint presentations about KAL between ESL specialists and higher education faculty are effective in dispelling lingering beliefs that KAL is theory unrelated to practice.

4. Teachers readily and easily grasp important KAL concepts associated with language acquisition and English proficiency stages and levels.

   a) Sheltered instructional techniques such as contextualizing vocabulary, promoting interaction, and adjusting content based on proficiency levels are also widely understood and utilized by teachers.

   b) Teachers need much more support before they can view their role as teaching specific linguistic forms that are difficult for ELLs.

   c) Teachers are more likely to be receptive to their need for KAL if they can develop it by exploring the language complexity, rhetorical organization, and specific forms needed to perform academic tasks that are contained in their own textbooks, assessments, and other instructional materials.

References

Abrams, J., & Ferguson, J. (2004). Teaching students from many nations. *Educational Leadership, 62*(4), 64–67.

Adger, C. T., Snow, C. E., & Christian, D. (2002). *What teachers need to know about language.* McHenry, IL: Delta Systems; and Washington, DC: Center for Applied Linguistics. (ERIC Document Reproduction Service No. ED482994)

Arkoudis, S. (2003). Teaching English as a second language in science classes: Incommensurate epistemologies? *Language and Education, 17,* 161–173.

Azzam, A. M. (2004). A look at language learning. *Educational Leadership, 62*(4), 7.

Bartels, N. (2004). Another reader reacts . . . Linguistic imperialism. *TESOL Quarterly, 38,* 128–133.

Capps, R., Fix, M., Murray, J., Ost, J., Passel, J., & Herwantoro, S. (2005). *The New demography of America's schools: Immigration and the No Child Left Behind Act.* Washington, DC: Urban Institute. (ERIC Document Reproduction Service No. ED490924)

Chamot, A. U. (1999). *The learning strategies handbook.* White Plains, NY: Longman.

Clegg, J. (Ed.). (1996). *Mainstreaming ESL: Case studies in integrating ESL students into the mainstream curriculum.* Bristol, PA: Multilingual Matters.

Creese, A. (2002). The discursive construction of power in teacher partnerships: Language and subject specialists in mainstream schools. *TESOL Quarterly, 36*, 597–616.

Cummins, J. (1984). Wanted: A theoretical framework for relating language proficiency to academic achievement among bilingual students. In C. Rivera (Ed.), *Language proficiency and academic achievement* (pp. 2–19). Clevedon, England: Multilingual Matters.

Dalton, S. S. (1998). *Pedagogy matters: Standards for effective teaching practice.* (Research Report No. 4). Santa Cruz, CA and Washington, DC: Center for Research on Education, Diversity, and Excellence (CREDE). Retrieved July 24, 2007, from http://crede.berkeley.edu/products/print/reports.html

Desimone, L. M., Porter, A. C., & Garet, M. S. (2002). Effects of professional development on teachers' instruction: Results from a three-year longitudinal study. *Educational Evaluation & Policy Analysis, 24*(2), 81.

Dutro, S., & Moran, C. (2003). Rethinking English language instruction: An architectural approach. In G. Garcia (Ed.), *English learners: Reaching the highest level of English literacy* (pp. 227–258). Newark, DE: International Reading Association.

Echevarria, J., & Graves, A. W. (2006). *Sheltered content instruction: Teaching English-language learners with diverse abilities* (3rd ed.). Boston: Allyn & Bacon.

Echevarria, J., Vogt, M., & Short, D. (2004). *Making content comprehensible for English learners: The SIOP model* (2nd ed.). Boston: Allyn & Bacon.

Ellis, R., Basturkmen, H., & Loewen, S. (2001). Preemptive focus on form in the ESL classroom. *TESOL Quarterly, 35*, 407–432.

Fillmore, L. W., & Snow, C. E. (2002). What teachers need to know about language. In C. T. Adger, C. E. Snow, & D. Christian (Eds.), *What teachers need to know about language* (pp. 7–53). McHenry, IL: Delta Systems; and Washington, DC: Center for Applied Linguistics.

Freeman, D. (2002). The hidden side of the work: Teacher knowledge and learning to teach. *Language Teaching, 35*, 1–13.

Freeman, D., & Johnson, K. E. (1998). Reconceptualizing the knowledge base of language teacher education. *TESOL Quarterly, 32*, 397–417.

Garcia, G. (2003). *English learners : Reaching the highest level of English literacy*. Newark, DE: International Reading Association.

Gibbons, P. (2002). *Scaffolding language, scaffolding learning: Teaching second language learners in the mainstream classroom*. Portsmouth, NH: Heinemann.

Glencoe/McGraw-Hill. (2005). *Mathscape: Seeing and thinking mathematically*. Blacklick, OH: Author.

Guskey, T. R. (2002). Professional development and teacher change. *Teachers and Teaching: Theory and Practice, 8*, 381–391.

Harklau, L. (1994). ESL versus mainstream classes: Contrasting L2 learning environments. *TESOL Quarterly, 28,* 241–272.

Hawkins, M. R., & Irujo, S. (2004). *Collaborative conversations among language teacher educators.* Alexandria, VA: TESOL.

Herrell, A. L., & Jordan, M. (2004). *Fifty strategies for teaching English language learners* (2nd ed.). Upper Saddle River, NJ: Pearson/Merrill Prentice Hall.

Hiebert, R., Gallimore, R., & Stigler, J. (2002). A knowledge base for the teaching profession: What would it look like and how can we get one? *Educational Researcher, 31*(5), 3.

Irujo, S. (2000). *Integrating the ESL standards into classroom practice.* Alexandria, VA: TESOL.

Johnson, K. E. (Ed.). (2000). *Teacher education.* Alexandria, VA: TESOL.

Johnston, B. (2000). Investigating dialogue in language teacher education: The teacher educator as learner. In K. Johnson (Ed.), *Teacher education* (pp. 157–173). Alexandria, VA: TESOL.

Larsen-Freeman, D. (2004). The nature of linguistics in a language teacher education program. In M. Hawkins & S. Irujo (Eds.), *Collaborative conversations among language teacher educators* (pp. 69–86). Alexandria, VA: TESOL.

Laturnau, J. (2003). Standards-based instruction for English language learners. In G. Garcia (Ed.), *English learners: Reaching the highest level of English literacy* (pp. 286–306). Newark, DE: International Reading Association.

Little, J. W. (1993). Teachers' professional development in a climate of educational reform. *Educational Evaluation and Policy Analysis, 15,* 129–151.

Mann, S. (2005). The language teacher's development. *Language Teaching, 38,* 103–118.

McLaughlin, B. (1992). *Myths and misconceptions about second language learning: What every teacher needs to unlearn.* (Educational Practice Report No. 5). Santa Cruz, CA: National Center for Research on Cultural Diversity and Second Language Learning. (ERIC Document Reproduction Service No. ED352806)

Muchisky, D., & Yates, R. (2004). The authors respond . . . Defending the discipline, field, and profession. *TESOL Quarterly, 38,* 134–140.

Platt, E. J., & Troudi, S. (1997). Mary and her teachers: A Grebo-speaking child's place in the mainstream classroom. *Modern Language Journal, 81,* 28–49.

Quality Utilization of Education, Support and Training (QUEST). (n.d.). A Title IV professional development program for content teachers. Retrieved July 24, 2007, from http://www.bsdvt.org/district/grants/quest/

Richardson, V. (1990). Significant and worthwhile change in teaching practice. *Educational Researcher, 19*(7), 10–18.

Richardson, V. (2002). Teacher knowledge about language. In C. T. Adger, C. E. Snow, & D. Christian (Eds.), *What teachers need to know about language* (pp. 85–101). McHenry, IL: Delta Systems; and Washington, DC: Center for Applied Linguistics.

Richardson, V., & Placier, P. (2001). Teacher change. In V. Richardson (Ed.), *Handbook of research on teaching* (4th ed., pp. 905–947). Washington, DC: American Educational Research Association.

Rintell, E. (2004). Can in-service professional development be authentic? In M. Hawkins & S. Irujo (Eds.), *Collaborative conversations among language teacher educators* (pp. 33–52). Alexandria, VA: TESOL.

Sharkey, J. (2004). ESOL teachers' knowledge of context as critical mediator in curriculum development. *TESOL Quarterly, 38,* 279–299.

Short, D., & Echevarria, J. (2004). Teacher skills to support English language learners. *Educational Leadership, 62*(4), 8–13.

Thomas, W. P., & Collier, V. P. (2002). *A national study of school effectiveness for language minority students' long-term academic achievement.* Santa Cruz, CA: Center for Research on Education, Diversity and Excellence. (ERIC Document Reproduction Service No. ED475048)

Tuchman, O. (2005, October). *Implementing ESL standards.* Paper presented at the Illinois Refugee Children School Impact Grant Conference, Chicago. Available from: www.doe.state.in.us/lmmp

Walqui, A. (2001). Accomplished teaching with English learners: A conceptualization of teacher expertise. *The Multilingual Educator, 2*(2), 51–56.

The Board of Regents of the University of Wisconsin System. (2005). World-Class Instructional Design and Assessment (WIDA) English Language Proficiency Standards. Retrieved September 4, 2007, from http://www.wida.us/standards/elp.aspx

Willet, J., & Miller, S. (2004). Transforming the discourses of teaching and learning: Rippling waters and shifting sands. In M. Hawkins (Ed.), *Language learning and teacher education: A sociocultural approach.* Bristol, PA: Multilingual Matters.

CHAPTER 4

Standards

(handwritten margin note: paper: state TESOL or WIDA)

Providing English Language Learners With Access to Standards: A Model of Collaboration for ESL and Content Area Teachers

Heidi Goertzen

(CASE STUDY)

Located in the rolling green hills of central Alabama, Shelby County School System serves more than 1,500 English language learners (ELLs), a number that continues to rise. It is the fastest-growing county in Alabama, with a population close to 200,000. Since 2003, there has been a 60% increase in the number of ELLs attending Shelby County Schools. Of the 39 languages and dialects spoken by the language learners, Spanish is dominant.

Stephanie, the lead ESL teacher at Oak Mountain High School, serves 42 of these ELLs—18 speak Spanish, 11 Japanese, 4 Chinese, 5 Korean, 3 Ukrainian, and 1 Vietnamese. The numbers of ELLs are increasing daily. Stephanie is implementing a sheltered instruction program at Oak Mountain HS through a collaborative partnership with her colleagues. Erika is an English language arts teacher at Oak Mountain HS who coteaches with Stephanie. Together they integrate the Alabama Course of Study for English Language Arts Standards and the state-adopted English Language Proficiency Standards for their ninth graders.

Since all Grade 9 students will be writing research papers in the spring, Stephanie and Erika decide that their students will first need to master the required state standards of writing and research skills. The standards these teachers have selected for their upcoming lesson are to (a) take notes, (b) synthesize information, (c) write sentences, (d) write narrative paragraphs, (e) demonstrate responsible use of others' ideas, and (f) read for comprehension. As Stephanie points out, they will need to refer to the English language proficiency standards to see how they can provide their ELLs with access to the English language arts standards considering that their English proficiency levels are at the early stages of development.

The sixth-period bell rings, and students enter English language arts class. Erika and Stephanie make some announcements and pass out a sample page on writing citations. "Today is the last day in the library, and on Monday the first draft of the research paper is due. We're passing out examples of what to do. At the top of the sheet is a grade rubric. Everyone put your finger on *Smith, 14*," Erika says, reading a citation while she and Stephanie model the commands and point out more examples. "After every sentence I've got to tell you about the author I got that idea from; that this isn't my own information," explains Erika. After checking for understanding, they lead their class to the Library Media Center, where students will continue taking notes from reference books.

These ELL students master the same academic content standards (Alabama Course of Study for English Language Arts) as their native-English-speaking peers. Erika and Stephanie's collaborative approach provides meaningful, standards-based instruction, bringing the ELLs a step closer to passing their graduation exam for language. The two teachers collaborate to develop their students' cognitive academic language proficiency (CALP; Cummins, 1979) with the guidance of the World-Class Instructional Design and Assessment English language proficiency (WIDA ELP) standards.

Prereading Questions

- Why do English language educators need standards?
- What do academic content and English language proficiency standards mean for secondary-level teachers?
- How are English language proficiency standards organized?
- What do content standards and English language proficiency standards mean for secondary level English language learners?
- How do secondary-level teachers collaborate to integrate content and language standards that improve academic achievement for English language learners?
- What contributes to sustained collaboration between ESL and content area teachers on standards?

WHY DO ENGLISH LANGUAGE EDUCATORS NEED STANDARDS?
The National Commission on Excellence in Education Report

The publication in 1983 of *A Nation at Risk* (National Commission on Excellence in Education) was a major landmark in the modern standards movement. In 1981 Secretary of Education T. H. Bell formed the National Commission on Excellence in Education and asked its panel of experts to report on the quality of education in the United States. They described an unacceptable level of mediocrity in the educational system with a potential for weakening the nation's ability to compete globally in business, science, and technology.

The report presents some of the following risk indicators about this country's ability to compete in the world of science and technology:

- U.S. high school students were lagging behind in academic test scores compared to students in other countries.

- Twenty-three million adults and 13% of 17-year-old high school students were illiterate in basic reading, writing, and math skills.
- Millions of dollars in remedial education costs were incurred by businesses and the military because of the ninth-grade reading level of their recruits.
- U.S. school-age children lacked higher order thinking skills.
- High school educational tracks surveyed in the study lacked rigor. (National Commission on Excellence in Education, 1983, pp. 8–9)

The report also laments that prior to 1983 each generation of students had academically outperformed its predecessors. Rather than identify scapegoats, the commission suggested steps to be taken to put education back on track, not simply by improving the effectiveness of teaching core subject areas, but through a comprehensive program of reform and excellence throughout schooling.

Equity and excellence in education became the vision. Recommendations were made about curriculum, time spent on learning, standards and expectations, teaching, leadership, and fiscal support. The commission charged national scholarly societies to join in the efforts to reform education. In addition to the National Council of Teachers of English and the National Council of Teachers of Mathematics (NCTM), the commission encouraged institutions of higher education and professional organizations from business, medicine, science, technology, and engineering to participate in reforming The U.S. educational system. The necessity of developing more rigorous standards and higher expectations for teachers, students, parents, educational leaders, and state and federal policy makers shifted the educational system into the standards movement.

The Response From National Educational Organizations

In 1987, the NCTM convened to draft academic standards in response to *A Nation at Risk*. In 1989, then President George H.W. Bush met with governors of all 50 states to discuss goals and objectives for science and mathematics education. One such goal was for U.S. students to rank first in math and science internationally by the year 2000. During the same year, the NCTM (1989) published *Curriculum and Evaluation Standards for School Mathematics*. Soon afterward, other professional education organizations representing specific content areas followed suit, and the standards movement was underway.

These professional educational organizations not only represented core subject areas of math, science, social studies, and English language arts, but also supported and were supported by the global organization Teachers of English to Speakers of Other Languages, Inc. (TESOL), whose mission is "to ensure excellence in English language teaching to speakers of other languages worldwide" (Liu, 2006, p. 5).

The National Commission on Excellence in Education's charge to the nation was to provide equity and excellence in education, and TESOL's charge was the same, but for ELLs. Standards developed and implemented nationally for language minority and immigrant students would provide those students with meaningful access to the curriculum. TESOL drafted its own standards for ELLs and published them in 1997. As a result of the U.S. No Child Left Behind Act of 2001 (NCLB, 2002), TESOL augmented these standards in spring 2006 to more adequately address the academic achievement of ELLs (TESOL, 2006). These new standards are dynamic in their structure and organization, because they integrate the four language domains (listening, speaking, reading, and writing), core subject areas, grade levels, and language proficiency definitions.

When compared to earlier federal legislation, NCLB[1] has proven more stringent, with mandates that states adopt and implement for all students, regardless of their background. Math and reading standards, coupled with an ambitious high-stakes accountability policy, create an extremely high bar for the academic achievement of these students.

The current policy impacts educators, administrators, and teachers alike. Though it is the toughest of educational legislation, and considered unfavorably by some, it has brought to the forefront a population—not to mention an entire discipline—that has traditionally been isolated and overlooked. All stakeholders involved in the education of ELLs are now held accountable for the academic achievement of language minority and immigrant students.

WHAT DO ACADEMIC CONTENT AND ENGLISH LANGUAGE PROFICIENCY STANDARDS MEAN FOR SECONDARY-LEVEL TEACHERS?

Accountability

Title I, Part A (hereafter referred to as Title I) of NCLB requires state education agencies (SEAs) receiving federal funds to develop core academic subject area standards. To close the achievement gap of disadvantaged youth, mastery of standards must be measured by standards-based assessments. Under Title I accountability policies, SEAs must develop and administer academic assessments in math; reading or language arts; and, by the 2007–2008 academic year, science. Therefore, the need to develop a rigorous set of standards that teachers can use consistently and easily is essential if students are to be expected to perform well at the classroom level and on large-scale assessments.

In an accountability system, SEAs must set annual measurable targets for all students on statewide tests for math, reading/language arts, and science. This process of measuring student achievement is referred to as *adequate yearly progress*[2] (AYP).

When accountability results are reported, SEAs determine which schools and local education agencies (LEAs) have met their targets. Those that have not met these state-determined targets for 2 consecutive years for the same component are placed on School Improvement status, whereby they must develop and implement a school improvement plan that directly addresses the reasons they did not make AYP. According to the Alabama State Department of Education (2005), "All schools that do not meet or exceed their annual measurable objectives are subject to progressively more

---

[1] Currently, No Child Left Behind is due for reauthorization whereby some of the regulations described in this chapter may be amended.

[2] Visit http://www.ed.gov/policy/elsec/leg/esea02/index.html for direct access to Title I legislation on AYP.

stringent sanctions" (p. 1). Schools and LEAs risk losing federal funds and staffing if these goals are not met over time.

Given that ELLs at beginning to intermediate proficiency levels experience difficulties comprehending statewide accountability assessments, the validity of statewide tests in math, reading/language arts, and science is questionable. Fortunately, alternative assessments are currently being developed to address this issue (Board of Regents of the University of Wisconsin System, 2007). As Gottlieb (2006) states, "if reliable, valid, and fair for our students, assessment can be the bridge to educational equity" (p. 1). Administering an assessment designed for English speakers to ELLs provides inaccurate data about the students' content knowledge because these data reflect the ELLs' lack of English skills required to comprehend test questions, not their lack of content knowledge.

Title III (Language Instruction for Limited English Proficient and Immigrant Students) of NCLB requires state education agencies to develop English language proficiency (ELP) standards aligned with core academic subject area standards in addition to an ELP test aligned with the ELP standards. Title III also requires state education agencies to set annual measurable achievement objectives and hold local education agencies and schools accountable for an acceptable percentage of limited English proficient (LEP) students making progress in English language proficiency, attaining English language proficiency, and meeting AYP under Title I. If schools do not meet these targets, they will be placed on School Improvement status, a process that parallels Title I. If local education agencies or schools do not meet Title III annual measurable achievement objectives, state education agencies must provide them with technical assistance.

Accountability and funding are key factors in the development of rigorous standards that can be applied to all children in U.S. schools (Gottlieb, 2004). The new TESOL PreK–12 Standards and the WIDA English Language Proficiency Standards facilitate the provision of an equitable education for ELLs in U.S. public schools because the standards are aligned with state and national content standards, and they provide insight on assessing ELLs. When provided with access to the curriculum through the implementation of these standards, equity is made possible because ELLs are given the tools to develop academic English and content knowledge.

A Shared Responsibility

Although it has been possible in the past, though perhaps unwise, for the ESL teacher to assume most of the responsibility for educating ELLs, new legislation and the sharp increase in the immigrant population make this practice unrealistic. When all teachers provide ELLs with access to the same academic content standards through high-quality, meaningful instruction, they can improve performance on high-stakes academic achievement tests (Echevarria, Short, & Powers, 2003) and help schools meet accountability goals. Well-designed English language proficiency standards help lead classroom teachers and their ELL students to academic success.

Those on the frontline, the teachers, are charged with implementing rigorous academic standards in their classrooms through well-designed lesson plans and classroom activities. With adequate training and education in ESL theory and methodology, ESL teachers understand the five stages of language development (see Table 1, p. 66) outlined by Krashen and Terrell (1983) and can plan units and lessons that meet the needs of ELLs according to their language proficiency levels and educational and cultural backgrounds. ESL teachers understand how to develop ELLs' new language and sociocultural awareness and assist them in applying this knowledge and skill in the classroom and beyond (Richards & Lockhart, 1996).

By the same token, well-trained content area teachers are knowledgeable and enthusiastic about their subject matter and apply content methodology to their practice. They know which content benchmarks their students must meet, and they successfully implement academic standards in their instruction.

Both groups of well-prepared teachers use a pedagogically sound approach relative to their fields and, ideally, have internalized the framework and theoretical underpinnings of the standards. However, in light of current education policy, both groups are now accountable for ELLs becoming proficient on standards-based, high-stakes academic assessments for reading, math, and science.

Experts from these traditionally distinct fields must cross each other's disciplinary paths to ensure the academic achievement of ELLs. These junctions should occur at the school level and state level, as well as in colleges of education. In some states, teacher certification programs are required to include ESL methodology courses as part of their overall program (Kaufman & Crandall, 2005). ESL pedagogy should be integrated with other content methodology courses to promote content-based instruction (Alabama State Department of Education, in press). The question is how teachers from distinct fields "whose views of teaching and learning are defined by their subject disciplines can maintain productive dialogue" (Arkoudis, 2005, p. 139).

The responsibility of educating ELLs must be shared by classroom teachers and language development specialists simply because ESL teachers alone cannot meet the needs of these students (Echevarria, 2006; Gottlieb, 2006). Circumstances require all educators to share the responsibility for the academic achievement of ELLs.

Bérubé (2000) points out that 56% of ELLs in the United States live in urban areas, leaving the other 44% in rural communities. In rural areas, there may be a range of 1 to 500 ELLs in a given school district, whereas more urban, high-incidence populations may enroll as many as 10,000 or more ELLs in one school district. These larger metropolitan areas typically receive more funding and resources than smaller, rural towns. In many small urban and rural areas, such as in Alabama, where there are low-incidence populations of ELLs, the availability of ESL teachers is low. At the same time, some high-concentration areas of ELL populations also lack qualified ESL teachers. Far too often, these ESL teachers are itinerant, placing the students with content area teachers who are untrained in working with ELLs for the majority of the school day. Clearly, these classroom teachers must be prepared to work with ELLs to develop both content and language knowledge and skills.

Finally, many ESL teachers are not, by the NCLB definition, highly qualified in core content areas, which prohibits them from teaching those subjects to ELLs. The caveat: Just as it may be inappropriate for math and science teachers with no formal training to work with language minority students, it is also unsuitable for a teacher certified in ESL to tutor or teach calculus or chemistry to ELLs. This underscores the importance of collaboration in helping professionals in both fields fulfill their responsibility to educate linguistically and culturally diverse students.

Understanding the Stages of Language Development

Different theories have emerged attempting to explain how a second language is acquired (e.g., Chomsky, 1968; Krashen, 1982; Vygotsky, 1978). Given that the ESL teacher cannot solely be responsible for educating ELLs, understanding second language acquisition in terms of the five stages of language development (Krashen & Terrell, 1983) and the two areas of language proficiency known as basic interpersonal communication skills (BICS) and cognitive academic language proficiency (CALP; Cummins, 1979) would enlighten core content area teachers working with ELLs (Crandall, 1998).

One of the challenges is for teachers to understand that BICS is not the same as CALP. Too often teachers and administrators mistake students' fluency in high-context, informal conversations with their peers for English fluency in academic language as well. They then prematurely discontinue language support services for ELLs. Cummins's (1979) model of academic language context and cognitive demand underscores the need to make cognitively demanding tasks comprehensible and accessible to ELLs.

To be effective, teachers must learn key concepts about educating language learners; these involve differences in cultures and values, the affective filter (Krashen, 1982), the role of the students' native language in acquiring second language literacy (August & Hakuta, 1997), individual differences (August & Shanahan, 2006), and cognitive theories of bilingualism (Baker, 2006; Thomas & Collier, 1997). Internalizing the stages of language development and their relationship to proficiency level is a practical starting place for classroom teachers to begin making appropriate accommodations and delivering instruction to develop students' academic language as they learn about various aspects of second language acquisition (see Table 1). The design of the WIDA ELP standards capitalizes on this concept (WIDA Consortium, 2004). A clear understanding of students' proficiency levels and language characteristics facilitates lesson planning that enables ELLs to comprehend and make progress in academic language development.

The five stages of language acquisition depicted in Table 1 illustrate the continuum of language development. As students progress through each stage, the level of technical language and discourse related to oral and literacy skills becomes more complex. The WIDA Consortium (2004) provides performance definitions that correlate to these five stages and guide educators with descriptive detail about the language students will be able to "process, understand, produce, or use," at each level (p. 6).

As ELLs go through stages of language development, their instructional needs differ. Differentiated instruction, an approach that enables all children in a classroom to participate in lesson activities regardless of their unique learning characteristics (Tomlinson, 1999), is necessary for the success of ELLs because it takes into consideration

Table 1. Five stages of language acquisition

Beginner	**Level 1** Preproduction *Entering**	• Minimal comprehension skills • Very little verbal production • Communicates with actions and gestures
	Level 2 Early Production *Beginning*	• Limited comprehension • One- to two- word responses • Uses short phrases
Intermediate to Advanced	**Level 3** Speech Emergent *Developing*	• Increased comprehension • Some errors in speech • Uses short sentences
	Level 4 Intermediate Fluency *Expanding*	• Very good comprehension • Complex sentences • Complex errors in speech • Engages in conversation and produces connected narrative
Advanced to Fluent	**Level 5** Near Proficient or Fluent *Bridging*	• Near proficient orally • Very good comprehension • Vocabulary approaches that of native speakers of same age
*Words in italics indicate terminology of the WIDA Consortium (2004) for English proficiency level.		

Source: Krashen & Terrell, 1983

each student's stage of language development. Students at different stages require varying degrees of comprehensible input (Dong, 2002; Krashen, 1982, 1985) that allow them to understand the concepts presented. Table 4 on page 69 illustrates language characteristics for each stage of language acquisition, making it easier for teachers to understand how to design appropriate instructional tasks for ELLs.

If teachers are differentiating instruction, they must also differentiate assessment (Gottlieb, 2006). Once content area teachers understand the stages of language proficiency, they can set reasonable expectations for students in terms of academic performance in classroom assessment; ELLs need alternative pathways to demonstrate knowledge of concepts taught (O'Malley & Valdez Pierce, 1996).

HOW ARE ENGLISH LANGUAGE PROFICIENCY STANDARDS ORGANIZED?
WIDA ELP Standards

Education departments in Alabama, 12 partner states (Delaware, Georgia, Illinois, Kentucky, Maine, New Hampshire, New Jersey, North Dakota, Oklahoma, Rhode Island, Vermont, and the lead state, Wisconsin), and the District of Columbia have recently formed the WIDA Consortium, a partnership designed to implement the NCLB federal mandates as they pertain to ELLs (Board of Regents, 2007). The standards developed by this consortium are shown in Table 2.

Table 2. The Five WIDA English Language Proficiency Standards

1. English language learners communicate in English for **social and instructional** purposes in the school setting
2. English language learners communicate information, ideas, and concepts necessary for academic success in the content area of **language arts**
3. English language learners communicate information, ideas, and concepts necessary for academic success in the content area of **math**
4. English language learners communicate information, ideas, and concepts necessary for academic success in the content area of **science**
5. English language learners communicate information, ideas, and concepts necessary for academic success in the content area of **social studies**

Source: adapted from the WIDA Consortium, 2004

The WIDA ELP standards are composed of five interrelated elements (see Appendixes A and B). These elements consist of English language proficiency standards; the four language domains of listening, speaking, reading, and writing; the five language proficiency levels; grade-level clusters; and model performance indicators (MPIs).

A central tenet of Title I and Title III is that schools must provide ELLs with access to state content standards for academic achievement and with English language instruction to facilitate progress in language development. The WIDA ELP standards allow educators to meet the requirements of Titles I and III because they address each core subject area and social and instructional language. As such, ELLs are able to develop academic language that facilitates academic achievement.

Through a partnership with the Center for Applied Linguistics and other experts in the field, the WIDA Consortium has developed ACCESS for ELLs, an assessment instrument that measures the level of academic and social English language proficiency in listening, speaking, reading, writing, and comprehension. ACCESS for ELLs is aligned with both the consortium states' content standards and the WIDA ELP standards. And the newly designed TESOL PreK–12 standards for ELLs use the same framework as the WIDA ELP standards, with minor modifications (TESOL, 2006).

A WIDA Consortium member since 2004, Alabama is continuing its efforts to implement these new standards. The standards provide content teachers with hundreds of model performance indicators that can be translated into standards-based activities for ELLs that develop academic English proficiency. These model performance indicators serve as an excellent starting place for collaboration between ESL and content area teachers.

The Frameworks of the WIDA ELP Standards

The WIDA ELP standards are divided into two frameworks: large-scale and class-room. The large-scale framework contains MPIs that provide examples of the knowledge and skills students are expected to demonstrate on large scale state assessments. The MPIs found in the classroom framework depict day-to-day procedural knowledge and hands-on tasks (WIDA Consortium, 2004). Table 3 shows examples of MPIs found in each framework. Note that the use of thermometers is appropriate for the classroom framework since these are tangible items that can be used in a hands-on classroom activity. Using thermometers in a standardized test setting would be impractical, however, which is why the large-scale framework depicts the use of photos or graphics instead.

Language Domains

The four language domains of listening, speaking, reading, and writing are integrated with the WIDA ELP standards. The WIDA Consortium (2004) defines the language domains as follows:

- **Listening:** process, understand, interpret, and evaluate spoken language in a variety of situations
- **Speaking:** engage in oral communication in a variety of situations for an array of purposes and audiences
- **Reading:** process, interpret, and evaluate written language, symbols, and text with understanding and fluency
- **Writing:** engage in written communication in a variety of forms for an array of purposes and audiences (pp. 3–4)

Teachers can access a particular matrix for each of the language domains, depending on their students' linguistic instructional needs. The ACCESS for ELLs test has four sections that assess students' language proficiency for each domain. Together, they give a composite, or overall score, and teachers use these results to inform instruction.

Language Proficiency Levels

The WIDA Consortium developers describe each stage of language development with specific performance definitions that address the level of discourse and technical language students demonstrate at each stage (see Table 4). The performance definitions play a critical role in terms of Title III accountability, which requires states to define progress in language acquisition and report the number of schools and local education agencies that show an acceptable percentage of ELLs making adequate progress in

Table 3. WIDA Consortium frameworks

Large-Scale Framework		Classroom Framework	
Domain	Level 1 Entering	Domain	Level 1 Entering
Speaking	Use words or phrases related to weather or environment from **pictures/ photographs** (such as seasons, temperatures, or precipitation)	Speaking	Use words or phrases related to weather or environment based on observation and instruments (such as **thermometers**)

Source: adapted from the WIDA Consortium, 2004

Table 4. WIDA language proficiency levels and performance definitions

At the given level of English language proficiency, English language learners will process, understand, produce, or use:	
5 **Bridging**	• the technical language of the content areas • a variety of sentence lengths of varying linguistic complexity in extended oral or written discourse, including stories, essays, or reports ➢ oral or written language approaching comparability to that of English proficient peers when presented with grade-level material
4 **Expanding**	• specific and some technical language of the content area • a variety of sentence lengths of varying linguistic complexity in oral discourse or multiple, related paragraphs ➢ oral or written language with minimal phonological, syntactic, or semantic errors that do not impede the overall meaning of the communication when presented with oral or written connected discourse with occasional visual and graphic support
3 **Developing**	• general and some specific language of the content areas • expanded sentences in oral interaction or written paragraphs ➢ oral or written language with phonological, syntactic, or semantic errors that may impede the communication but retain much of its meaning when presented with oral or written, narrative or expository descriptions with occasional visual and graphic support
2 **Beginning**	• general language related to the content areas • phrases or short sentences ➢ oral or written language with phonological, syntactic, or semantic errors that often impede the meaning of the communication when presented with one to multiple-step commands, directions, questions, or a series of statements with visual and graphic support
1 **Entering**	• pictorial or graphic representation of the language of the content areas • words, phrases, or chunks of language when presented with one-step commands, directions, WH-questions, or statements with visual and graphic support

Source: adapted from the WIDA Consortium, 2004

language acquisition. Member states of the WIDA Consortium use these performance definitions to set their Title III annual measurable achievement objectives.

The performance definitions are expressed numerically on the ACCESS for ELLs test. For example, students' scores may appear as 2.5, indicating that their proficiency level is between the beginning and developing stages of English language acquisition. When students reach level 6, they are considered fluent academic English speakers. However, states in the WIDA Consortium may define their own English fluency levels.

Model Performance Indicators

The focal point of the WIDA ELP standards are the MPIs, which contain information about how to develop and assess language skills in the context of the content area. Each cell in the WIDA ELP tables (see Appendixes A–C) contains an MPI composed of three elements: content stem, language function, and level of support (see Table 5).

Table 5. Elements of a model performance indicator

Identify distribution of natural resources around the world from maps or graphs and oral statements	
1. Content stem	distribution of natural resources around the world
2. Language function	identify . . . from oral statements
3. Level of scaffolding	maps and graphs

Source: adapted from Gottlieb, 2006

The MPIs serve as an excellent collaborative tool for content and ESL teachers (Gottlieb, 2006).

Alignment of the WIDA ELP Standards

The MPIs listed in Appendixes A–C depict gradual increases in language development from proficiency level 1, Entering, through proficiency level 5, Bridging, forming the horizontal alignment of the standards. This component of the WIDA ELP standards is the point of collaboration between ESL and content area teachers because it illustrates reasonable expectations teachers have for students' particular proficiency levels in the context of content area standards. Teachers are able to plug their own curriculum into MPIs and use the same or similar language functions and sample scaffolding techniques provided in each cell.

Grade-Level Clusters and Vertical Alignment

The WIDA Consortium developers have organized grade-level clusters into K–2, 3–5, 6–8, and 9–12, which are listed vertically on the matrix. ACCESS for ELLs is organized by these grade level clusters. K–12 ESL teachers or district-level curriculum specialists can see the function of MPIs in terms of age and grade level within the context of both content area and language domain.

A Conceptual Framework of the WIDA ELP Standards and Assessment

The conceptual framework of the WIDA ELP standards is depicted in Figure 1. Classroom and large-scale assessment frameworks and MPIs for listening (L), speaking (S), reading (R), and writing (W) are derived from ELP standards. The classroom MPIs exemplify classroom activities and hands-on projects that build ELLs' academic language skills and are measured by the large-scale assessment.

Accessing the WIDA ELP Standards

The WIDA Consortium developers have facilitated the use of these standards for teachers by making them available in a variety of configurations. Teachers can select a matrix for a particular content area and grade-level cluster for each of the four language domains. A tenth-grade science teacher who would like suggestions on how to build his or her students' language skills for each domain might select a matrix

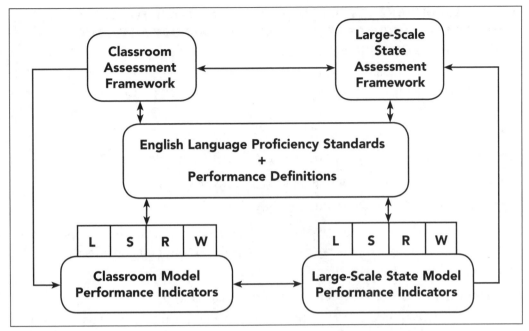

Figure 1. Classroom and large-scale assessment
Source: adapted from the WIDA Consortium, 2004

pertaining to that content area and view the different language strands of MPIs (see Appendix C). Depending on the student's instructional needs, teachers can access a variety of tools to assist with lesson planning and assessment.

WHAT DO CONTENT STANDARDS AND ENGLISH LANGUAGE PROFICIENCY STANDARDS MEAN FOR SECONDARY-LEVEL ENGLISH LANGUAGE LEARNERS?

Credit Accrual and Graduation

With more rigorous standards and higher learning expectations, ELLs in U.S. high schools require meaningful instruction that takes their English proficiency level and educational background into account. The primary goal is to increase the high school graduation rate of ELLs and improve their educational opportunities beyond secondary school.

ELLs in high schools who spend instructional time in noncredit courses fall behind their peers in their rate of credit accrual, which results in fewer students receiving diplomas. In many states, students are required to take an exit exam in each core subject area. A large percent of ELLs do not pass these graduation exams simply because they have not mastered content standards. Many teachers are not trained to teach content concepts to ELLs in a manner they can comprehend. In short, if ELLs are not provided access to content area standards in an instructionally meaningful way, the academic achievement gap will widen and contribute to the educational system's failure to respond to the warnings spelled out in *A Nation at Risk* (National Commission on Excellence in Education, 1983).

HOW DO SECONDARY-LEVEL TEACHERS COLLABORATE TO INTEGRATE CONTENT AND LANGUAGE STANDARDS THAT IMPROVE ACADEMIC ACHIEVEMENT FOR ENGLISH LANGUAGE LEARNERS?

Successful, sustained collaboration between secondary-level content teachers and ESL teachers providing ELLs with access to content standards can be attained through the following:

- a collaborative culture fostered by effective leadership
- sustained, scientifically research-based professional development
- coteaching models for standards-based instruction
- meetings and lesson-debriefing sessions

Each of these efforts is described below in greater detail, and all of them attest to the hard and sustained work that is needed to undertake meaningful and effective teacher collaboration in ELL instruction.

A Collaborative Culture Fostered by Effective Leadership

The principal at Oak Mountain High School recognized the implications of NCLB, especially in terms of accountability, and he responded by researching and developing an effective, standards-based ESL program. Because the school district as a whole was experiencing significant annual increases in the ELL population, the principal was determined to establish an ESL program that would be a model for the state. In addition to selecting ESL as the professional development project, he asked the lead ESL teacher, Stephanie, to visit other schools and speak to experts in the field to research innovative approaches to successful ESL programming.

Meanwhile, Stephanie was going through an intensive ESL certification program at a leading state university, where she learned about a systematic approach to sheltered instruction (SI). Stephanie felt strongly that this was the path her school should take. She proposed the idea of implementing an SI program that involved content and ESL teachers coteaching. The principal asked her to prepare a report detailing its theoretical framework and how it would be applied in practice. He was well aware that to comply with NCLB, schools must implement scientifically research-based instructional programs. When he read Stephanie's proposal, he agreed that SI was the approach their school should take.

The principal wanted to ensure that the implementation of the school's ESL program involved the whole faculty. Through consultation with their ELL coordinator and experts in the field, a comprehensive training project began to unfold.

Sustained, Scientifically Research-Based Professional Development

The principal assigned Stephanie to handle an integral part of the professional development program at Oak Mountain High School. At the beginning of each school year, she trains the faculty on the WIDA ELP standards. Before the in-service training she determines the English proficiency levels of her students using scores from the ACCESS for ELLs test and the WIDA ACCESS Placement Test (WAPT). She then develops a folder for each student, which she gives to the content area teachers, that includes the following documents:

- the WIDA ELP standards table for the teachers' particular content areas and grade levels
- the table for ELP Standard 1, Social and Instructional English
- the ACCESS for ELLs Teacher Report, which indicates a student's performance on each of the four language domains, oral and literacy proficiency levels, and composite score
- an FAQ sheet with questions that include *What do I do when I get my first ELL? How do I make content comprehensible? How do I grade ELLs?*
- a grade-monitoring sheet that allows teachers to identify assessment accommodations

During the training, Stephanie explains how to interpret and use each page in the folder. She describes differences in the linguistic ability of ELLs at each proficiency level and demonstrates how to use the MPIs in specific subjects when differentiating instruction.

Before implementing the SI program, Oak Mountain faculty and administrators engaged in a yearlong professional development project to learn new instructional strategies that would help ELLs improve achievement by developing their academic language proficiency. Teachers were committed to using two or more strategies in their classroom activities during the first year. Two professors of ESL education provided training for the entire faculty, and breakout sessions were held for the various academic departments, organized as learning communities. During these sessions the presenters gave lesson demonstrations using a traditional, decontextualized format followed by one that used context-embedded instruction so that the faculty could experience what ELLs experience in the classroom.

Based on this training, teachers were then expected to annotate the strategies they were using in their lesson plans and submit them to the assistant principal every 2 weeks. The schoolwide training made it feasible for administrators to review effective lesson plans with ELL accommodations and strategies, since they had also been learning about ELL methodology. During the school year teachers were evaluated by supervisors via classroom observations and lesson plan reviews.

Coteaching Models for Standards-Based Instruction

During the first year of the SI program, Stephanie found a collaborative partner in Dominique, an effective biology teacher who was experienced in a special education inclusion model. Aware of Dominique's sensitivity to the unique characteristics of special populations, Stephanie reiterated how SI would allow ELLs to fully participate in the same standards-based curriculum offered to native English speakers and asked Dominique if she would be interested in teaching an SI class. After giving it some thought, Dominique volunteered to teach Sheltered Instruction Biology 10 with

Stephanie. They cotaught this course for one year until the additional ESL teacher, Kristal, was hired; now Kristal and Dominique coteach the SI biology class, allowing Stephanie to begin a new partnership with Erika, the English language arts teacher.

In the current school year, Stephanie and Erika coteach ninth-grade English language arts. Stephanie understands that this is Erika's first experience with teaching a large group of beginning-level ELLs, so she is taking small steps in implementing the same type of model that she and Dominique established last year in their SI biology class, which was composed exclusively of ELLs. For now, Stephanie's role in the English language arts classroom is to collaborate with Erika to promote and deliver standards-based, differentiated instruction aligned with the ELLs' English proficiency level and to use and model teaching strategies that make content comprehensible.

During the next 2 weeks, Erika and Stephanie's class is working on writing skills that will help them next semester when they begin their research projects. The two teachers have integrated some key English language arts standards with WIDA ELP standards in their lesson activities (see Table 6), which will prepare students for writing their term papers and for their more immediate goal of reading *To Kill a Mockingbird*, by Harper Lee (1960), the following week.

Meetings and Lesson Debriefing Sessions

The school bell dismisses classes for the day, and the hallways fill up with students rushing toward the exit doors. The two teachers convene in Erika's classroom to discuss how their activity went and what direction it will take in the next few days.

"I didn't see Mario taking one note in the library. What if I let him use the Internet in Spanish so he can take notes and learn more about his topic?" Erika asks. Stephanie agrees with Erika's suggestion and plans to have him work on that during his ESL class. ELLs at these levels need support in their first language (L1) so they have access

Table 6. Integration of English language arts and English language proficiency objectives

English Language Arts Objectives	WIDA English Language Proficiency Objectives	Language Domain
Read and discuss *To Kill a Mockingbird* . . .	. . . using books in the first language (L1) and with intensive vocabulary instruction and visual support	Reading and Speaking
Take notes from reference materials . . .	. . . using materials with visual support, simplified language, and when necessary, added support in the L1	Reading and Writing
Write sentences from notes taken . . .	. . . using simple sentence structures through interactive group work and teacher support	Writing
Write paragraphs and essays . . .	. . . through interactive group work, teacher support, and by limiting the required number of paragraphs	Writing

to content material in the L1, which helps them maintain knowledge of their native language.

Having students take notes from text and write sentences based on those notes prompts Stephanie to share information about a writing rubric she found in one of the WIDA assessment instruments, which describes Entering and Beginning levels of student writing. The rubric explains that it is not uncommon for students at these levels to copy from original source material and that they tend to use simple sentence structures or phrases that can often impede meaning. Stephanie emphasizes that they need to make sure students understand what plagiarism is, which is one of the standards they had selected for their lesson.

"We need to teach them sentence patterns, give them simple structures that we can build on in terms of vocabulary and syntax so they can expand their level of writing—and communication in general. As long as students at this level are writing meaningful simple sentences that come from their notes, they are meeting the WIDA standards and the English language arts standards," says Stephanie. She tells Erika that she and her students had actually been working on that particular skill during their English language development class that morning: "We practiced generating ideas and jotted them down, then we constructed simple sentences from those notes."

Erika was glad to hear that students had been practicing these skills with Stephanie and considered how they would then leap from writing simple sentences to paragraphs, which was another standard they had planned to teach. "Instead of having them write four paragraphs like the rest of the kids, why don't they write just three while working in groups?" suggests Erika.

"Okay, then we can take turns working with them in their groups, and I can continue to give them extra support during ESL class," replies Stephanie. Erika recalls Stephanie's comment about building vocabulary and takes out a vocabulary handout she uses with her other general education classes, which Erika hopes might help with comprehension skills when students begin reading *To Kill a Mockingbird* (Lee, 1960).

"In terms of the timeline for reading the book, my other classes will be reading the first five chapters by Tuesday when we'll have a quick assessment and one day to discuss the story," explains Erika. "It seems fast, but for our class we'll keep adjusting, and we have copies of the book in their native languages, so they will be able to read them in their ESL class and this weekend at home."

These teachers exemplify collaboration based on the integration of content and English language proficiency standards through coteaching. Entering- and Beginning-level students have extra time in Stephanie's classroom to practice language skills and master the standards. They learn new vocabulary words, practice note-taking skills using simplified text, and learn how to write sentences and paragraphs while working in interactive groups in both of their classes. Stephanie and Erika's collaboration ensures that students are focused on both content area and ELP standards.

Lessons Learned and Next Steps

WHAT CONTRIBUTES TO SUSTAINED COLLABORATION BETWEEN ESL AND CONTENT AREA TEACHERS ON STANDARDS?

The quality of leadership demonstrated by the Oak Mountain High School principal provided the school's ELLs with the instructional support and appropriate resources necessary to foster academic achievement. The principal's proactive approach enabled the faculty to develop an equitable standards-based curriculum. Accepting the challenge presented by NCLB, he was determined to design a model ESL program for the state, and he expressed this vision to his faculty.

Oak Mountain High School views professional development as an ongoing, dynamic process. The school's practice aligns with national staff development standards in terms of context, process, and content (see National Staff Development Council, 2001). The context in which professional development occurs shapes the extent to which teachers and administrators can work collaboratively in learning communities where they can discuss and implement standards-based curriculum and address related issues to promote achievement.

Professional development is long term (Clair, 2000). The ESL professional development training lasted an entire school year, allowing more time for teachers to internalize and implement concepts related to educating ELLs. Because of the long-term nature of professional development, this process can proceed gradually. SI is an evolutionary process at Oak Mountain High School leading to the development of additional SI content area courses. The principal ensured that a scientifically research-based ESL program would be implemented by taking time and effort to inquire about effective practice in ESL education. This new model of instruction was introduced step by step, giving teachers time to practice new strategies with support through a collaborative model and constructive feedback.

Finally, leadership provided appropriate resources to content teachers in the form of well-trained ESL teachers and outside experts. These resources made it possible for sustained collaboration to take place between Stephanie and classroom teachers to provide ELLs with access to content standards.

Increased Outreach

Outreach is needed by professionals from both mainstream and language education. Schools that are successful in helping ELLs succeed in meeting standards are encouraged to share their practice with other schools. One way to do so is to present at both ESL and mainstream education conferences. Stephanie and her colleagues will present at the annual state conference to share their successes with other interested colleagues. Also, schools can send teams to other schools to investigate innovative practice just as the principal at Oak Mountain High School had suggested to Stephanie. In the current semester, a team from a northeast Alabama high-incidence school district with limited experience and resources will visit Oak Mountain High School to learn about solutions that enable ELLs to achieve success with regard to standards.

Collaboration at All Levels

To level the playing field for ELLs and all students, teachers are encouraged to work together; however, professionals at all levels in the field of education should also collaborate on behalf of these students. Institutes of higher education, state departments of education, and district-level administration are all accountable in some respect and should work together to strengthen the educational system for these students.

Questions for Discussion

Review the case study at the beginning of the chapter. Discuss the following questions that aim to extend the discussions included in the chapter.

1. Under the collaborative model they use, how do you suppose Stephanie and Erika view their roles as ESL and English language arts teachers?

2. How can Stephanie and Erika's collaboration around the standards lead to equal roles in the classroom?

3. Imagine you are Stephanie. List some of the strategies you might use to develop a collaborative partnership with Erika. Now change roles; what approach would you take if you were in Erika's position?

4. National policy requires states to develop both English language proficiency standards and content area standards. How are these two types of standards connected, and what are their implications?

Summary of Main Ideas
1. The standards movement
a) was a response to the findings from *A Nation at Risk* (National Commission on Excellence in Education, 1983)
b) resulted in academic achievement and performance standards published by national educational organizations for the content areas
c) continues to impact federal legislative policy in education
2. Secondary-level teachers are impacted by academic content and English language proficiency standards
a) through the accountability policy under No Child Left Behind
b) through the need to share the responsibility for educating ELLs
c) through the subsequent need for content area teachers to understand the stages of language development

3.	The framework of the WIDA ELP standards

3. The framework of the WIDA ELP standards
   a) includes several elements that can be accessed as a classroom instructional framework or a large-scale state assessment framework
   b) includes content area standards for math, science, social studies, language arts, and social and instructional English
   c) is designed to develop the four language domains of reading, writing, listening, and speaking
   d) is based on performance definitions illustrating the five stages of English language proficiency
   e) contains model performance indicators that guide content and ESL teachers in planning classroom instruction and assessment and large-scale state assessments
   f) is aligned vertically by grade-level cluster and horizontally to show progression in language acquisition
   g) is Web based and can be downloaded in a variety of configurations that assist teachers in planning instruction and assessment

4. State academic standards and ELP standards impact secondary-level ELLs by equipping them with the academic English required for achievement and prospects for high school graduation

5. Successful sustained collaboration between secondary-level content and ESL teachers providing ELLs with access to content standards can be attained through
   a) a collaborative culture fostered by effective leadership
   b) sustained, scientifically research-based professional development
   c) coteaching models
   d) meetings and lesson-debriefing sessions between ESL and content area teachers

References

Alabama State Department of Education. (2005). Rewards and sanctions plan—Alabama accountability system. Retrieved August 27, 2006, from ftp://ftp.alsde.edu/documents/57/Rewards%20and%20Sanctions%20Plan.doc

Alabama State Department of Education. (in press). English language learner comprehensive needs assessment.

Arkoudis, S. (2005). Frilled up science: Developing practices within collaboration. In D. Kaufman & J. Crandall (Eds.), *Content-based instruction in primary and secondary school settings* (pp. 133–141). Alexandria, VA: TESOL.

August, D., & Hakuta, K. (Eds.). (1997). *Improving schooling for language-minority students: A research agenda.* Washington, DC: National Academy Press.

August, D., & Shanahan, T. (2006). *Developing literacy in second language learners: Report of the national literacy panel on language minority children and youth.* Mahwah, NJ: Lawrence Erlbaum.

Baker, C. (2006). *Foundations of bilingual education and bilingualism collaboration* (4th ed.). Buffalo, NY: Multilingual Matters.

Bérubé, B. (2000). *Managing ESL programs in rural and small urban schools.* Alexandria, VA: TESOL.

Board of Regents of the University of Wisconsin System. (2007). *English Language Proficiency (ELP) Standards.* Retrieved July 1, 2007, from http://www.wida.us /standards/elp.aspx

Chomsky, N. (1968). *Language and mind.* New York: Harcourt Brace Jovanovich.

Clair, N. (2000). Teaching educators about language: Principles, structures, and challenges (Report No. EDO-FL-00-08). Washington, DC: Center for Applied Linguistics. Retrieved July 24, 2007, from http://www.cal.org/resources/digest /0008teaching.html

Crandall, J. (1998). Collaborate and cooperate: Teacher education for integrating language and content instruction. *English Teaching Forum Online,* 36(1), 2. Retrieved July 24, 2007, from http://exchanges.state.gov/forum/vols/vol36/no1/p2.htm

Cummins, J. (1979). Linguistic interdependence and the educational development of bilingual children. *Review of Educational Research,* 49, 221–251.

Dong, Y. R. (2002). Integrating language and content: How three biology teachers work with non-English-speaking students. *International Journal of Bilingual Education and Bilingualism,* 5(1), 40–56.

Echevarria, J. (2006). How do you ensure that the mainstream teachers and English as a second language teachers collaborate with each other to effectively address the content and language needs of the English language learners? In E. Hamayan & R. Freeman (Eds.), *English language learners at school: a guide for administrators* (pp. 114–117). Philadelphia: Caslon.

Echevarria, J., Short, D., & Powers, K. (2003). *School reform and standards-based education: How do teachers help ELLs?* (Technical Report). Santa Cruz, CA and Washington, DC: Center for Research on Education, Diversity & Excellence.

Gottlieb, M. (2004). *WIDA Consortium English language proficiency standards for English language learners in kindergarten through grade 12: Frameworks for large scale state and classroom assessment overview document.* WI: State of Wisconsin.

Gottlieb, M. (2006). *Assessing English language learners: Bridges from language proficiency to academic achievement.* Thousand Oaks, CA: Corwin Press.

Kaufman, D., & Crandall, J. (2005). Standards- and content-based instruction: Transforming language education in primary and secondary schools. In D. Kaufman & J. Crandall (Eds.), *Content-based instruction in primary and secondary school settings* (pp. 1–7). Alexandria, VA: TESOL.

Krashen, S. D. (1982). *Principles and practice in second language acquisition.* New York: Pergamon Press.

Krashen, S. D. (1985). *The input hypothesis: Issues and implications.* New York: Longman.

Krashen, S. D., & Terrell, T. D. (1983). *The natural approach: Language acquisition in the classroom*. London: Prentice Hall Europe.

Lee, H. (1960). *To Kill a Mockingbird*. New York: J. B. Lippincott.

Liu, J. (2006). Advocacy and professional development: Key issues in TESOL's strategic plan. *Essential Teacher, 3*(3), 5.

National Commission on Excellence in Education. (1983). *A nation at risk: The imperative for educational reform*. Washington, DC: U.S. Department of Education.

National Council of Teachers of Mathematics. (1989). *Curriculum and evaluation standards for school mathematics*. Reston, VA: Author.

National Staff Development Council. (2001). NSDC's standards for staff development. Retrieved July 25, 2007, from http://www.nsdc.org/standards/index.cfm

No Child Left Behind Act of 2001 (NCLB). Public Law 107–110, 107th Congress. (January 8, 2002).

O'Malley, M. J., & Valdez Pierce, L. (1996). *Authentic assessment for English language learners: Practical approaches for teachers*. New York: Addison-Wesley.

Richards, J. C., & Lockhart, C. (1996). *Reflective teaching in second language classrooms*. New York: Cambridge University Press.

TESOL. (1997). *ESL standards for pre-K–12 students*. Alexandria, VA: Author.

TESOL. (2006). *PreK–12 English language proficiency standards: An augmentation of the WIDA English language proficiency standards*. Alexandria, VA: Author.

Thomas, W. P., & Collier, V. (1997). *School effectiveness for language minority students*. NCBE Resource Collection Series, No. 9. Washington, DC: National Clearinghouse for English Language Acquisition and Language Instruction Educational Programs. Retrieved July 25, 2007, from http://www.ncela.gwu.edu/pubs/resource /effectiveness/

Tomlinson, C. A. (1999). *The differentiated classroom: Responding to the needs of all learners*. Alexandria, VA: Association for Supervision and Curriculum and Development.

Vygotsky, L. S. (1978). *Mind in society: The development of higher psychological processes*. Cambridge, MA: Harvard University Press.

WIDA Consortium. (2004). English language proficiency standards for English language learners in kindergarten through grade 12. Retrieved July 26, 2007, from http://www.wida.us/standards/elpoverview.pdf

Appendix A. Framework for Large-Scale Assessment

English Language Proficiency Standard 5: English language learners communicate information, ideas, and concepts necessary for academic success in the content area of SOCIAL STUDIES.

Domain: LISTENING — process, understand, interpret, and evaluate spoken language in a variety of situations

Grade Level Cluster	Level 1 Entering	Level 2 Beginning	Level 3 Developing	Level 4 Expanding	Level 5 Bridging
K–2	locate reference points on local or world maps or globes from oral commands (such as around the school and community)	identify major physical features of the earth on local or world maps or globes based on oral statements (such as mountains and oceans)	identify directions and cardinal points on local maps or scales based on a series of oral directions (such as the compass rose or legends)	distinguish among geographic locations on local or regional maps based on oral descriptions that include directionality	follow travel routes on maps based on a series of directionality and sequence statements
3–5	identify information from oral statements supported visually such as points on timelines or other visual aids	arrange information on timelines, graphs, charts, maps or other visual aids according to oral directions	order or sequence information on timelines, graphs, charts, maps or other visual aids from oral directions	interpret information on timelines, graphs, charts, maps or other visual aids from oral directions	draw conclusions from information on timelines, graphs, charts, maps or other visual aids read aloud
6–8	identify icons on maps or graphs from oral statements (such as natural resources, products; e.g., "Locate corn on the map.")	locate resources or products on maps or graphs from oral descriptions (e.g., "Show where corn is grown.")	categorize resources or products of regions (on maps or graphs) from oral descriptions (e.g., "IL grows corn and wheat; AR produces cotton and rice.")	find patterns associated with resources or products of regions described orally (e.g., "The Northeast and Midwest manufacture more goods than the South.")	draw conclusions about resources or products in various regions based on oral descriptions (e.g., "There is more manufacturing near rivers.")
9–12	identify regions or countries of political, economic, or historical significance to U.S. or world history from oral statements and maps	match regions or countries with similar political, economic, or historical significance to U.S. or world history from oral descriptions and maps	find examples of regions or countries that have similar economic, political or historical significance to U.S. or world history from oral scenarios and maps	compare/contrast countries and regions that have similar economic, political, or historical significance to U.S. or world history from oral reading	distinguish between rationales (economic, political, or historical) for significant events in U.S. or world history from oral reading or tapes representing varying perspectives

Source: adapted from the WIDA Consortium, 2004

Appendix B. Framework for Classroom Instruction and Assessment

English Language Proficiency Standard 5: English language learners communicate information, ideas, and concepts necessary for academic success in the content area of SOCIAL STUDIES.

Domain: LISTENING — process, understand, interpret, and evaluate spoken language in a variety of situations

Grade Level Cluster	Level 1 Entering	Level 2 Beginning	Level 3 Developing	Level 4 Expanding	Level 5 Bridging
K–2	identify neighborhood signs from pictures (such as traffic lights, schools or railroad crossings)	identify buildings in neighborhoods from pictures (e.g., "Firefighters work here.")	locate places in neighborhoods from maps (e.g., "The house is next to the park.")	find locations using maps of neighborhoods (e.g., "The school is at the corner of First and Oak.")	construct maps or reproductions of neighborhoods based on field trips or oral directions
3–5	identify prehistoric animals or tools from pictures and oral statements (e.g., "This animal looked like a horse.")	identify prehistoric animals or tools from pictures and oral descriptions (e.g., "This animal was taller than a 5 story building.")	match pictures of prehistoric animals or tools and their environments with oral scenarios	re-enact the lives of prehistoric animals or events surrounding the creation or use of tools based on videos or movies	interpret the work of paleontologists and anthropologists through oral readings, videos, or movies
6–8	locate places using a variety of geographic representations (such as globes, maps, aerial photos, or satellite images) from oral commands	select appropriate maps to identify regions, countries, or land forms from oral statements	select appropriate maps based on oral information about regions, countries, land forms, or highways	compare and contrast different types of maps from oral descriptions	evaluate the usefulness of different types of maps for different purposes from oral descriptions
9–12	identify distribution of natural resources around the world from maps or graphs and oral statements	indicate availability of natural resources from oral statements by constructing graphs or maps	compare availability of natural resources of two or more countries from maps or graphs and oral statements	analyze distribution of products from natural resources among global markets from maps or graphs and oral descriptions	interpret implications of distribution of products from natural resources among global markets from maps or graphs and oral descriptions

Source: adapted from the WIDA Consortium, 2004

Appendix C. Framework for Classroom Instruction and Assessment

English Language Proficiency Standard 4: English language learners communicate information, ideas, and concepts necessary for academic success in the content area of SCIENCE.

Domain	Level 1 Entering	Level 2 Beginning	Level 3 Developing	Level 4 Expanding	Level 5 Bridging
Listening	collect and prepare real-life materials needed for **scientific** experiments based on oral directions	replicate **scientific** experiments using real-life materials based on oral directions	build different hypotheses based on oral descriptions of **science** issues	match different oral explanations of the results with evidence of the findings	conduct **scientific** inquiry using multimedia resources that include oral input
Speaking	create and present collages or depictions of **scientific** issues	brainstorm ideas based on illustrations of **scientific** issues that affect everyday life (e.g., "What are some examples of pollution?")	describe ways in which **scientific** issues can be resolved (e.g., "How can we reduce pollution?")	discuss pros and cons of **scientific** issues using graphic organizers	engage in debates on **scientific** issues (such as genetic engineering, nuclear energy)
Reading	match pictures of **scientific** equipment with their uses (such as telescope–see stars)	match pictures of **scientific** equipment with descriptions of kinds of scientists (e.g., "Biologists use this tool to see cells.")	identify **scientific** equipment needed for **scientific** investigations (e.g., "You are examining the migratory patterns of birds. Which **scientific** tools will help you?")	identify **scientific** equipment associated with descriptions of **scientific** investigations	evaluate relative use of **scientific** equipment based on readings from **scientific** investigations (e.g., "Which works best to predict weather patterns and why?")
Writing	use drawings, words, and phrases to answer WH-questions on lab reports based on experiments	use phrases, sentences, and diagrams to answer questions on lab reports based on experiments	complete lab reports following step-by-step procedures based on experiments	produce lab reports from outlines or learning logs based on **science** experiments	produce narrative lab reports based on grade level **science** experiments

Source: adapted from the WIDA Consortium, 2004

CHAPTER 5

Assessment

Collaboration in Assessment: Secondary and ESL Teachers Teaming Together

Trish Morita-Mullaney

(CASE STUDY)

Caroline is a middle school science teacher in Indiana. Her school district has experienced a great influx of immigrants from Mexico, and she is now teaching a growing number of immigrant students whose first language is Spanish. She has 10 years of teaching experience and is highly regarded by her peers. Recently, her confidence in her ability to teach has been shaken because of the difficulty she has had helping her ESL students. A disproportionately high number of these students have failed her class, and she wonders if they are failing due to their limited English or difficulties in understanding science content. She knows that their limited English may preclude them from expressing what they know about the content. She wonders if the ESL staff might have ideas about how to overcome this dilemma.

However, Caroline is unsure and somewhat insecure about seeking assistance from her colleagues or from the ESL staff on how to assess her ESL students. First and foremost, she is confident in her skills as a teacher and is not sure that anyone outside her area is knowledgeable enough to understand what she needs. Also, she has limited time and many students under her charge, and she does not want to waste any time searching for additional help unless she is sure it is going to make a difference.

Meanwhile, on the other side of the hallway from Caroline, Jason is an ESL teacher who has recently completed an in-service training seminar on teaching ESL students for all content area teachers. He was excited when Caroline recently expressed an interest in addressing ESL student needs in her instruction. He has noticed that she seems generally interested in creating a positive climate for ESL students at the school. However, he wonders why Caroline seldom seeks him out to ask about specific modifications and tools that would help her ESL students. He is disappointed that they do not collaborate more. Jason wonders if Caroline considers him unqualified to provide ideas because he is an ESL teacher and not a science teacher.

Prereading Questions

- What are the reasons and bases for sound assessment of English language learners?
- How do secondary and ESL teachers work together in English language learner assessment?

WHAT ARE THE REASONS AND BASES FOR SOUND ASSESSMENT OF ENGLISH LANGUAGE LEARNERS?

The case study demonstrates dilemmas faced by both the content area teacher and the ESL teacher. The two teachers namely struggle with (a) ways they can accurately assess both the content and language knowledge of their ELL students and (b) ways to overcome their fear of inadequacy in each other's area of specialty so that they can collaborate as equal partners to better assess ELLs. For all teachers, continuing with their existing instruction and assessment practices is often easier than attempting something that may not be successful (Costa & Garmston, 1994). The status quo is safer than venturing into the unfamiliar and uncomfortable. Yet the growth in number of ELLs over the past decade and the testing of ELLs mandated by the No Child Left Behind Act (NCLB) has moved content area and ESL teachers into reconsidering their instruction and assessment practices.

Collaboration between ESL and content area teachers in assessment can be a powerful way to help teachers understand the specific needs and differences that linguistically diverse students bring to the content area classroom. The goal of this chapter is to explain how collaboration can support and transform assessment frameworks in order to bring about greater access and equity for ELLs. Therefore, this chapter focuses on reasons and bases for assessing ELLs and collaborative models of assessment for ESL and content area teachers.

The reasons for assessing ELLs have expanded since the implementation of academic standards (Reeves, 2002) and the creation of ESL standards (Echevarria, Vogt, & Short, 2004; Gottlieb, 2006). Instead of focusing only on decisions regarding ESL services and identification of English language proficiency levels, assessment must also measure students' mastery of ESL and content area standards.

While the importance of assessing ELLs is evident, the way in which to effectively assess is problematic. August and Pease-Alvarez (1996) have identified five qualities of sound assessment practices for ELLs:

1. Assessing both content knowledge and English language proficiency
2. Assessing content knowledge and abilities in the first language (L1)
3. Using a variety of measures that are more formative in nature
4. Promoting and developing teacher awareness of assessment purposes
5. Understanding the students' backgrounds

Assessing Both Content Knowledge and English Language Proficiency

Traditionally, English is taught first and then content second based on a general misconception that content can be learned in an English-only environment after acquiring minimal levels of English proficiency (LaCelle-Peterson & Rivera, 1994). This problem has been compounded by the historic teaching of English in discrete domains of listening, speaking, reading, and writing. However, this practice is being challenged by proponents of content-based instruction (CBI), who argue that language and content are inextricably linked. English is used to convey students' learning and thinking about content. The CALLA model of instruction (Chamot & O'Malley, 1996) and the Sheltered Instruction Observation Protocol (SIOP; Echevarria et al., 2004) both explicitly link the teaching of content and language. In addition, the longitudinal findings of Thomas and Collier (2002) claim that it generally takes 5–7 years to become fully English proficient (and in some cases, 10–12 years). Suspending content instruction for such a long period would further disenfranchise the ELL community from academic access and equity.

Though CBI gives students important access to academic content, it also challenges the assessment process, so the issue of assessment must be addressed. In short, if instruction is changed then assessments must reflect that instruction. One possible solution is to align academic standards by grade level or grade-level cluster. Content area standards remain the same, but the performance indicator changes based on the students' English proficiency level. Table 1 demonstrates how this can be achieved. The English language arts standards explain what students must master, and the English language proficiency standards explain how ELLs can demonstrate this knowledge (performance indicators).

Performance indicators differ based on a student's level of English proficiency, giving ELLs, regardless of their level of proficiency, the opportunity to demonstrate their mastery of rigorous and appropriate content in a variety of ways. This correlation provides a framework for instruction and assessment. Both content instruction

Table 1. Alignment of content and language proficiency standards

English Language Arts Standards	English Language Proficiency Standards
Standard	***Performance Indicator by English Proficiency Level***
What?	**How?**
Grade 8: Writing Processes and Features Create compositions that have a clear message, have a coherent thesis (a statement of position on the topic), and end with a clear and well-supported conclusion.	**Grade 8: Writing Processes and Features** **Level 1:** Convey a main idea by expressing nonverbally (e.g., pictures, charts, tables, graphic organizers) or with simple spoken or written phrases or sentences. **Level 4:** Develop a clear thesis, and support it appropriately with analogies, quotations, and facts.

Source: adapted from Majercak, 2004

and assessment must be differentiated in dynamic ways. For example, a teacher who teaches students to write a clear and compelling composition purely by lecturing about the expectations of the given standard is unlikely to engage level-1 ESL students in a way that enables them to produce a product for assessment. However, if a teacher models the expectations and uses graphic organizers and visuals to illustrate the parts and purposes of a solid composition, the level-1 ESL students can then convey the standard with a graphic organizer that includes drawings and supporting key words that are related to content.

Though performance indicators can vary by level, they must be closely aligned with grade-level standards (Carr & Lagunoff, 2006). The content standards cannot be lowered to a lower elementary grade simply due to the student's limited English proficiency. For example, if a student is a beginner in his or her level of English proficiency as an eighth grader, reducing the academic content expectation to fifth grade is unacceptable because this would reduce the developmentally appropriate rigor and content standards.

When introducing the SIOP (Echevarria et al., 2004) and the CALLA (Chamot & O'Malley, 1996) curriculum models, it is necessary for teachers to reinforce the models with academic standards. The curriculum that results should not be a watered-down version of the original (Smith, 1998) but instead should be directly related to mastery of academic content and the state's academic standards.

Assessing Content Knowledge and Abilities in the L1

Cummins (1981) argues that a common underlying proficiency (CUP) exists, which means that the L1 positively impacts knowledge and understanding in the second language (L2). The strengths of L1 and L2 complement each other, rather than one precluding the other (Hakuta, 1990). Therefore, it may be appropriate to assess content knowledge in students' L1 because that knowledge will also be accessible in the students' L2 after their L2 language skills have further developed.

The opening case study posed the question of why ELLs perform poorly in academic areas: Is it the English or the content that is difficult for them? A frequently used strategy at the secondary level is to use translated resources in the L1 to model and solicit the content objectives for ELLs. In the absence of strong English skills, the L1 is used to understand and convey content. However, there are caveats to this practice. Although L1 use can be a powerful tool, it is important to remember that not all students are literate in their L1, so use of the L1 for testing may not prove helpful. Additionally, assessment based on situations that the learner has never experienced will not be helped by use of the L1. Learners may also have difficulty being assessed in their L1 if they only received instruction in their L2. For example, in a biology class, students must learn a great deal of specialized vocabulary that they are unlikely to know in their L1. Assessing content knowledge in their L1 will be of no value because they do not have that content or language knowledge available to them in their L1. Finally, teachers must consider what L1 resources are available to them in their building and whether it will be possible to interpret what the students express in their L1.

Using a Variety of Measures That Are More Formative in Nature

Standardized measures of student achievement do hold a place in the assessment of ELLs. This is due in part to the voice such standardized measures give them in the U.S. educational system (Butler & Stevens, 2001); however, many questions regarding their appropriateness still remain. Often, school buildings and districts follow the lead of large-scale assessment practices, fully including ELLs in standardized assessments because all ELLs will participate after one year in high-stakes state-level tests for accountability purposes. Unfortunately, large-scale assessments are more likely to have linguistic and cultural bias that impacts the performance of ELLs (Boals, 2001). These measures alone remain insufficient for ELLs who may be unfamiliar with both standardized testing formats and the content in them (O'Malley & Valdez Pierce, 1996).

Depending on an ELL's placement within content area classrooms, he or she may be taking a heavy load of courses that are mostly focused on standardized measures at the classroom level. The test is then the final and predominantly used measure for academic assessment. This is problematic because standardized tests often rely more heavily on an ELL's level of English acquisition in order to be successful than other alternative assessments. As Abedi (2001) explains, "if ELL performance is low, we may not know whether the cause is due to limited language skills, low content knowledge, or a combination of both."

Alternative assessments, such as performance and authentic assessments, may be a more realistic way for students to express what they have learned. Performance assessments can include a variety of techniques for documenting and assessing the performance of ELLs in content areas. They include, but are not limited to, oral interviews, story or text retelling, writing samples, projects and exhibitions, experiments and demonstrations, constructed-response items, teacher observations, and portfolios (O'Malley & Valdez Pierce, 1996).

By broadening the scope of how educators frame assessment for ELLs at the classroom level, assessment can become more responsive to students' English language learning needs. The challenge of comparability and reliability is an area that requires consideration. However, this challenge should not preclude educators from recognizing a wide body of research supporting the use of alternative assessments. Authentic performance assessments can create a bridge for ELLs to show what they have mastered in varied and different ways (Gottlieb, 2006; O'Malley & Valdez Pierce, 1996). The inclusion of such assessments within content area classrooms generally provides a more holistic picture of performance that includes both content and language objectives that are aligned with state academic standards (Gottlieb, 2006).

Promoting and Developing Teacher Awareness of Assessment Purposes

Teachers must be aware that discussions about assessment should not immediately guide them to the final stage of grading (i.e., summative assessment); a discussion about the complexity and diversity of assessment is merited. What do grades really represent? Teachers need to reflect on what factors are reflected through grades. Ancillary rationale that affect grades often includes effort, behavior, and attendance, but these secondary measures may give a false perception of students' academic capacity. Marzano (2000) asserts that grades should solely look at the academic achievement of students, though Short (1993) disagrees and proposes assessment on eight levels: problem solving, content area skills, concept comprehension, language use, communication skills, individual behavior, group behavior, and attitudes. She argues that looking at these levels is of particular importance when students are learning both content and language because they give students an opportunity to use their strengths and demonstrate their abilities in different ways.

Teachers must also be aware that differentiated instruction affects assessment. Differentiation refers to the dynamic cycle of instruction and assessment that is inclusive of the myriad of needs within a classroom setting. Tomlinson (2001) describes differentiation as having three critical elements: Content is the curriculum that is offered to students, process is the way in which that content is delivered, and product is what educators ask students to produce to demonstrate their performance level. In a differentiated classroom, these three elements are interrelated, responsive, and dynamic. The process is cyclical and responds to the unique needs of each student. If a student product demonstrates that the student missed several key elements of the intended content, this information is regarded as worthy by the teacher, who identifies a different way to present the content. Otherwise, the product or the final assessment measure conveys incomplete information about the student's level of content understanding.

For teachers to go beyond the final destination of a grade, they need to be encouraged to consider what the student product or work tells them about their teaching. Darling-Hammond (1994) explains a model in which the student assessment product can have a positive impact on the process of teaching and learning. It forces teachers to inquire and ask what this product tells them about the students' learning and, subsequently, their teaching. The teacher would then redirect how the intended content is delivered to ELLs. Through further investigation the teachers may find that the students do not possess the same background knowledge as many of their classmates, and schemata in that content area need to be built before understanding can be established. Furthermore, the ELLs' level of English proficiency may be precluding them from accessing the content effectively.

One challenging element of this model is that teachers often assume they are differentiating their instruction as long as the expected product from a student is changed. This instructional accommodation that changes the product and not the process is often suggested in special education and ESL programs. Sometimes the product becomes so vastly changed that it doesn't reflect the originally intended content, nor is it standards based. Instead of offering ELLs content in social studies, for example, it becomes an exercise in keeping students occupied, which can be seen in one teacher's reflection: "I wanted them to label different countries, but in the end, the student just colored in the map. It really didn't reflect the same standard of identifying and finding countries" (personal communication, September 2, 2006). If a product expectation is shifted, it must also be reflected in the process component of Tomlinson's (2001) framework.

Additionally, students must understand the process by which they are being assessed. For students to demonstrate their content mastery, they must be explicitly taught how to demonstrate their ability. Supplying ELLs with a different product and then expecting a miraculous connection to content objectives is unrealistic without a toolbox of strategies. These new methods that may be less demanding of students' language skills must still be explicitly taught through modeling by the teacher.

Understanding Students' Backgrounds

Cummins (1986) believes that "widespread school failure does not occur in minority groups that are positively oriented toward their own and the dominant culture, that do not perceive themselves as inferior to the dominant group, and that are not alienated from their own cultural values" (p. 32). This sociocultural variable must be discussed and understood by ESL and content area teachers in order for ELLs to feel that they are an integral part of the school community. The lowering of students' affective filters (Krashen, 1985) is a collective effort that extends beyond the ESL program. ESL and content area teachers are partners in inquiring about and discovering ELLs' backgrounds. When ELLs feel that their background is recognized, represented, and honored beyond the ESL setting and fostered within content area classrooms, their filter is lowered at a faster pace, and engagement in learning is more quickly fostered (Krashen, 1985; Schlechty, 2002).

HOW DO SECONDARY AND ESL TEACHERS WORK TOGETHER IN ENGLISH LANGUAGE LEARNER ASSESSMENT?

Collaboration in Indianapolis

In the Midwestern School District's middle schools, ESL teachers and content area teachers have entered into an informal collaborative agreement. The process began when the ESL coordinator, who assumed the head coach role, conducted individual coaching sessions with ESL teachers. In these sessions, the ESL coordinator purposefully modeled effective coaching techniques. Cognitive coaching is a way of thinking and working with one another that is based on problem solving rather than a stand-and-deliver mode of advising and consulting (Dieckmann & Montemayor, 2004). It is coaching from within the setting rather than advising from an outside perspective (see Table 2).

After modeling coaching, the ESL coordinator then encouraged the ESL teachers to partner with content area teachers. The ESL teachers subsequently identified

Table 2. Differences between consulting and coaching

Consulting	Coaching
Furnishes information so that a person *may* become more effective in his or her profession	Inspires a person's effectiveness in his or her profession through encouragement
Considers a person's challenges and offers a *solution* on their behalf	Facilitates a person's challenges and motivates self-generated *resolution*

specific content area teachers to collaborate with on the basis of instructional need, time availability, and expressed interest in working with the ESL teachers. In selecting content area teachers to collaborate with, the ESL teachers referred to Bandura's (1971) social model as a guide in partner selection. They sought individuals whom they felt they and others could trust, confide in, and seek counsel from. Once they had identified those individuals, the ESL teachers assumed their role as peer coaches to the content area teachers. The pairs of teachers then met approximately once a month.

As the process started, the ESL coordinator undertook action research through which she discovered that coaching was more effective if interwoven with consulting sessions in which there was direct dissemination and sharing of information (Morita-Mullaney, 2004). For example, a substantial number of secondary content area teachers in the district had just begun to learn about ELLs. These teachers had limited background in teaching and assessing ELLs, so the ESL coordinator decided it was necessary to first organize workshops for content area teachers in which explicit professional knowledge about ELLs could be disseminated. Once the ESL and content area teachers were able to share a common foundation of professional knowledge and strategies, the former could more effectively engage in peer coaching and collaboration with their content area colleagues.

Another element that came to light as the coaching/consulting sessions got underway was the important role of substitute teachers. ESL and content area teachers relied upon the substitutes to free up large chunks of time for the coaching/consulting sessions.

The ESL and content area teachers came to a joint decision as they began the coaching/consulting sessions that they would end each session by agreeing to try something that emerged from the session before they met again the next time. Finally, after all the pieces were put into place, the informal but frequent sessions became routine, as collaborative monthly events in which ESL and content area teachers came together to support and share ideas with each other. The following sections provide a look into three sessions that focused particularly on assessment.

Collaboration Into Action: Three Journeys of Learning

Collaboration on Integration of Academic Standards and
English Language Proficiency (ELP) Standards

The collaboration began with ESL teachers meeting in the summer of 2004 to study and review the ELP standards. The ESL teachers were excited about the standards that would now formalize their profession, and they soon realized that connecting these language standards to content area standards would be an important step in helping them connect and collaborate with content area teachers. The ESL teachers first resolved to create sample lessons that demonstrated the integration of ELP and academic standards for content area teachers. However, they quickly realized with the help of coaching sessions led by the district-level ESL coordinator that this approach would not guarantee their colleagues' understanding of the integration of standards in a way that would result in joint instruction and assessment of language and content. While working together both in the summer and then at two full-day ESL staff meetings during the school year, the ESL teachers created a blank template with guidance from Ainsworth's (2003) process of *unwrapping the standard*, which could be used to facilitate collaboration between the ESL and content area teachers.

The ESL teachers then headed to their buildings and chose one content area teacher with whom they could work to make the ELP standards comprehensible, connected, and relevant to their teaching. The first step was a consulting step in which the ESL teachers discussed the thrust of the ELP standards and shared the examples they had developed in the summer regarding how to integrate the standards with academic standards. The next step was to peer-coach and support the content area teachers in finding ways to relate their academic standards to the ELP standards. Table 3 is the product of one such dialogue between an ESL and a language arts teacher.

Table 3 reflects the process outlined in Table 1 (page 87), in which the ELA standards are the content goals to be attained and the ELP standards are the processes and steps by which ELLs can demonstrate achievement of those goals. The instructional component is included for the reference of both ESL and content area teachers in terms of relevant, multimodal strategies that could elicit assessable student output. The coaching sessions led to a change in thinking of both the ESL and content area teachers. In this case, both groups of teachers realized that furnishing a plan for implementation in isolation increased the likelihood that it would be misunderstood and unexecuted in the instruction and assessment cycle.

Collaboration Regarding the Use of Students' Native Languages in Assessment

Content Area Teacher: I gave my ESL students my content area test in Spanish. I was thrilled to have this as a resource! After they completed the assessment, I had a bilingual assistant help me interpret the outcome of the test. The results were dismal. They didn't get much right. The assistant asked me, "Did you teach this in Spanish?" That really got me. No, I had not. I had taught in English, but expected an assessment in Spanish. This disjuncture became apparent and made me really rethink my approach.

ESL Teacher: When I found out about the teacher's dilemma, I first encouraged her to talk about how she modeled her lessons to students, her use of manipulatives, and oral speech. We then moved on to the issue of using the L1. I shared with her that her two ELLs didn't read and write in their L1 with grade-level proficiency. We both realized through our conversation that content knowledge foundation is the missing element that cannot be overcome with the use of students' native languages in assessment.

The ESL teacher was engaging the content area teacher in conversation rather than telling her what to do. This is an example of peer coaching that took place during monthly collaborative conversation sessions. These meetings provided a forum in which questions of assessment, such as the role of the L1, could be addressed. The two teachers decided to share this conversation with the ESL coordinator and their school principal. The direct result of this sharing are four guiding questions that are used as a heuristic in their school when teachers are considering the use of the L1 in assessment of ELLs:

Table 3. Combining content area and ELP standards

Grade 7: ESL Standards

READING: Word Recognition, Fluency, and Vocabulary Development
ELA 7.1.1 Identify and understand idioms and comparisons—such as analogies, metaphors, and similes—in prose and poetry.
ELA 7.1.2 Use knowledge of Greek, Latin, and Anglo-Saxon roots and word parts to understand subject-area vocabulary (science, social studies, and mathematics).
ELA 7.1.3 Clarify word meanings through the use of definition, example, restatement, or through the use of contrast stated in the text.

English Language Proficiency Standards
Language minority students will listen, speak, read, and write to convey knowledge of sounds, words, word parts, and context clues.

		Verbs	How Performed	Instruction
ELP Standard for Level 1				
ELP 7.1.1	Begin to produce most English phonemes while reading one's own writing or simple texts.	Produce Identify	Points, nods, gestures; Matches word to print; Repeats; Takes dictation of high-frequency words and phrases; Uses simple words or phrases.	Model decoding strategies. Use visuals before reading activity. Use predictable books with simplified vocabulary and repeated sentence structure. Use a small-group emergent reading approach to lower anxiety level.
ELP 7.1.2	Identify common English phonemes and morphemes.			
ELP Standard for Level 2				
ELP 7.1.3	Use common English morphemes while reading.	Use Identify	Reads simple text with fluency; Illustrates similes and metaphors.	Provide decodable text. Support instruction with visuals and graphic representations. Choral reading. Chants.
ELP 7.1.4	Identify use of similes and metaphors in simple literary works and poetry.			

Source: adapted from Ainsworth, 2003; the Indiana Department of Education, 2003; Majercak, 2004

- *Are the students sufficiently literate in the L1 to read and access the content if translated?* One element that always requires consideration is the literacy level of the students. If they do not read at the level at which the document has been written and do not have resources within immediate proximity (people or materials), then every assessment conducted is more an assessment of their reading level in the L1 than of the given content objective and standard.

- *Was oral and written instruction offered in the L1?* If an exam or assignment in the L1 is offered to students for the purpose of assessing their content mastery and it is only offered in a written form, teachers again are relying on the students' literacy levels in their L1 to match the literacy level at which the assessment is written. If students' reading level in their L1 is lower than that which the assessment requires, understanding can be scaffolded with oral communication. If the oral information and/or exchange is absent, opportunity for understanding is reduced. Translating test items into a student's native language has been found to have a limited impact on performance if the instruction is not also in the student's native language (Abedi, 2001).

- *Has sufficient background knowledge been developed so that students can understand the concepts?* If students have no prior knowledge in a given area of study, then no matter what language content is expressed in, they are less likely to make connections related to the content objective and standard. Teaching has to reflect solid instruction that includes the building of background, comprehensible input, strategies development, interaction, practice, and application (Echevarria et al., 2004).

- *Are there sufficient L1 resources in the building to interpret what the students expressed in the L1?* If the responses to the aforementioned questions are a resounding *yes*, then practically and philosophically it makes sense to use the L1 to express what ELLs have understood and mastered.

These guiding questions have helped Midwestern School District move beyond relying exclusively on the L1 in assessment. As the ESL and content area teachers learned through their purposeful, collaborative conversation, questions such as these can help teachers make decisions about future steps regarding the use of students' native languages.

Collaboration via Focused Discussion on Teacher Roles in Assessment

ESL Teacher: I gave the content area teachers in the building a list of adaptations and accommodations they could make for their students in assessment and instruction, just like I do each year. I wondered why everyone was having such a hard time implementing these suggestions. After thinking about this and talking with other ESL teachers, I realized that because content area teachers saw me as the expert in the area of ESL, they didn't see adaptations and accommodations for instruction and assessment as their responsibility to implement in their classrooms. I realized that I sometimes did the same to them. I didn't know all of the teachers' content, so I just deferred to them to assess their own content area.

This teacher's comment illustrates the classic dilemma about assessment. Whose responsibility is it? Is it the ESL program's? Is it the content area teacher's? One of the ways Midwestern School District addressed this dilemma was through focused discussion sessions at the building level, particularly at the meeting that focused on assessment and assessment responsibilities. The session resembled a modified version of the Issaquah coaching protocol (McDonald, Mohr, Dichter, & McDonald, 2003), which combines consulting and coaching approaches. The protocol combines information sharing with intensive deconstructing of ideas so that the ideas can be understood and applied to specific situations. The protocol thus fit well into the district's existing infrastructure. The stages of the protocol were adhered to in the following way:

1. Presentation: The ESL coordinator provided content area teachers with a basic overview of what types of assessment could be offered to ELLs based on their English proficiency. This gave teachers permission to implement different strategies when assessing ELLs. The overview was followed by explicit modeling of a content area lesson and its subsequent assessment.

2. Clarifying questions: In a small-group conversation, content area and ESL teachers asked questions of one another and developed strategies and ideas that would enhance the "model lesson" and the assessment of student performance.

3. Active listening/reflection: Content area teachers were asked to take the discussion to the next level with their ESL counterparts, namely to reflect on how the model could be customized to fit their own situation. This was undertaken so that teachers could answer questions such as "What does it look like for my social studies unit, and how do I assess students' performance in it?" Follow-up guaranteed greater implementation and sustained practice that promoted ELL learning.

4. Check-in: The ESL coordinator checked to see whether the content area teachers, in collaboration with their ESL colleagues, were able to identify workable ways of incorporating the model lesson and assessment modifications into their lesson plans.

5. Probing questions: The ESL and content area teachers engaged in a discussion with each other and with the ESL coordinator regarding the pitfalls and resources available (personnel and material) to undertake assessment and assessment modifications for ELLs.

6. Connections and suggestions: The two sets of teachers, along with the ESL coordinator, engaged in a discussion of options beyond what was presented.

7. Responses and debriefing: Everyone in the meeting engaged in discussion of next steps. There were two reasons for this final stage, which began with one-on-one discussions and ended with an all-group meeting. One reason was to develop the opportunity for content area teachers to seek help and reassurance from colleagues in undertaking ELL assessment. The other was to develop an awareness of areas of overlap between ESL and content area teachers' assessment roles and joint responsibilities. Through the focused discussion, it became apparent that ESL and content area teachers have equal responsibilities and opportunities to assess ELLs. Table 4 illustrates the new awareness that emerged from the discussion during this phase.

Table 4. Responsibility for ELL assessment

Reason for assessment	Teacher(s) presently responsible for assessment of ELLs	Desired teachers responsible for assessment of ELLs	Rationale
Placement in ESL services	ESL teacher	Content area and ESL teacher	ESL proficiency assessment determines eligibility for ESL services.
Exiting from ESL services	ESL teacher	Content area and ESL teacher	Feedback from content area teachers provides multiple assessment measures about students exiting from program.
Monitoring for ESL services	ESL teacher	Content area and ESL teacher	Overall student achievement and English proficiency level need consideration and decisions on whether monitoring is merited.
Identification of English language proficiency level	ESL teacher	ESL teacher and guidance personnel	English proficiency assessments are standardized in each state.
Academic mastery of ESL standards	ESL teacher	Content area and ESL teacher	Understanding of ESL and content area standards provides mutual understanding and explicit connections between the two sets of standards, which ensure rigorous and appropriate academic content.
Academic mastery of content area standards	Content area and ESL teacher	Content area and ESL teacher	ESL services are designed to support the learning needs of ELLs in grade-level content areas.

Source: adapted from Gottlieb, 2006, p. 9

Lessons Learned and Next Steps

Midwestern School District emerged from its efforts with the understanding that ESL and content area teachers must all be part of a joint interdisciplinary team. Often, learning communities are organized by content area. ESL teachers have limited opportunities within this framework to engage with teachers across content areas in which ELLs spend most of their day. The coaching-consulting sessions that were initiated in this district have been successful in engaging ESL teachers and their content area counterparts in teamwork and collaboration. Being on a team helps each set of teachers grow in their sense of self-efficacy by having the opportunity to engage in collective inquiry with others (Bandura, 1971). Consequently, the students are better served because of the merging of not only the teachers' knowledge, but also their sense of the mission to undertake fair and equitable assessment.

The next step is to align collaborative efforts at the high school level with those at the elementary level within the district. The high schools plan to adopt the collaborative analysis of student learning (CASL; Langer, Colton, & Goff, 2003) that has been successfully adapted by the district at the elementary level. CASL collaboration begins with joint analyses of student work. Teachers take turns sharing student work with colleagues and eliciting input on assumptions underlying their assessment, the myriad of conclusions that could be drawn from the assessment from various perspectives, and the actions to be taken toward more equitable assessment.

The word *assessment* comes from the Latin *assidiēre*: to sit beside, to gather data in order to make informed decisions (Wormelli, 2006). The different ways that teachers assess students mean that the feedback teachers receive from students about their mastery or misunderstanding of content is solid input for how teachers may need to readjust their instructional delivery. In short, it becomes an exchange that allows educators to adjust midstream and seek alternative ways of teaching their content. Ultimately, this is most equitably seized when they enter into earnest discourse (Fullan, 2001) with all involved.

Questions for Discussion

Review the case study at the beginning of the chapter. Discuss the following questions that aim to extend the discussions included in the chapter.

1. What are some barriers that prevent ESL and content area teachers from collaborating? What ideas do you have to overcome these barriers?

2. What concrete steps could be taken by ESL teachers to develop a collaborative relationship with content area teachers? Use ideas from the chapter or from your own experience.

3. How could linking academic and ELP standards help content area teachers assess their ELLs' progress?

4. If the L1 is considered for use in assessment, what questions do content area and ESL teachers need to consider?

Summary of Main Ideas
1. The addition of ESL and content area standards has expanded the reasons for assessment beyond focusing only on decisions regarding ESL services and identification of English language proficiency levels.

2. Five qualities of sound assessment that can be promoted through collaboration are
  a) assessing both content knowledge and English language proficiency
  b) assessing content knowledge and abilities in the L1
  c) using a variety of measures that are more formative in nature
  d) promoting and developing teacher awareness of assessment purposes
  e) understanding the students' backgrounds

3.	Coaching facilitates and impacts teacher change more effectively than typical stand-and-deliver methods because it is provided by a social model with which teachers can identify.
4.	One productive area for collaboration regarding assessment is linking content area and ELP standards.
5.	Four guiding questions can be used in collaboration and provide a heuristic for deciding whether the L1 should be used in assessment: a) Are the students sufficiently literate in the L1 to read and access the content if translated? b) Was oral and written instruction offered in the L1? c) Has sufficient background knowledge been developed so that students can understand the concepts? d) Are there sufficient L1 resources in the building to interpret what the students expressed in the L1?
6.	Collaboration via coaching and consulting sessions can push teachers toward shared responsibility for assessment.
7.	ESL teachers must be part of a content area or interdisciplinary team.

References

Abedi, J. (2001). *Assessment and accommodations for English language learners: Issues and recommendations*. Los Angeles: National Center for Research on Evaluation, Standards and Student Testing.

Ainsworth, L. (2003). *Unwrapping the standards: A simple process to make standards manageable*. Denver, CO: Advanced Learning Press.

August, D., & Pease-Alvarez, L. (1996). *Attributes of effective programs and classrooms serving English language learners*. Santa Cruz, CA: National Center for Research on Cultural Diversity and Second Language Learning.

Bandura, A. (1971). *Social learning theory*. New York: General Learning Press.

Boals, T. (2001). *Academic assessment of limited English proficient (LEP) students in an era of accountability: A review of the literature*. Madison: Department of Public Instruction of Wisconsin.

Butler, F. A., & Stevens, R. (2001). Standardized assessment of the content knowledge of English language learners K–12: Current trends and old dilemmas. *Language Testing*, 18, 409–427.

Carr, J., & Lagunoff, R. (2006). *The map of standards for English learners, 6–12: Integrating instruction and assessment of English language development and English language arts standards in California*. San Francisco: WestEd.

Chamot, A., & O'Malley, M. (1996). *CALLA: Cognitive academic language learning approach*. New York: Longman.

Costa, A., & Garmston, R. (1994). *Cognitive coaching: A foundation for renaissance schools*. Norwood, MA: Christopher-Gordon.

Cummins, J. (1981). The role of primary language development in promoting educational success for language minority students. In California State Department of Education (Ed.), *Schooling and language minority students: A theoretical framework* (pp. 3–49). Los Angeles: California State University, Los Angeles, National Evaluation, Dissemination, and Assessment Center.

Cummins, J. (1986). Empowering minority students: A framework for intervention, *Harvard Educational Review, 56*(1), 18–36.

Darling-Hammond, L. (1994). Performance-based assessment and educational equity. *Harvard Educational Review, 64*(1), 5–30.

Dieckmann, J., & Montemayor, A. (2004, January). Planning for English language learner success. *IDRA Newsletter.* Retrieved July 25, 2007, from http://www.idra .org/IDRA_Newsletters/January_2004_Self_-_Renewing_Schools_Bilingual _Education/Planning_for_English_Language_Learner_Success/

Echevarria, J., Vogt, M., & Short, D. (2004). *Making content comprehensible for English learners: The SIOP model.* New York: Allyn & Bacon.

Fullan, M. (2001). *Leading in a culture of change.* San Francisco: Jossey-Bass.

Gottlieb, M. (2006). *Assessing English language learners: Bridges from language proficiency to academic achievement.* Thousand Oaks, CA: Corwin Press.

Hakuta, K. (1990). Language and cognition in bilingual children. In A. M. Padilla, H. H. Fairchild, & C. M. Valadez (Eds.), *Bilingual education: Issues and strategies* (pp.47–59). Newbury Park, CA: Sage.

Indiana Department of Education. (2003). *Indiana English Proficiency Standards.* Indianapolis: Author.

Krashen, S. (1985). *The input hypothesis: Issues and implications.* New York: Longman.

LaCelle-Peterson, M., & Rivera, C. (1994). Is it real for all kids? A framework for equitable assessment policies for English language learners. *Harvard Educational Review, 64*(1), 55–75.

Langer, G. M, Colton, A. B., & Goff, L. S. (2003). *Collaborative analysis of student work.* Alexandria, VA: Association for Supervision and Curriculum Development.

Majercak, J. (2004). *Template for integrating ELP and content standards.* Unpublished handout.

Marzano, R. J. (2000). *Transforming classroom grading.* Alexandria, VA: Association for Supervision and Curriculum Development.

McDonald, J. P., Mohr, N., Dichter, A., & McDonald, E. C. (2003). *The power of protocols: An educator's guide to better practice.* New York: Teachers College Press.

Morita-Mullaney, T. (2004). *ESL coaching vs. consulting: An action research project.* Unpublished manuscript.

O'Malley, M., & Valdez Pierce, L. (1996). *Authentic assessment for English language learners.* New York: Addison-Wesley.

Reeves, D. (2002). *A leader's guide to standards: A blueprint for educational equity and excellence.* San Francisco: Jossey-Bass.

Schlechty, P. (2002). *Working on the work: An action plan for teachers, principals and superintendents.* San Francisco: Jossey-Bass.

Short, D. (1993). Assessing integrated language and content instruction. *TESOL Quarterly, 27,* 627–656.

Smith, F. (1998). *The book of learning and forgetting.* New York: Stenhouse.

Thomas, W., & Collier, V. (2002). *A national study of school effectiveness for language minority students' long term academic achievement.* Santa Cruz, CA and Washington, DC: Center for Research on Education, Diversity and Excellence.

Tomlinson, C. (2001). *How to differentiate instruction in mixed-ability classrooms.* Alexandria, VA: Association for Supervision and Curriculum Development.

Wormelli, R. (2006). *Fair isn't always equal: Assessing and grading in the differentiated classroom.* Portland, ME: Stenhouse.

CHAPTER 6

Assessment of English Language Learners With Disabilities

Content Area and Special Education Teacher Collaboration in English Language Learner Identification and Assessment

Michael W. Dunn and Trenia Walker

CASE STUDY

Goldstone High School is located in an urbanized area of the northwestern United States. The school is located in a district that has a total enrollment of between 30,000 and 35,000 students, yet only 1% of students are considered to be English language learners (ELLs). Due to the low number of ELLs, the district only employs between five and eight ESL teachers to service all schools in the district. In an inclusive classroom, this often means that a special education teacher must provide assistance to ELLs along with students who have learning disabilities (LDs).

Mr. Carson's ninth-grade civics class is an inclusive classroom with a sufficient level of academic need and number of students with identified LDs to merit having a special education teacher in the classroom. Ms. Trahan, the special education teacher, is also able to help Abdullah, an immigrant who arrived from eastern Africa 2 years earlier. Abdullah and his immediate family members spoke very little, if any, English upon their arrival in the United States. Although the use of a special education teacher to assess ELLs is not ideal, Ms. Trahan has 5 years of experience working with ELLs and is considered reliable and informed in the appropriate assessment and placement of ELLs.

Prereading Questions

- What are the defining characteristics of students who are English language learners versus English language learners with learning disabilities?

- How are English language learners with learning disabilities identified?

- What does the collaboration between Ms. Trahan and Mr. Carson look like? Does it lead to the appropriate classification of Abdullah?

WHAT ARE THE DEFINING CHARACTERISTICS OF STUDENTS WHO ARE ENGLISH LANGUAGE LEARNERS VERSUS ENGLISH LANGUAGE LEARNERS WITH LEARNING DISABILITIES?

The task of defining ELLs who may also have a learning disability is a challenge that the special education community struggles to clarify. Ms. Trahan, who is both a special education teacher and an ESL teacher, is charged with the responsibility of making the distinction clear for everyone working with Abdullah and, more important, for Abdullah himself. In that regard, Ms. Trahan, like others who are responsible for both ELLs and students with LDs, has to keep in mind three categories of students: (a) non-ELLs with learning disabilities, (b) ELLs without learning disabilities, and (c) ELLs with learning disabilities. In the third case, when a student is an ELL and has a learning disability, appropriate assessment is more difficult.

This chapter focuses on factors for special education teachers to consider in assessing an inclusive classroom of ELLs and students with LDs. The discussion is based on practices in the Riverview School District in Vancouver, Washington, including the joint efforts made by a social studies teacher and a special education teacher to appropriately assess and assist an ELL.

How Are Students With Learning Disabilities Identified in This District?

The Individuals with Disabilities Education Improvement Act of 2004 (IDEA, 2004) defines federal guidelines and provides partial funding for the education of students with disabilities; the 2004 reauthorization includes an increased focus on early identification of disabilities. One method that is being considered in this district as a means to assess for LDs is *response to intervention* (RTI; Gresham, 2002).

In RTI, a student struggling with literacy skills is considered as possibly having an LD if he or she is dually discrepant, that is, he or she has low achievement levels, and makes little or no progress in a three-tiered intervention program. In the first tier, students participate in reading instruction activities that are similar to those used with students generally across the nation (Fuchs, Mock, Morgan, & Young, 2003). Each student's rate of reading growth is evaluated periodically throughout the year. A student who is dually discrepant is designated as possibly having a learning disability. This student moves to the second tier in the RTI process, in which progress monitoring is conducted again—this time in a small-group or individual instructional format. The aim of the second tier is twofold: (a) to prevent reading difficulty by delivering a more intensive intervention that improves reading development and (b) to assess the level of responsiveness to intensive instruction from which most students should improve. If progress occurs, the student returns to the regular classroom program and is no longer viewed as dually discrepant. If the student does not make appreciable progress over time, an intrinsic deficit is implied. Failure to improve at the second tier of instruction indicates the need for the third and final RTI tier: special education placement following a condensed special education evaluation (Donovan & Cross, 2002; Fuchs et al., 2003; Heller, Holtzman, & Messick, 1982).

How Are English Language Learners Identified in This District, and Why Is Proper Identification Critical?

In the Riverview School District, ELLs undergo two placement tests: the Comprehensive Inventory of Basic Skills (Brigance, 1999) and the Washington Language Proficiency Test (WLPT; Washington Office of Superintendent of Public Instruction, 2006). The assessments reveal a gradient of English language ability within the ELL population that can often be directly related to the students' various backgrounds. Some students may be born in countries other than the United States and speak languages other than English at home, some may attend English language schools for years before coming to the United States, and some may come to the United States with some formal instruction in their first language (L1) but not in English. This education may have been very different from U.S. education, so it may be difficult for the student to adjust to a new style of education. In other situations, such as that of Abdullah's, formal education in his native country may not have been available or accessible. Further complicating the situation is that some ELLs, like other students, come from low-income families and have parents who work long hours, which increases the complexity of the task of learning at school (Catts & Kamhi, 2005). The descriptions above are by no means comprehensive, but they do provide a view of the great diversity of educational and linguistic backgrounds of ELLs within the district.

When ELLs demonstrate great difficulty with academic tasks, the question of the presence of an LD can be posed. There is awareness in the teaching profession that it can take 5 to 7 years for an ELL to attain academic English skills (Chamot & O'Malley, 1994; Cummins, 2000). Thus, the idea of identifying a student with a disability in the early elementary grades is problematic. Yet the earlier students' academic difficulties are identified and addressed, the less pronounced their skill deficits are by middle and high school (Lyon et al., 2001). As with all districts, Riverview School District encounters situations in which some ELLs are prematurely referred for special education services and are consequently classified as having an LD. This leads to an overrepresentation of ELLs in special education classes, a situation that is attested to in many studies. For example, Wilkinson, Ortiz, Robertson, and Kushner (2006) found that Spanish-speaking ELLs were receiving special education support in reading because they had been referred for assessment of an LD without proper attention being paid to factors such as documentation of general education interventions, sufficient attendance at school, and other prereferral intervention practices. This could easily happen in a school like Goldstone, where lack of ELL services could lead to incorrect referrals of ELLs. Fortunately for Abdullah, the experience and expertise of Ms. Trahan, as well as the collaboration between Ms. Trahan and Mr. Carson, played a significant role in helping to steer him toward the type of education he deserved.

HOW ARE ENGLISH LANGUAGE LEARNERS WITH LEARNING DISABILITIES IDENTIFIED?

Students who are ELLs are distinctly different from students with LDs, yet certain cases in which persistent difficulties with language skills are involved may indicate that a student's difficulties are due to both being an ELL and having an LD. IDEA (2004) states that ELLs should be excluded from LD identification; however, school teams receive referrals in which language difficulty appears to be attributable to something beyond having an L1 other than English. This happens when the following factors are present:

- Ability/achievement discrepancy: Based on observation of what the student comprehends and does in class, he or she appears to have ability, but has difficulty actually demonstrating that knowledge when asked, even in a conversational format.

- Processing difficulties: Part of the theoretical model of LD is that these students do not process information the way normally achieving students do. There is no specific assessment to test for this characteristic. Rather, teachers may make conclusions about behavior and peer relationships noticed over time, which indicate processing difficulties of the student in question.

- Expressive (oral language and writing) and receptive (reading and listening comprehension) difficulties in both the student's L1 and English.

- Difficulties with reading in both the student's L1 and English.

When these factors are present, teachers are asked to consider them carefully in conjunction with input from all involved with the student in order to facilitate an informed decision about possible classification.

The imperative to address students' needs at an early point in school is often in conflict with the need to allow language proficiency to develop before assessing a student as having an LD. As previously mentioned, it can take ELLs 5 to 7 years to develop academic English language skills (Chamot & O'Malley, 1994; Cummins, 2000). Theoretically, an ELL could participate in middle and high school programming for 6 years and not know if he or she has an LD until adulthood—long after the opportunity for public school remediation has passed. Therefore, it is imperative to define at the earliest point in a student's life whether special education services are needed (Lyon et al., 2001) while allowing for typical language difficulties that ELLs face. Given the situation, it is also imperative that ESL, content area, and special education teachers collaborate to help differentiate ELLs who are experiencing natural language acquisition development from those with special needs.

How Can ESL Teachers, Special Education Teachers, Content Area Teachers, and Parents Collaborate to Appropriately Diagnose English Language Learners With Learning Disabilities?

Given that most students who are referred by their classroom teachers for assessment of a possible LD have a high likelihood of being formally identified as having an LD, the power of the classroom teacher to make the initial referral and the subjectivity of that process should be considered (Thurlow, Christenson, & Ysseldyke, 1983; Ysseldyke & Algozzine, 1981; Ysseldyke, Algozzine, Regan, & McGue, 1981). The classroom teacher's evaluation can have immediate and long-term implications. For a general education classroom teacher, the difficulty of distinguishing the characteristics that separate an ELL who has a possible LD from an ELL who does not makes the task exceedingly challenging. Collaboration between teachers becomes very important when making proper diagnoses because a great deal of information is needed to make a correct assessment.

A team of teachers, in contrast to an individual teacher, can provide and consider a more comprehensive set of information. The information could include a student's background experiences, home life, personal interests, and strengths and weaknesses across the different subject areas and how these factors relate to academic performance. A team of teachers, because of the broader view of the students who are accessible to them through their combined knowledge of the students, can more likely prevent the premature referral of students such as Abdullah, whose primary challenge is due to limited exposure to schooling and instruction in English. Although categorically denying an ELL for referral should not be accepted practice, the referral should be considered as a last option if the student's difficulties are pronounced. The referral should also be considered if a student's difficulty cannot be attributed to other contextual factors (Wilkinson et al. , 2006) such as those that could emerge if two principal questions are asked: Can the student read and write in his or her L1? Can the stress of a new culture, language, and learning environment be provoking the difficulty with academics and cause the difficulties to appear worse than they really are?

To gather the appropriate background information, collaboration must exist between teachers. The team of teachers must also be able to centrally record questions and problems, such as students' current levels of performance and other extenuating factors, that remain after educational interventions. Doing so would enable teachers to make informed and unified decisions about ELLs so that their misclassification as students with LDs can be avoided, as it is unethical for the students, the family, the school, and the education system to incorrectly identify students as having a disability when it is not warranted. To facilitate a fair and judicious process, multidisciplinary school teams need to work together.

WHAT DOES THE COLLABORATION BETWEEN MS. TRAHAN AND MR. CARSON LOOK LIKE? DOES IT LEAD TO THE APPROPRIATE CLASSIFICATION OF ABDULLAH?

As mentioned in the case study, Abdullah is a student in Mr. Carson's ninth-grade civics class who speaks little English. Ms. Trahan is the special education teacher assigned to the room as well as the designated ESL teacher for the one ELL, Abdullah. These two teachers coteach, focusing on making the civics instruction accessible to students of varying abilities in the same classroom (Dettmer, Thurston, & Dyck, 1993). Together they address the three major components of coteaching: planning, instruction, and assessment. The planning component included a joint agreement early in the school year to become more knowledgeable about the geography, history, and political situation in Abdullah's home country so that they could share the information with other students in the class. Also, because of their joint concern for Abdullah, the teachers decided to collaborate in advocating for him and identifying ways to assist him in realizing his potential.

Mr. Carson and Ms. Trahan's class was one of the classes periodically observed by the district's special education teacher candidates as a part of a teacher education training program. In their observations of the classroom, the candidates saw that neither teacher dominated nor led the class in a direction that the other partner was not expecting. It is critical for this balance to exist because ESL and special education teachers are often misconceived as service providers to content teachers. Mr. Carson and Ms. Trahan worked with an administrator to schedule a common planning time, and they continually asked two questions during that time, which has been a key element to their success as partners: Is what we're doing working for us? Is it good for the students?

In the case of Abdullah, the teachers provided him with activities in the classroom to dialogue with peers about topics, to participate in small-group discussions, and to contribute to group writing assignments. When reading was required, Mr. Carson or Ms. Trahan would paraphrase the content and have Abdullah note key vocabulary in his notebook. The nature of topics in the civics class provided for this highly interactive learning of academic material.

Collaborating to Adjust Referral

Abdullah was referred by the English teacher, Mrs. Fitzgerald, in January of his ninth-grade school year, to the in-school academic support (ISAS) team for consideration for special education services due to possibly being dually discrepant. Mr. Carson and Ms. Trahan received the referral notice and made plans to join Abdullah's other teachers in this discussion about next steps. The ISAS team was scheduled to meet on a Thursday during lunch to discuss Abdullah's case. Mrs. Fitzgerald commented about Abdullah's low reading ability. She had administered the Slosson Oral Reading Test (Slosson & Nicholson, 1994), a series of word lists organized by grade level, which can be administered in about 3 minutes and provides a quick gauge of a student's oral decoding ability. Abdullah's score was 2.4 (second grade, fourth month). However, she noticed that he was able to contribute in small-group discussions. To accommodate for his low English literacy skills, Mrs. Fitzgerald offered Abdullah oral tests and quizzes. Mr. Veinot, Abdullah's math teacher, commented that Abdullah was having real difficulty. While the civics class facilitated a very communicative format for class activities and assignments, math terminology and word problems posed a serious challenge for Abdullah. Mrs. Tate, Abdullah's chemistry teacher, was not able to attend, but the ISAS team agreed that he was probably experiencing similar difficulties in science as he was in math. Because regular education programming (tier one of the RTI conceptual model discussed earlier) with accommodations did not appear to be addressing Abdullah's academic needs, Mr. Carson and Ms. Trahan suggested that they follow up by having a meeting with Abdullah and his parents in order to create an intervention plan for him (a tier-two RTI intervention to explore the possibility of an underlying disability). The ISAS team would reconvene in one week. In the meantime, Ms. Trahan would send Mrs. Tate an e-mail including the notes from the meeting and notice of the group reconvening the following Thursday.

Ms. Trahan and Mr. Carson quickly took action after the meeting and worked together to gather information regarding Abdullah so that they could decide on appropriate teaching interventions. They collaborated to identify and implement interventions that could help in distinguishing ELLs who are struggling with second language acquisition from those who have learning disabilities. Furthermore, Wilkinson et al. (2006) suggest that there needs to be documentation of the interventions used to help the ELLs improve before consideration for special education services should be formally considered. Also, an extensive review of all documentation and people involved with the student both at school and at home must be completed before the student can be referred for special education services.

Gathering Information and Garnering Parental Support

Mr. Carson and Ms. Trahan met after school to review Abdullah's scholastic record, including all assessment information to date. The previous year's teachers found him pleasant and cooperative. He appeared to understand much of what was presented and spoken to him, but expressive language (oral language and writing) posed an ongoing challenge. With accommodations in the classroom such as modified assignments and oral tests, Abdullah attained passing grades in seventh grade, and his eighth-grade year produced similar teacher remarks and grades. In physical education, he got an A.

Mr. Carson and Ms. Trahan then consulted with Abdullah's parents. This is a key step in the assessment process in terms of attaining up-to-date information about a student's language skills in the home, or L1 environment. His family gave the following report about Abdullah's early years: They had come to know a group of humanitarian workers while living in Africa. It was this organization that had arranged for Abdullah's family to come to Vancouver so that they could help teach African languages and provide social-customs training for U.S. citizens planning to work in African countries. Given their involvement with the humanitarian workers, the parents had learned some English. However, at home with Abdullah, they spoke mostly in the L1. Because the family had lived in a remote rural area, Abdullah's schooling had been noncontinuous; consequently, he was unable to read and write in his L1.

Mr. Carson asked the parents about Abdullah's home life in Vancouver. The parents described Abdullah as a quiet boy who was very helpful at home with cleaning, cooking, and yard work. They also explained that one of the neighbors was a police officer; he had shown Abdullah the police car and functions of the car's computer and communications systems. Last year for career day at Abdullah's school, this police officer had come to the school to speak to the students. They said that Abdullah was fascinated with policing. They told Mr. Carson and Ms. Trahan that Abdullah had also developed a group of friends in the community with whom he liked to play soccer. He often commented that he liked school, given the variety of experiences and people with whom he could interact. Nevertheless, the parents went on to say that many of the tasks at school posed a challenge for Abdullah, and he was becoming more frustrated as time passed. They felt that Abdullah knew far more than he could express by speaking and writing. They also commented that he sometimes did not seem to understand everything, even in his L1.

Through an interpreter, Ms. Trahan and Mr. Carson discussed with the parents the next steps the school would take in helping Abdullah. The purposes of this discussion were to allay the parents' fears that their son would be neglected and, more important, to create buy-in as well as support for the teachers to undertake the interventions. Ms. Trahan and Mr. Carsen indicated to Abdullah's parents that they were going to gather from and share information with his teachers so that everybody would have a complete profile of Abdullah's academic progress.

Additionally, the parents were informed that before any interventions were made, Abdullah would be given two tests so that baseline information about him would be available for comparison: the WLPT and the Comprehensive Inventory of Basic Skills. The WLPT involves listening, reading, writing, writing conventions, and speaking subtests. Mr. Carson and Ms. Trahan described to Abdullah's parents the intervention types:

- Radio reading: This activity is derived from Crawley and Merritt's (2004) extensive lists of intervention ideas for students having difficulty with reading skills. Mr. Carson and Ms. Trahan would provide Abdullah with audio books to help improve his reading sight vocabulary and oral reading fluency skills. Both teachers would consistently spend 10 minutes a day providing Abdullah with the opportunity to repeatedly hear a story/chapter and vocalize the sentences along with the voice recording. Ms. Trahan, Mr. Carson, or a peer tutor in the class would ask Abdullah to retell the story in his own words and answer questions relating to the story's structure (see Table 1).

- High-interest/low-vocabulary textbook version: To help Abdullah study the Civic Engagement unit, Abdullah would use the high-interest/low-vocabulary version of the textbook, which reduces both the amount of text per page and the difficult vocabulary. The text also has a CD-ROM, which would give Abdullah the opportunity to listen to the text outside of class and at home. (For additional information on high-interest/low-vocabulary books and free activity sheets, see Tea Leaf Press, n.d.) Ms. Trahan and Mr. Carson noted that Abdullah's interest in policing

Table 1. Getting at a story's structure: WWW, W = 2, H = 2 Questions

W, W, W	Who is the main character?
	Who else is in the story?
	When/where does the story take place?
W = 2	What do the main character and other characters do or want to do?
	What happens when the main character and/or other characters do or try to do it?
H = 2	How does the story end?
	How do the main character and other characters feel?

Source: adapted from Graham & Harris, 2005

would be a great match for this unit, and they could include the police work in their discussions with him.

- Assistive technology software: To assist Abdullah with reading handouts, notes, texts, computer files, or Web sites, he would be taught to use Kurzweil 3000 (2000), an assistive technology software program that reads text on the computer screen to the student. The program would help Abdullah access aurally the information provided in the classroom and would help support his developing English reading skills.

- Interactive and multimedia assistance with composing written text: While assessing Abdullah orally, the teachers would also provide interactive means to support Abdullah in developing writing skills. They would use the ask, reflect, text (ART) strategy. The first step in the strategy is the review of the question prods identified as WWW, W = 2, H = 2 questions (Graham & Harris, 2005). After considering the answers, Abdullah would draw, paint, or sculpt from play dough to illustrate the components of the story. After presenting the story ideas in art form, Abdullah would write or type the text with the use of a computer. This strategy provides a preplanning stage in which Abdullah could illustrate his ideas before generating text. To assist with writing the actual text, Abdullah would also be provided with the option of using CoWriter:SOLO (1992) writing-assistance software. With a word-processing program such as Microsoft Word, this application appears along the bottom of the computer's monitor to assist with word choices. The application can also read the words aloud.

- Oral assessment: Since writing has continually posed a challenge for Abdullah because of his limited experience with formal writing, Ms. Trahan and Mr. Carson would provide him with an oral assessment while other students complete written tests. Given the written expectations at the high school level, Abdullah would need more time to develop composing strategies in order to be able to begin composing text. To give him that time, the two teachers would utilize oral assessment during the first 5 weeks of the interventions.

Ms. Trahan and Mr. Carson were planning to use multimodal and differentiated approaches to assist Abdullah in learning language and content. He would be given the opportunity to engage in learning and to access information in various formats that address several aspects of his multiple intelligences and his interests. Abdullah's parents were impressed with these ideas to help him improve his academic skills. Mr. Carson and Ms. Trahan stated that they would keep the parents updated every 2 weeks about Abdullah's progress.

Implementation Approaches

Ms. Trahan and Mr. Carson planned to implement the interventions in their own classroom and in their colleagues' classrooms. In their own classroom, they first considered three variations of coteaching models available at Gladstone between the special education/ELL teacher and the content area teacher: (a) teaching alongside the general education teacher (parallel teaching), (b) working with a small group of students in the special education classroom while the general education teacher teaches the remainder of the class (one teaching/one helping), and (c) the special education/ELL teacher operating a pull-out resource room program. Mr. Carson and Ms. Trahan preferred the parallel teaching model that would enable them to equally rotate among small groups in the class, as this was their established practice. As they moved from one group to another, Mr. Carson and Ms. Trahan took turns working individually with Abdullah on the intervention activities.

To advocate for the use of the interventions in their colleagues' classrooms, Mr. Carson and Ms. Trahan attended the ISAS team meeting about Abdullah the following Thursday as planned. All of his teachers were present. Mr. Carson and Ms. Trahan discussed the results of their review of Abdullah's school record, past assessment results, the parent meeting earlier that week, and their suggested intervention ideas. Mrs. Fitzgerald posed a question about the intervention's timeline, and Ms. Trahan indicated that it was 5 weeks, in accordance with the Washington state guidelines. All of Abdullah's teachers chose to undertake the interventions 10 days after the meeting. Additionally, also in accordance with state guidelines, the teachers collected progress-monitoring data. Progress monitoring involves measuring student progress not only with periodic formative and summative assessments such as unit quizzes and tests, but also with daily measurements of progress—commonly referred to as curriculum-based measurement (CBM). (For a thorough discussion of CBM, see Curriculum-Based Measurement Warehouse, n.d.)

Lessons Learned and Next Steps

In math, Kurzweil 3000 helped Abdullah with his ability to hear the word problems (multiple times, if he wished). He found writing numbers on paper easier than writing words. He could use the computer to type his answers if he wished. Mr. Veinot provided Abdullah with a peer tutor to help explain vocabulary when needed. Mrs. Fitzgerald used the oral reading assessment described previously along with the WWW, W = 2, H = 2 questions to assess reading comprehension. Kurzweill 3000 and Co:Writer SOLO made a significant difference for Abdullah in English class as well as in science. To type science experiments, Abdullah found CoWriter:SOLO to be essential; his terminology may not have been as elaborate as that of the other students, but Mrs. Tate could see substantial progress during the 5 weeks.

At the end of the fifth week, all of the ISAS team members reconvened to consider the progress-monitoring/CBM results. The school psychologist joined the group to offer insight. Due to Abdullah's progress during the 5-week intervention, he was no longer considered as dually discrepant (low academic skills and little/no progress over time). As a result of this intensive strategy instruction, Abdullah's difficulty with processing language was less pronounced. He had demonstrated his ability to make progress, which indicated that no underlying disability was present. These strategies would be continued given the degree to which Abdullah benefited. Abdullah's parents were very pleased with his progress and with the fact that he would not need further identification or special education placement at that time. The processing problem noted by his parents had not made itself evident in terms of interventions and assessments. The teachers valued the new strategies and their own availability to assist other students who needed assistance. The interventions were appropriate for an ELL like Abdullah because they directly addressed his academic needs in a practical way.

Nevertheless, lingering questions remained after the successful collaboration between Ms. Trahan, Mr. Carson, and their colleagues to assist Abdullah. These questions and their responses follow:

- *Were 5 weeks sufficient to determine the nonexistence of a dual discrepancy with academic skills?* There is no definitive answer to this question given that response to intervention is a new conceptual assessment model. In intervention research, a minimum timeline to determine the effectiveness of an intervention is 25 days, one hour per day. Reading Recovery (Clay, 2002), a first-grade literacy skills intervention program, uses a 12- to 20-week timeline (30 minutes per day). Some states and districts provide no timeline at all, resulting in some schools considering a tier-three intervention assessment for classification after 3 years; however, to provide an informative and timely assessment, this may be too long. While the student is receiving the benefit of a targeted intervention during this 3-year period, there should be a point long before the completion of 3 years when the ISAS team can feel confident that an underlying disability is present, warranting consideration for long-term classification and placement.

- *How does one exactly define dual discrepancy?* Though generally it is defined as low ability and little/no progress over time, these are conceptual terms that, like the issue of a timeline, have no definitive agreed-upon answer; for example, one cannot universally define how much progress is "little" progress. The essential component in considering whether a student continues to be dually discrepant is whether or not progress has been made during the intervention. If even a small amount of progress has been made, does that indicate the student's capability to improve given that no special education services have yet been provided? Each ISAS team's student case data will need to be reviewed to determine whether or not the team agrees that the student has made progress.

- *If Abdullah's assessment had resulted in a dual discrepancy following the 5-week intervention, would he then be immediately assessed for a tier-three intervention?* As the practice of intervention becomes more widely implemented, there seems to be a growing preference for two or more intervention attempts before moving on to tier three. If Abdullah had not made progress, the team could have considered other interventions from the intervention/assessment Web sites and books mentioned previously.

- *Why not provide Abdullah with an intensive one-on-one intervention with a paraprofessional, literacy coach, or resource teacher?* RTI interventions typically occur in the regular education classroom; they are often referred to as problem-solving RTI models, which, depending on the state or district, may or may not result in official classification and placement in special education—some districts no longer officially classify students. An alternative RTI format to the classroom-based problem-solving model is the *standard protocol* approach in which, for example, students with a specific need (e.g., difficulty with reading decoding) receive a targeted intervention with one paraprofessional, literacy coach, or resource teacher (who is trained in the intervention strategy targeting the skill in question) in a resource room for 30 minutes a day. In Abdullah's case, he was comfortable in the regular classroom, and the intervention components could be implemented there without much adjustment for him or the rest of the class. For ELLs, maintaining a supportive and interactive environment facilitates their exposure to academic and functional language, which promotes their practice and use of English.

Questions for Discussion

Review the case study at the beginning of the chapter. Discuss the following questions that aim to extend the discussions included in the chapter.

1. What complications do you anticipate when the special education teacher is also the ESL teacher?

2. Goldstone's district reports that only 1% of its student population are ELLs. How are ELLs identified in your district? What is their percentage in relation to the total student population, and what services and resources are available to ELLs, given their number, in your community?

3. Abdullah and his parents speak very little English and are from Somalia, in East Africa. To your knowledge, what are the special needs of African immigrants in your district, if it contains any immigrants from that region of the world? In addressing these needs, who have you and your colleagues collaborated with, or who do you plan to collaborate with and why?

Summary of Main Ideas
1. It can take 5 to 7 years for an ESL student to attain academic English skills.
2. The reauthorization of the Individuals with Disabilities Education Improvement Act calls for an increased focus on early identification of learning disabilities—referred to as *response to intervention* (RTI).
3. ELL and special education teachers must collaborate to help differentiate between ELLs with learning disailities and ELLs who are experiencing acquisition difficulties that are part of the natural process of second language developmental stages.
4. The classroom teacher has a pivotal role in initiating special education referrals.
5. For ELLs, nomination for special education services may occur if prereferral intervention has not been successful, exclusionary factors have been considered, formal and informal assessment in the student's first language and English has been provided, a synthesis of all available student data has been compiled, families have been consulted, and an ESL teacher is included in a multidisciplinary team.

6.	At Goldstone High School there are three general coteaching arrangements:
	a) Parallel teaching: the special education teacher teaching alongside the general education teacher
	b) One teaching/one helping: the special education teacher working with a small group of students in the special education classroom while the general education teacher teaches the remainder of the class
	c) Pull out: the special education teacher operates a pull-out resource room program
7.	The collaboration between Mr. Carson and Ms. Trahan had several benefits:
	a) They had a mutual commitment to advocate for Abdullah.
	b) They developed the intervention component ideas together and displayed leadership in collaboration by taking the initiative to employ the interventions in their own classroom for Abdullah's benefit.
	c) Their collaborative example encouraged Abdullah's other content area teachers to use the same intervention components and report back with their own findings—collaboration was catching on!
	d) Finally, their collaborative effort resulted in an appropriate determination of Abdullah not being classified as having a learning disability.

References

Brigance, A. H. (1999). *Comprehensive inventory of basic skills*. North Billerica, MA: Curriculum Associates.

Catts, H., & Kamhi, A. (2005). *Language and reading disabilities* (2nd ed.). Boston: Pearson.

Chamot, A., & O'Malley, J. (1994). *The CALLA handbook*. Reading, MA: Addison-Wesley.

Clay, M. (2002). *Reading recovery: A guidebook for teachers in training*. Portsmouth, NH: Heinemann.

CoWriter: SOLO [Computer software]. (1992). Wauconda, IL: Don Johnston Developmental Equipment.

Crawley, S. J., & Merritt, K. (2004). *Remediating reading difficulties*. Boston: McGraw Hill.

Cummins, J. (2000). *Language, power, and pedagogy: Bilingual children in the crossfire*. Clevedon, England: Multilingual Matters.

Curriculum-based measurement warehouse: A world of CBM resources under one roof. (n.d.). Retrieved August 20, 2007, from http://www.interventioncentral.org/htmdocs /interventions/cbmwarehouse.php

Dettmer, P., Thurston, L., & Dyck, N. (1993). *Consultation, collaboration, and teamwork: For students with special needs*. Boston: Allyn & Bacon.

Donovan, M., & Cross, C. (2002). *Minority students in special and gifted education*. Washington, DC: National Academy Press.

Fuchs, D., Mock, D., Morgan, P., & Young, C. (2003). Responsiveness-to-instruction: Definitions, evidence, and implications for learning disabilities construct. *Learning Disabilities Research & Practice, 18*(3), 157–171.

Graham, S., & Harris, K. (2005). *Writing better: Effective strategies for teaching students with learning difficulties.* Baltimore: Paul H. Brookes.

Gresham, F. (2002). Responsiveness to intervention: An alternative approach to the identification of learning disabilities. In R. Bradley, L. Danielson, & D. Hallahan (Eds.), *Identification of learning disabilities: Response to treatment* (pp. 467–519). Mahwah, NJ: Lawrence Erlbaum.

Heller, K., Holtzman, W., & Messick, S. (1982). *Placing children in special education: A strategy for equity.* Washington, DC: National Academy Press.

Individuals with Disabilities Education Improvement Act of 2004. Public Law 108-446, 108th Congress. (December 3, 2004).

Kurzweil3000 [Computer software]. (2000). Bedford, MA: Kurzweil Educational Systems.

Lyon, G. R., Fletcher, J. M., Shaywitz, S. E., Shaywitz, B. A., Torgensen, J. K., Wood, F. B., et al. (2001). Rethinking learning disabilties. In C. E. Finn, C. R. Hokanson, & A. J. Rotherham (Eds.), *Rethinking special education for a new century* (pp. 259–287). Washington, DC: Thomas B. Fordham Foundation.

Slosson, R. L., & Nicholson, N. L. (1994). *Slosson oral reading test—revised (SORT-R).* Columbia, MO: Hawthorne Educational Services.

Thurlow, M., Christenson, S., & Ysseldyke, J. (1983). *Referral research: An integrative summary of findings.* Minneapolis, MN: University of Minneapolis.

Tea Leaf Press. (n.d.). *Reviews.* Retrieved August 20, 2007, from http://www.tealeaf-press.com/reviews.html

Washington Office of Superintendent of Public Instruction. (2006). *Washington Language Proficiency Test.* Retrieved October 30, 2006, from http://www.k12.wa.us/assessment/WLPTII/default.aspx

Wilkinson, C. Y., Ortiz, A. A., Robertson, P. M., & Kushner, M. I. (2006). English language learners with reading-related LD: Linking data from multiple sources to make eligibility determinations. *Journal of Learning Disabilities, 39*(2), 129–141.

Ysseldyke, J., & Algozzine, B. (1981). Diagnostic classification decisions as a function of referral information. *Journal of Special Education, 15,* 429–435.

Ysseldyke, J., Algozzine, B., Regan, R., & McGue, M. (1981). The influence of test scores and naturally occurring pupil characteristics on psycho-educational decision making with children. *Journal of School Psychology, 19,* 167–177.

CHAPTER 7

Community

Collaborating to Develop Partnerships With Parents and the Wider School Community

Thomas H. Levine and George C. Bunch

---(**CASE STUDY**)---

Bethune-Chavez Academy's six teachers are splayed across floor pillows and chairs. Sunlight filters through tall pines, lighting the large open cabin where the group is holding its summer retreat. The easy banter and earnest discussions that filled this space earlier in the day give way to a purposeful quiet. The teachers are each writing in response to an important question: What are the things we will do that will make a difference?

All of these teachers, save the new biology teacher, Jennifer, worked at Liberty High School last year. They are familiar with key challenges of working at a large comprehensive school in the inner city: high dropout rates; low attendance; limited school resources; cross-cultural misunderstandings and mistrust between school staff and the Latino, African American, and Asian American families that send their students to the school; and the need to adapt instruction to support content mastery and language acquisition for the 38% of students whom the state categorizes as English language learners (ELLs).

These teachers do not seem daunted by these challenges as they prepare to "make a difference" by opening a new, autonomous, small school on the campus of Liberty. The group will do some things differently this year as they break away from a large, impersonal high school. First, every student will have an academic advisor, a staff member who will get to know them through various activities during the week. Second, each advisor will become the primary point of communication with an advisee's family, with the hope of developing a two-way flow of communication and trust. Third, in joining the school, both teachers and students understand that every family will be visited by one teacher, sometimes accompanied by a bilingual interpreter. Finally, teachers have agreed to teach the equivalent of four classes of 32 students rather than five somewhat smaller classes, as would be required at Liberty. By carefully managing their school budget, teachers will have a period of daily release time that they will use to contact families; to work on curriculum; and three times a week, to collaborate.

The teachers finish their freewriting. Jennifer shares her answer first. "I think everything we're going to do will make a difference—it's such a new model!" she says.

Diane, the ESL teacher, goes next. "What's really going to make a difference for me is teacher support and administrative support, knowing that you've got my back," she declares. Rebecca, the special education teacher, agrees. "Team work," James echoes.

On paper, these teachers' plans and commitment to teamwork comprise a promising approach to working with traditionally underserved students and families, including those with home languages other than English. Will working as an intensive, ongoing community of teachers help these professionals overcome barriers of language, mistrust, and differing values to connect with and involve the school community? Will the involvement of teachers with each other, with parents, and with other partners in the school community make a difference for the teaching and learning of ELLs at the school?[1]

Prereading Questions

- What is teacher professional community?
- How does teacher professional community matter for the teaching and learning of English language learners?
- How do families and community organizations matter for teaching and learning in schools?
- What are traditional views on how parents and the community should be involved in students' education? How do teachers need to rethink these views when working with language minority families?
- What can teachers do to develop trust, communication, and collaboration with language minority families?
- What does collaboration between content area teachers and ESL teachers look like in one real-life setting? How does such collaborative work help teachers partner with parents and the wider school community in this setting?

This chapter is about two kinds of communities that matter for the teaching and learning of ELLs: the professional community that exists among both mainstream and ESL teachers responsible for instructing English language learners and the broader school community, including students' families. These are the key messages of this chapter:

---

[1] *Regarding the cases in this chapter*: The first author of this chapter observed collaboration and teaching among both ninth grade-teams of teachers described in this chapter and did not play a role himself in contributing to their work or professional development. The second author, while not involved in the original research, contributed to the chapter by providing expertise regarding the pedagogical and sociocultural contexts of working with linguistically diverse students and their families and communities.

- Building a more collaborative professional community requires patience, intentional effort, and an openness to learn from others; the results can improve the teaching and learning of ELLs.

- Collaboration between ESL teachers and content area teachers can facilitate access to rigorous curriculum and promote learning opportunities for ELLs.

- Collaborating with language minority families and communities requires patience, intentional effort, and an openness to learn from others; the results can improve the teaching and learning of ELLs.

- Building a more collaborative professional community inside schools helps teachers build stronger partnerships with families and communities outside of schools.

WHAT IS TEACHER PROFESSIONAL COMMUNITY?

All schools have teacher professional community. It comprises the norms, attitudes, and practices that teachers develop together and which guide how teachers relate to colleagues and students. Norms are unstated rules or typical patterns that guide behavior among a group of people. Most groups develop a set of norms regarding what individuals do or don't do with each other, such as how they talk or what they discuss when they are together. Research on teacher communities has found that in most schools, teachers' relationships with their colleagues are governed by norms of privacy, autonomy, noninterference, and harmony (Achinstein, 2002; Little, 1990; Lortie, 1975; McLaughlin & Talbert, 2001). Teachers avoid discussions that would reveal too much of their own teaching. They also avoid discussion likely to provoke conflict or suggest how others should teach.

What might lead a group of teachers to break the norms that traditionally isolate teachers? Why would they trade some of their autonomy for the opportunity to influence each other? Teachers' concerns with academic achievement as measured in testing—and with students' limited learning and progress more broadly defined—often lead them to seek each other out as they try to change what they do (McLaughlin & Talbert, 2006). Teachers' frustration with the limits of their current ability to improve students' academic achievement can spur them to join colleagues to address problems. Problems in student achievement may also show up in standardized test scores or observable student behavior, galvanizing teacher collaboration to address student needs (McLaughlin & Talbert, 2006).

HOW DOES TEACHER PROFESSIONAL COMMUNITY MATTER FOR THE TEACHING AND LEARNING OF ENGLISH LANGUAGE LEARNERS?

In school communities characterized by traditional notions of teacher autonomy and isolation, ELLs clearly do not benefit from the potential advantages of collegial collaboration. Since ESL teachers are often relegated to subordinate roles, they sometimes work at the periphery of a school's curricular and instructional efforts in the content areas. An ESL teacher may be working essentially alone, either due to the traditional notions of independence and isolation described above or because he or she is the only ESL teacher at a given school. In fact, some ESL teachers travel from school to school, teaching at each site only a few days per week or a few hours per day.

It is important, however, to consider not only the professional community and collaboration within ESL departments or within the content area departments of teachers who teach ELLs, but also the interaction and collaboration between ESL and content area teachers. Even in schools with a highly regarded and thriving community of ESL teachers, those who are responsible for teaching core content to ELLs through sheltered content classes may be sealed off from a school's community of mainstream content area teachers. Thus the collective knowledge and experience of content area specialists, who themselves may meet regularly to discuss curriculum and instruction, coplan lessons, and engage in professional development activities, do not benefit ESL teachers and their students. Reciprocally, those mainstream content area teachers responsible for educating ELLs may have little contact with ESL teachers who could be collaborators.

The potential benefits of communities of content area and ESL teachers working together are profound. ESL teachers can help content teachers understand the linguistic and social backgrounds of particular ELLs, and content teachers can help ESL teachers understand the areas in which current or former ESL students are succeeding and struggling. ESL teachers trained in sheltering instruction can offer important insight to mainstream content teachers, whose teacher education may have prepared them to teach their discipline primarily to monolingual English speakers who come from a dominant middle-class U.S. culture (Commins & Miramontes, 2006). Working together, ESL and content area teachers can unpack the linguistic demands—and language learning opportunities—inherent in instruction, assignments, and assessment. These teachers together can discuss appropriate strategies for helping students acquire academic English and succeed with tasks and texts. And ESL teachers can help content area teachers design instruction to build on students' cultural knowledge and resources. Throughout this process, ESL teachers gain access to the content knowledge, pedagogical content knowledge[2], and curricular goals in specific disciplines, so that their own efforts to promote language and content mastery are grounded in a richer and more authentic disciplinary context. At the same time, content teachers gain a larger repertoire of strategies for meeting the needs of linguistically and culturally diverse students. In sum, teachers working together can help students achieve outcomes that would be much more difficult if teachers' efforts were to continue in isolation. Ideally, these potential rewards are great enough to encourage content area and ESL teachers to yield some of their traditional autonomy over their respective domains.

Teacher professional community may also benefit ELLs by promoting teachers' health and happiness. Teachers who say that they work in cohesive and highly collegial

---

[2] Pedagogical content knowledge is the knowledge of how to teach specific disciplinary subject matter and skills and of the typical student misconceptions or difficulties that need to be addressed to succeed in teaching such subject-specific content (see Shulman, 1987).

professional communities report higher levels of commitment to teaching all students, higher levels of energy and enthusiasm, and higher levels of innovation (McLaughlin, 1993). Given the multiple challenges and stresses of working in schools, community may provide teachers with emotional support as well as intellectual resources that help them succeed. Later in the chapter, it will be shown how work within a professional community can also add stress and challenge. Nevertheless, there can be tremendous satisfaction, humor, and camaraderie in working as part of a team, sharing students, and finding common cause with others.

How Do Families and Community Organizations Matter for Teaching and Learning in Schools?

Colleagues are not the only community that matters for the teaching of ELLs. According to the U.S. Department of Education (1995), "thirty years of research make it clear: parents and families are pivotal to children's learning" (p. 19). There is evidence that parent involvement improves students' academic achievement and lowers students' dropout rates regardless of racial, cultural, or socioeconomic background (Flaxman & Inger, 1991). Parent involvement is associated with higher rates of homework completion and high school graduation (U.S. Department of Education, 1997), and specific practices to partner with parents have also been associated with a reduction in absenteeism (Epstein & Sheldon, 2002).

Parent involvement, however, generally diminishes after elementary school (Epstein, 2001). Many factors contribute to the additional challenges of sustaining parent and community involvement in the education of secondary students. Parents may be less comfortable with more advanced academic content and with the challenges of relating to adolescent children. Secondary teachers have more students than elementary teachers, and thus more parents with whom to partner. Conversely, parents often find it easier to communicate with one main elementary teacher who knows their child well rather than with a collection of teachers. In spite of these extra challenges, research shows that middle schools and high schools that implement well-designed partnership programs can help all families support their children's academic progress (Epstein, 2002).

While research has often focused on parents as primary points of contact, in many families grandparents, aunts and uncles, or other guardians may be the appropriate partners. Especially among immigrants and other language minority families, the extended family provides multiple sources of strength and resources that teachers should consider in their outreach (Inger, 1992).

Meanwhile, families are not the only members of the community with an interest in schools' work or the potential to further that work. Community organizations can be valuable partners in supporting the academic, social, physical, and cultural development of students, especially in settings where schools or families lack financial or human resources. Local businesses, social service organizations, government agencies, universities, and cultural organizations can provide expertise, resources, and opportunities for enrichment that teachers, on their own, could not provide for their students.

WHAT ARE TRADITIONAL VIEWS ON HOW PARENTS AND THE COMMUNITY SHOULD BE INVOLVED IN STUDENTS' EDUCATION? HOW DO TEACHERS NEED TO RETHINK THESE VIEWS WHEN WORKING WITH LANGUAGE MINORITY FAMILIES?

The Center on School, Family, and Community Partnerships has identified six types of involvement that are desirable and effective as part of a comprehensive program of community partnership (Epstein, 2001). The National Parent Teacher Organization has endorsed and published these categories, and they have continued to be published—with some modifications—for the past 3 decades:

1. Parenting: Teachers and schools establish programs to help all families build home environments that support children as students. Examples include workshops on relating to an adolescent son or daughter or a newsletter article about teen health.

2. Communicating: Teachers design effective, two-way forms of conveying information about class activities, school programs, and student progress. Examples include parent conferences, report cards, and phone calls from teacher to parent or parent to teacher. In most schools, teachers provide one-way communication with families informing them about a problem. More ideal but less common is communication that conveys positive accomplishments and that is truly reciprocal. This means that both partners learn from the other to inform their respective work.

3. Volunteering: Teachers recruit and organize parents as speakers, activity leaders, advisors, chaperones in extracurricular projects, and so on. An example would be a grade-level team's efforts to keep a database of parents willing to help in various ways.

4. Learning at home: Teachers provide information about how families can help students with homework or other curriculum-related activities. Examples include a summer reading list or a letter about an upcoming project and how parents can support students' work on this project.

5. Decision making: Parents can help make key decisions about policy and curriculum. Examples include active parent-teacher organizations, parental representation on committees, and surveys sent home to get input.

6. Collaborating with the community: Teachers and schools identify and integrate resources and services from the community to strengthen student learning and development. An example would be providing families with information about—or access to—community health organizations, cultural programs, or social and recreational opportunities.

As promising as these practices are, teachers' efforts to promote such involvement from language minority families may be ineffective—or even create conflict—if teachers are not aware that relationships between schools and families are impacted by complex historical, cultural, political, and linguistic factors. Teachers need to examine their own assumptions and beliefs about what constitutes effective parent participation for each of these categories of involvement, and they need to learn about how students' families may understand these issues. Teachers must be thoughtful about what roles and supports family and community can best provide and how to implement traditional categories of parental involvement in productive and culturally responsive ways.

Parenting

A school's role in supporting parenting becomes more complex when educators acknowledge that models of good parenting vary, especially across cultures (Rogoff, 2003). Valdés (1996), for example, has explored how Mexican women whose children attended U.S. schools demonstrated childrearing practices that were "grounded in deeply held views about parent-child relationships and about maternal roles in particular" (p. 139), that differ from those practiced and valued by middle-class U.S. women. For instance, dedicated Mexican mothers may do wonderful jobs teaching their children culturally specific meanings of *respect*—not bothering adults when they are busy, not speaking out of turn, not boasting or demanding attention in ways that would distract from the well-being of the family—without realizing that most middle-class U.S. mothers also teach children colors, letters, and numbers before and while they attend kindergarten. School staff may either be ignorant of such differences or may view them as deficiencies; as a result, they may misinterpret Mexican students' apparent passivity and parents' degree of interest in their children's education. Such cultural misunderstanding and misinterpretation may explain why "schools often tell parents what they must do," resulting in "a negative perception that the school is demanding and not family-friendly" (Trumbull, Rothstein-Fisch, Greenfield, & Quiroz, 2001, p. 12).

Communication

A number of language issues obviously impact efforts to foster the kinds of two-way communication advocated above. Teachers and parents may not speak a common language, in which case bilingual staff or volunteers are needed to help facilitate communication and translate school documents. In addition, families' cultural preferences regarding modes of communication may vary. For instance, face-to-face, one-on-one meetings may in some cases be a culturally appropriate way to begin a relationship, so an impersonal photocopied letter to all parents or a phone call home without previous introduction may not seem friendly. Teachers may misunderstand communication conveyed in unfamiliar ways. For example, in some immigrant families, it is quite common for children to be reliable conduits of information between adults and school personnel, a practice that might not be taken seriously by teachers accustomed to dealing directly with parents (Valdés, 1996).

When teachers communicate with parents about individual student progress, teachers may feel that they are doing what is in parents' best interest and that good parents will appreciate this. However, some language minority families, especially those from Hispanic and Asian backgrounds, may emphasize care and concern for groups like the family or fellow classmates more than for individual achievement, the primary focus of many U.S. educators (Onikama, Hammond, & Koki, 1998; Valdés, 1996). Some parents thus may feel that U.S. schools are promoting their children's self-centeredness and self-assertion while eroding respect for elders (ESCORT, 2001). It is reasonable and appropriate for educators to seek parent involvement in students' academic learning and school assignments, but educators should also ask about—and value—parents' aims for their children's development.

Volunteering

Getting parents to volunteer to come into school raises issues about whether families have the time and means to come to the school building. If teachers hope parents will volunteer in schools or attend parent conferences and open houses, they must consider immigrant families' economic situations. Families may have difficulty finding time, child care, and transportation in order to come to school to volunteer or talk on site with teachers (Sosa, 1997). Teachers also must consider whether family members would be comfortable volunteering or speaking with a teacher. Expectations and norms for parental involvement in schools vary from country to country and from culture to culture. Furthermore, parents who have had limited or negative experiences with their own schooling may not have the confidence or desire to volunteer, communicate with teachers, or participate in decision making. Differences in social class can play a role as well. Lareau (2000) has found that working-class families, while equally desirous of a quality education for their children as their upper-middle-class counterparts, are less likely to view themselves as responsible for monitoring or intervening in the academic life of their children's classrooms. Working-class parents who encounter school practices more aligned with upper-middle-class norms may feel uncomfortable in traditional parent participation activities and events. When working-class families do interact with teachers, they are less likely than middle-class families to ask questions and make requests of teachers, thus limiting their ability to influence change that might lead to improved school success for their children (Lareau, 1987).

Learning at Home

Research examining the practices of families of immigrant and other language minority youth consistently points to the fact that these families care deeply about their children's education and that a wide variety of learning activities occur inside the home (e.g., González, Moll, & Amanti, 2005; Schecter & Bayley, 2002; Valdés, 1996). However, immigrant and language minority families' beliefs about what it means to be "well educated" and how learning should be organized in the home may diverge from mainstream, middle-class U.S. ideals (de Carvalho, 2001; Pease-Alvarez, Angelillo, & Chavajay, 2005; Rogoff, 2003; Valdés, 1996).

Language minority parents may see their role as primarily one of nurturing children, and they may delegate to schools more responsibility for formal education than is often customary among middle-class Caucasian families (ESCORT, 2001; Onikama et al., 1998). Valdés (1996) found that immigrant Latino families focus less on school lives and academic performance, and more on their children's physical survival and health, their opportunities to make a living, and their enactment of core cultural values in their daily lives. For the families that Valdés studied, "prestige, intellectual achievement, and even wealth were less important than morality and family loyalty" (p. 189). This is not to say that language minority parents do not care deeply about their children's success in school. Schecter and Bailey (2002) demonstrate the wide range of ways in which immigrant and language minority families explicitly attempt to support their children's schoolwork, even when parents have very limited skills in English. In fact, in the Latino families profiled by Schecter and Bailey, "the school's agenda serves as primary organizer of the educational work of caregivers and, in particular, mothers" (p. 141). Naturally, parents who are less experienced with formal schooling in English may not understand teachers' expectations or be able to provide the kind of support desired by teachers. In this case, teachers may need to work with parents to discuss ways in which students can be supported with homework and other aspects of their formal school learning.

Decision Making

Having family and community stakeholders contribute to decision making in schools is a laudable goal. The idea of joining with a group of fellow (but unknown) citizens in civic organizations is particularly common in mainstream U.S. culture and history (de Tocqueville, 1969). The ways in which families contribute to the public good and connect with communities, however, differs considerably around the world. For example, the idea of a parent-teacher organization might be quite foreign to many families of ELLs. Once again, teachers will need to consider the traditions, experiences, and skills of potential parents when trying to construct such opportunities or support parental involvement.

Collaborating With the Community

When their efforts to include language minority parents in conferences, volunteer programs, or school decision making do not result in widespread participation, teachers often interpret this as a lack of interest or support. Teacher professional communities can thus sustain unexamined assumptions that view the homes and communities of ELLs as part of a "culture of deficit" (González et al., 2005, p. 34) or a "culture of poverty" (González et al., 2005, p. 34; Valdés, 1996, p. 17). This view puts the responsibility for students' academic achievement on their families and community resources rather than on the school. Instead of focusing on the school's failure to meet the needs of linguistic and cultural minority students, teachers sometimes shift the blame to students' home and cultural contexts, arguing that students have deficiencies in terms of knowledge, skills, attitudes, and behaviors that can only be addressed by teaching students to think and behave in ways consistent with mainstream cultural expectations (Valdés, 1996). This culture-of-deficit model lets teachers avoid looking more critically at their teaching or their efforts to collaborate with parents across language, traditions, and goals. Thinking in terms of what students lack also misses the cultural resources, dispositions, and knowledge children do bring to school and the ways in which educators might build on these.

The alternative, as suggested throughout this section, is for teachers to focus on the cultural, linguistic, and intellectual resources that students bring with them, recognizing the unique cultural capital that minority families bring to U.S. schools (Yosso, 2005). Furthermore, these families are already involved in their children's education, but in ways that might challenge teachers' assumptions about what such involvement should look like (Lopez, 2001). As teachers attempt to foster the kind of participation that is often valued in U.S. schools, they also need to build on these already-existing forms of involvement.

The following section explores strategies for reaching out to parents of secondary ELLs, challenging teachers to rethink their assumptions about parent involvement in schools, which are often based on monolingual and monocultural norms. By using these strategies, teachers are likely to learn more about the cultural resources and traditions on which they might build academic instruction. They may also experience greater success and satisfaction in their work when they allow their goals to be informed by a potentially complementary but different set of aims and hopes from parents. When teachers are true partners, willing to listen, learn, and respect as well as seek influence, family members may become key allies in promoting the academic and personal development of their children.

WHAT CAN TEACHERS DO TO DEVELOP TRUST, COMMUNICATION, AND COLLABORATION WITH LANGUAGE MINORITY FAMILIES?

Perhaps the most important step teachers can take to improve their work with language minority families is to see themselves as aiming to be equal partners with those families: to seek two-way communication, learning, and influence. Parents are not subjects to be managed, and teachers gain rather than lose influence by choosing to include parents in the process of education (Epstein et al., 2002). Some starting points are provided in this section, and resources listed at the end of the chapter provide more suggested approaches. This list progresses from strategies teachers might use on their own toward strategies that can more easily be implemented by collaborating teachers.

Find Paid or Volunteer Interpreters and Translators

One of the most basic and powerful strategies for including parents of ELLs is to find ways to communicate with them in their own language, sending a powerful message about teachers' desire to connect. When schools have difficulty finding (or paying) individuals who can help with an uncommon language, a community organization may be able to provide a volunteer translator (Moles, 1996). Often, older children from language minority families serve as bilingual interpreters between parents and school staff, which is a challenging task for youngsters but an opportunity to recognize and build on the linguistic, cultural, and intellectual skills required (Valdés, 2003). Although the use of youngsters as interpreters raises some important ethical issues, schools can recognize the linguistic talents that students utilize in these encounters, establishing programs that allow students to use their strengths in interpretation to further develop their bilingual abilities and to transfer some of these strengths to academic tasks (Valdés, 2003).

Parent Workshops

Workshops can help parents learn about the expected roles, concerns, and communication styles of U.S. teachers and can help teachers learn about parental expectations and concerns. These gatherings for newcomers and teachers can be led by other immigrant parents in a native language and translated into English (ESCORT, 2001), thus allowing teachers to understand what it is like to have to wait for the translation.

Meeting Parents Halfway in Face-to-Face Communication

When communicating face-to-face with parents whose culture and first language differ from one's own, some teachers have found it helpful to let parents voice concerns and set the agenda first before rushing in with their usual concerns and communication styles (see Trumbull et al., 2001). Teachers can also make a conscious attempt to perceive parents' body language or ask questions to understand whether parents understand and agree with what a teacher is saying.

Experiences in the Community

Teachers may find ways to participate in organizations, special events, or everyday life in the school community. The presence of "insiders," or people who can answer questions, increases the odds that such experiences will be useful rather than misinterpreted.

Home Visits, With Teachers as Learners Regarding Funds of Knowledge

Home visits, which provide direct contact with families, are a powerful way for teachers to ground their thinking about specific students and families, clarifying the resources and potential for support teachers can find in students' families. Such visits can be particularly valuable when working with parents who would traditionally be uncomfortable or mistrustful contacting teachers at school. On the other hand, home visits with little orientation for teachers could reinforce a deficit model unless teachers are prepared to engage in reciprocal communication and look for the resources that exist in families and communities. The aim is not to overlook the real challenges that students and families experience, but to recognize sources of strength and support on which teachers can draw.

For example, González et al. (2005) have helped teachers prepare interview questions they could bring into homes to stay focused on the "funds of knowledge" (p. ix) that exist in language minority families and communities. One participating teacher described the impact of such visits on a group of teachers.

> The types of information we gathered prompted us to change our perspectives of our students' homes and communities from, at best, being irrelevant to the educational process and, at worst being the cause of our students' lack of educational progress, to being rich resources for teaching and learning. (p. 14)

This teacher believed that debriefing after the home visits (making sense of them in collegial conversation back at the school) helped her make sense of what she saw and allowed what she had learned to begin informing her work with students.

Advisors or Parent Liaisons

ESL teachers are sometimes positioned well to be a liaison to parents, facilitating two-way flows of information between homes and content area teachers. A team of teachers working with the same group of students—with every student having one designated advisor—can coordinate and simplify parental communication. The cases presented in the following sections illustrate what advisors can do and how this system responds to the challenges of facilitating communication between families and multiple content area teachers in middle and high schools.

WHAT DOES COLLABORATION BETWEEN CONTENT AREA TEACHERS AND ESL TEACHERS LOOK LIKE IN ONE REAL-LIFE SETTING? HOW DOES SUCH COLLABORATIVE WORK HELP TEACHERS PARTNER WITH PARENTS AND THE WIDER SCHOOL COMMUNITY IN THIS SETTING?

To answer these questions, consider the case of Bethune-Chavez Academy (B-C). In the case study at the beginning of the chapter, B-C teachers were at the end of their summer retreat, full of hope for how their work together would make a difference. The process of starting a new small school from scratch—and of learning how to work together—proved to be more difficult than staff members had foreseen; nevertheless, by the end of the year, the staff succeeded in developing intentional structures that helped teachers in their work with ELLs and their families.

B-C is located in a major urban area in California. The student population is identified as just over two-fifths Hispanic and two-fifths African American. The majority of the remaining student body is of Asian descent. Almost three quarters of the students qualify for free or reduced-price meals, and the state identifies almost two fifths as ELLs.

The staff, with the exception of the biology teacher, Jennifer, had already taught on the campus of Liberty High School, where B-C Academy was now opening its doors. As the principal picked from among current Liberty High staff who applied to join the school, she chose a balance of veteran and new teachers, as shown in Table 1.

Table 1. Bethune-Chavez Academy teacher characteristics

Name, Subject(s) Taught	Years of Prior Teaching Experience
Diane, ESL and English	1.5
Jennifer, Biology	2.5
Rebecca, Resource/SPED	4
Zardos, Algebra	21
James, Social Studies	31
Guy, Social Studies	32

Advising

The teachers agreed on a schedule that allowed them to teach the equivalent of four classes of students during the year, with a typical class having 28 to 32 students, if all attended. In addition, teachers spent 30 minutes most days meeting with their advisees. Each student had one advisor who followed his or her academic progress, ran activities that promoted growth in social skills and study habits, and facilitated communication between the school and students' parents or guardians. This system allowed each teacher to form relationships with 17 families while relying on other teachers to communicate with families about students who were not their advisees. Teachers also conveyed an invitation for parents to visit the school at any time; some parents accepted this invitation, making planned or impromptu visits to the school.

Home Visits

All teachers, just before school started or at the beginning of the year, made home visits. The core purpose of these visits was to facilitate the building of trust, though teachers also used them as a chance to make families aware of the school's specific curriculum and expectations. One advisor said in an interview that these home visits to parents "gave us a lot of leverage before school even started; they knew a little bit of what we were about and began work on that wall of trust issues that parents and teachers have with each other."

Intentionally Structured Collaboration

When the teachers met to collaborate during school hours, they engaged in three types of activities:

1. Using protocols to prompt reflection on instruction
2. Participating in workshops that dig deeper into instructional issues
3. Sharing information about students

In the descriptions of these activities below, note how the teachers chose to intentionally structure and focus their work, creating routines and consistency that allowed them to make more progress and achieve goals that informal talk probably would not have achieved. Each type of collaboration contributed something different to the teachers' ability to work with parents and/or to improve their own instruction of ELLs.

Using Protocols to Prompt Reflection on Instruction

To deepen their work together, B-C teachers sometimes used protocols, or conversational tools, which list phases of a conversation and provide specific expectations regarding who should say what, and for how long. The critical-friends protocol described in Table 2 provides an illustration of this work.

The teachers also developed a protocol to help teachers talk about modifications for students with special needs. The protocol required attentiveness to students' strengths as well as deficiencies and to specific modifications teachers had tried or could try in their classroom.

Consider this example of how protocols helped teachers deprivatize their work

Table 2. Summary of the critical-friends protocol used at Bethune-Chavez Academy

Does What	For How Long?
Participants volunteer for key roles: presenter, facilitator, timekeeper, process checker	—
Presenter shares a teaching dilemma with descriptive detail	7 minutes
Colleagues ask clarifying questions	2 minutes
Colleagues discuss dilemma in ways that might help presenter rethink, reframe, or consider alternative courses of action	13 minutes
Presenter reflects aloud on what he or she heard, learned, or will try	5 minutes
Process checker leads group reflection on the process	5 minutes

and assist others. Jennifer opened one critical-friends protocol by explaining to her colleagues, "I've been struggling with a project for second semester." She described the complex concepts in genetics that she wanted her students to grasp and said that she was unsure how to design a project that would convey, and assess student comprehension of, such complex material.

Having the protocol gave Jennifer permission—indeed, the requirement—to speak publicly about a problem in her teaching and gave peers permission to get involved. Colleagues asked clarifying questions, and then James announced the beginning of the phase in which the presenter sits back, listens, and takes notes. Rebecca, the special education teacher, confirmed with the group, "Okay, so we talk about how to solve the problems?" The group agreed, so she said, "I'm all ready. I've been holding this one for a few minutes." Rebecca proceeded to make a suggestion regarding how Jennifer could help B-C students with complex content and a complex project:

> I mean, they're pretty sophisticated ideas. And it's just going to have to be a really really structured thing. It's going to have to lead the kids—really lead the kids—on all the pieces that they need to have, all the pieces that they need to show. I mean, you're going to have to definitely have some kind of template that's going to lead them through it. . . . The more structured—the more "okay, now I've got to do this, this, this"—the better it's going to be.

A template, a tool Rebecca championed in her work with her peers, is any sheet that identifies a challenging goal and breaks it down into pieces, such as a worksheet preparing students for essay writing by asking them to state their main idea and main points before they begin writing. Explicit teaching of such transferable skills, such as essay writing or carrying out an experiment, can be particularly helpful for ELLs (Echevarria & Graves, 2003), as long as they do not foreclose access to the rich intellectual work at the center of the learning task (Bunch, Abram, Lotan, & Valdés, 2001; Bunch, Lotan, Valdés, & Cohen, 2005).

Diane proceeded to offer additional suggestions for improving instruction, for both ELLs and other students, proposing the use of a timeline and peer tutoring. Such direct suggestions to a colleague for instructional improvement are unusual acts among teachers (Little, 1990; McLaughlin & Talbert, 2001). All teachers who were participants in this conversation (not just Jennifer) had the opportunity to learn new ways of adding such structure and visual reminders as well as to understand the reasons it is important to do so.

The group was not yet using protocols that focused on student work or teacher curriculum (see McDonald, Mohr, Dichter, & McDonald, 2003, Resources). Such discussions raise even more difficult questions of teaching and learning, and ask teachers to take even greater risks in deprivatizing their work and gaining others' help with it. The group would have found such discussions difficult during its first year. If the group develops sufficient trust and a sustained focus on improving instruction over time, such protocols would be a logical next step.

Participating in Workshops That Dig Deeper Into Instructional Issues

In addition to protocol-guided discussions, B-C teachers participated in workshops organized by the principal, a school coach, and a specialist on language learning issues. Manuela, an ESL specialist and site coordinator for the small schools at Liberty High School, led the workshops training teachers to administer individual tests of speaking and listening to ELLs. Manuela also helped teachers learn how to use state test results for English proficiency, introduced key research findings on language learning, and modeled strategies for applying theory while actually teaching the teachers a math lesson.

This type of collaboration allowed teachers to sustain attention to one problem over several consecutive sessions; for instance, there were four consecutive sessions on ELLs. In contrast to other types of collaboration, the content of these workshops sometimes included theory or research-based insights that teachers might apply to their classrooms. After presenting research and modeling a lesson, Manuela announced, "Let's look at routines you could include in your own curriculum that you see, hear, or observed today. What's a practice I did that would address second language learners?" The group assembled a list on the board and discussed each briefly:

- graphic organizers
- front-loading vocabulary
- breaking down vocabulary
- prefixes, synonyms
- contrastive analysis [across languages]
- practice together
- positive reinforcement
- writing
- checking for understanding
- guided practice, independent practice

- summarize
- putting objectives on board

In the following years, the teachers used such structured workshops to consider and prepare exhibition assignments (i.e., student presentations) that both opened and closed the year. In the opening to this exhibition, students presented a personal educational empowerment plan that they had formulated with their advisor. They told their parents and advisor about their goals and what they would do to accomplish them. At the end, students asked parents or guardians what role they would like to play in helping the students achieve their goals or in helping the school. In this way, the school recruited more volunteers and elicited some parents' involvement in their children's school work. Teachers needed structured collaboration to deepen their own learning and to design such new structures for the school and its outreach to families.

Sharing Information About Students

On Data Mondays—each Monday morning while students took physical education—teachers met to share and analyze data regarding students. Teachers gave their colleagues sheets providing data about student grades, attendance, or behavior. Each teacher looked over the grades they got from colleagues and filled out a page for each of their 18 advisees. They would share this sheet during one-on-one meetings with students once every other week during the advisory class. These short meetings let teachers discuss students' academic progress and convey suggestions or requirements for improvement.

On occasion, these meetings provided an opportunity for teachers to share knowledge that would influence the school experience of ELLs. For instance, Diane, the ESL teacher, advocated for Jennifer, the biology teacher, to slow down her speaking pace and to add visuals to her presentation of content. On another occasion, Diane convinced the group not to send a student named Eliana to the Student Attendance Review Board. Diane explained that the student was helping her family by staying home and caring for young children, and that this behavior was valued by families of Mexican heritage. While such behavior did present an obstacle to Eliana's education, the group agreed to hold a meeting with her mother instead of taking an impersonal route that risked triggering legal proceedings and alienating the family. The teachers had the chance to learn about the students facing the most challenges, their families, and their social lives during these meetings.

These meetings also helped teachers connect students with community resources. After teachers discussed one student's anger, the principal, Sarah, brought the discussion to a close, stating, "He won't come to Saturday school or do any of our interventions." She then suggested drawing on resources available through an Asian American counseling service and asked Zardos, the student's advisor, to follow up with a referral. Guy, another teacher, had urged the group to take advantage of this community resource, given the special challenges of engaging families of Asian descent in any kind of counseling.

Finally, in this setting, colleagues occasionally talked about phone calls they would make to a student's home or how they could communicate with families. For instance, colleagues urged Jennifer to have students make phone calls to their parents or guardians immediately—if briefly—during advisory. This way, she could hear that students were communicating the most recent news on their academic progress even if she could not speak the parents' language. She did this and used her professional judgment to determine whether students were really talking with their parents.

B-C teachers also moved beyond the traditional informal "teacher talk" about a student that is common around lunch tables or after school. In contrast, the teachers committed to looking at three specific types of student data—attendance, academic, and behavioral—with the intention of using what they learned to inform their work with their advisees, their advisees' families, and their approach to working with students in the classroom. In their roles as advisors, teachers did make phone calls to parents, especially when there were problems, and were able to convey information about a student's work in all classes and, if relevant, relate information about the student's social life or behavior in class.

The time teachers spent talking together about students was more effective in some areas than others. Such talk fostered communication with families and helped teachers focus on the students whose behavior or academic progress demanded more immediate attention. On the other hand, though, it was not as helpful for quieter students or those who were passing but falling short of their potential. Nor did this kind of informal conversation lead teachers to reveal or reflect on their own teaching the way that structured protocols or workshops did. It seemed that without some kind of intentional structure, teachers would not break the norms of privacy and noninterference. Teachers weren't comfortable sharing their work directly or providing constructive criticisms or suggestions to colleagues regarding instruction unless the nature of an activity provided prompts and permission for this (Little, 1990; Lortie, 1975). If collaboration consisted only of informal, unstructured conversation, it might never put teachers in a position to identify problems, consider solutions, and publicly grapple with the hardest questions of how content area and ESL teachers can change their own work to better support content mastery and language acquisition.

Successes in Improving Instruction

Though the demands of intensive collaboration and starting a new school were considerable, the staff's work together seemed to result in observable improvements in teaching. Jennifer's work with students provides a clear illustration of instructional shifts that would help ELLs and students with learning disabilities.

In the fall, there were three predominant ways in which Jennifer sought to help students learn biology. The most common method Jennifer used to help students learn content was direct instruction, or teacher-directed presentation of concepts interspersed with occasional questions. Jennifer occasionally used a second method— organized lab activities—to reinforce concepts. A third method for conveying content was homework, which Jennifer wanted to be "meaty . . . so that students would feel it is important."

Most students did not bring in their homework assignments, perhaps due to the linguistic challenges facing ELLs who have to work alone at home without the opportunity to ask questions, request guidance, or check understanding with either a teacher or peers. By the spring, Jennifer understood the challenges of homework assignments that required student comprehension of reading in English that was done independently at home. She emphasized class work and participation to convey the "meat" of the content and shifted away from traditional lectures toward more hands-on and visually oriented classwork to provide greater access to core concepts. A glimpse of Jennifer's teaching at the end of the year illustrates how her new efforts gave ELLs and others greater access to academic content.

At the end of the school year, Jennifer taught the concept of *meiosis*.[3] The period opened with a quick-write prompt on the board reviewing previous material: "What is needed to make a baby? Be specific. Include pictures if you want." As students produced their answers with text and pictures, Jennifer walked around the room taking attendance and providing feedback. When she finished, she asked for eight volunteers. At the front of the class, she lined up four boys and four girls facing each other, each holding plastic bags rolled up to represent the spindle fibers that connect paired chromosomes. Jennifer choreographed a story of meiosis one—of spindle fibers shortening—followed by meiosis two, leading to new cells forming with only half of the original genetic material in each. She made diagrams on the board corresponding to what students had acted out, explaining key concepts both orally and in these pictures. Jennifer used several strategies identified as desirable for the instruction of ELLs, including encouraging multiple means for students to express their thoughts, progress checks on previous understanding, graphics and visuals in conjunction with English text to convey key concepts, and live demonstrations (Echevarria & Graves, 2003; Téllez & Waxman, 2006). Note that these strategies were integrated into, rather than substituted for, an intellectually rigorous biology lesson.

Jennifer had changed not only in behavior but also in attitude. She felt more responsibility to make challenging academic content accessible to students. While she showed the greatest instructional shift with implications for ELLs, other teachers also shifted their instruction in ways that would benefit ELLs.

Successes in Partnering With Parents and the Community

By collaborating, B-C teachers could work together to learn and make sense of attendance and academic data. They used this information in their new role as advisors to communicate with families and to bring information from families back to their colleagues. Structured collaboration also helped them learn to reflect on their own practice, learn from others' work, and make suggestions to peers that might improve instruction of ELLs and others. Collaboration also allowed the teachers to organize events for parents, such as an open house or students' presentation of their own goals and academic work.

---

[3] Meiosis is a cellular process leading to the division of chromosomes in order to produce gametes; a gamete can combine with a gamete from the opposite sex to produce a full set of chromosomes and new life.

The staff agreed on a schedule allowing daily release time that could be used both for teacher collaboration and for individual teachers making phone calls home.

Home visits, phone calls, parent conferences, and the open house helped teachers communicate to families that their participation was valued and helped create a two-way flow of information about students. All of the efforts to connect with families and to develop individualized connections between students and faculty may account for the striking success in promoting attendance. Although B-C is located in a part of the city where attendance rates are usually lower than the district average, the school had a 91% attendance rate compared to the district average of 82%.

The school also energized Hispanic parents, who otherwise might not have felt comfortable or welcome in schools. With the school's blessing, and in an atmosphere in which parents had already received welcoming communication from teachers, a Hispanic parents' group coalesced that included most of the Hispanic families at some level of participation. The parents learned more about what the school was doing, but also provided constructive criticism regarding the 30-minute advisory class and the need for more counseling resources for students. The staff used that critical feedback to rethink the purpose of advisories in later years and generated suggestions from parents about professionals in the community that the school could hire to provide additional counseling services.

Finally, at the beginning of the school's second year, when ELLs were retested, 10% of the school's population—more than one fourth of all ELLs—were redesignated as fluent English proficient, signifying the school's belief that they were no longer in need of special language support. It is possible, though, that the school's efforts to get students to take the test seriously accounted for part of the progress.

Lessons Learned and Next Steps

The Advantages and Challenges of Structured Collaboration

Collaboration may be most effective when teachers identify specific goals and intentionally choose structures or activities that address these goals. At B-C, teachers' use of protocols helped them stay focused on questions of instruction, talk about their own teaching in depth and detail, and offer ideas to each other. Structured workshops had clear foci, such as helping teachers acquire and apply theory about English language learning. Informal conversation may be particularly powerful for some purposes, such as brainstorming and developing curriculum together; teachers can certainly achieve things without tightly organized workshops or protocols. Adding structures, however, can help teachers learn and do things that would be very difficult in informal conversation.

It is beyond the scope of this chapter to fully explore challenges to collaborative work. However, this kind of intensive collaboration was difficult, especially for veteran teachers who had been used to working in isolation. One veteran said he felt defensive while presenting an instructional challenge during a protocol-guided discussion, and two of the three veteran teachers seemed to withdraw from active participation in the collaboration over time. All of the teachers on occasion experienced additional stress, demands, the need to compromise, and hurt feelings. Others have observed how intensive collaboration asks teachers to risk sharing areas in which their teaching or content knowledge is weaker (Wilson & Berne, 1999) and have the potential to prompt tension and bitterness among teachers unused to such collegiality (Achinstein, 2002; Grossman, Wineburg, & Woolworth, 2001). Teachers can achieve ends together that they couldn't do alone, but effective collaboration may require them to develop new skills, compromise, and try new pedagogies or curriculum.

The Need for Patience and Time for Groups to Function Well Together

If teachers do not already have a specific project or shared goal, it is unreasonable to expect them to achieve significant shifts in instruction in the first year of working together. Most teachers will not have as much time and professional support as the B-C teachers had; thus, others may need even more time to develop routines, interpersonal familiarity, trust, and consensus regarding the goals for collaboration.

The Need for Patience and Time for Individuals to Grow in Their Teaching

Nobody can change immediately; like students, teachers usually need multiple chances to understand and practice new skills. Even Jennifer, who demonstrated the greatest shift in one year, still had additional room to grow. For instance, at the end of the year, Jennifer still wrote daily lesson objectives concerned solely with academic outcomes and biological concepts. She was not yet designing her instruction around language learning goals as well as academic content goals, a core notion of successful instruction for ELLs and a concept the group had discussed once.

The Potential and Challenges of Teachers as Advisors

One strategy for supporting teachers in building relationships with families and students is for teachers to serve as advisors to individual students. Whether schools do this formally or simply seek to increase informal communication with parents, that communication will be richer if teachers have the chance to share what they learn about students and families with each other. Teachers will also be more likely to learn about and use community resources if they talk with one another about such resources and about the specific students who might take advantage of their services. At B-C Academy, some advisors adopted the role of advisor more easily and energetically than others. Teachers might have benefited from more explicit training about connecting with diverse families.

Questions for Discussion

Review the case study at the beginning of the chapter. Discuss the following questions that aim to extend the discussions included in the chapter.

1. At B-C, there has traditionally been some mistrust between families and school staff. Why might this mistrust exist?

2. How could involving parents—at B-C or in your own school—make a difference for ELLs' success in school?

3. In the case study, Jennifer is excited for the "new model" of working with colleagues and the school community. Could you imagine your school adopting this model? What might be the benefits and challenges?

4. What joys and difficulties might you, personally, find in collaborating intensively with other teachers to improve the schooling of shared students?

Summary of Main Ideas
1. Two kinds of community can influence the teaching and learning of ELLs: the professional community that exists among teachers and the wider school community, including students' families and others.

2. Teacher professional communities
  a) comprise the shared norms and practices that guide how a group of teachers interact with others and work with students
  b) are traditionally defined by norms of privacy, autonomy, noninterference, and harmony; these norms reinforce teachers conducting their work in relative isolation

3. When ESL and content area teachers break through the norms of typical teacher professional community, their collaboration and complementary expertise can enhance ELLs' learning of rigorous academic and language content.
4. ELLs' parents and communities can provide teachers with additional resources and support for acquiring knowledge and mastering academic content in school.

5. Teachers are more likely to develop effective and reciprocal partnerships with families and communities of ELLs if they do the following:
  a) become aware of the different expectations, assumptions, and experiences that teachers and language minority families bring to the process of education
  b) learn about and build on the cultural strengths and practices that language minority families and communities provide to English language learners
  c) take into account the needs of families when seeking to partner with parents (e.g., lack of time or means to come to school during the work day, the need for two-way interpretation and translation.)
  d) view parents as equal partners engaging in mutual influence and learning as well as the shared enterprise of promoting students' success in school

6. A variety of strategies might help teachers succeed in partnering with parents and the wider school community. Many of these strategies are easier and more effective when implemented in the context of a collaborative professional community.
7. Working more closely with colleagues can entail some loss of individual autonomy and reveal areas for personal improvement. Work done among a community of teachers is more likely to be personally satisfying, improve instruction, and promote better connections with parents and the wider community if teachers agree on clear aims and have the time and patience to develop trust and routines.

8. Intentionally structuring collaboration can increase the odds that teachers
  a) stay focused on their shared aims
  b) deprivatize their practice, reflect on it, and provide examples of teaching that might help others
  c) feel they have both permission and encouragement to become involved in each other's work

References

Achinstein, B. (2002). Conflict amid community: The micropolitics of teacher collaboration. *Teachers College Record, 104*, 4212–4455.

Bunch, G. C., Abram, P. L., Lotan, R. A., & Valdés, G. (2001). Beyond sheltered instruction: Rethinking conditions for academic language development. *TESOL Journal, 10*(2/3), 28–33.

Bunch, G. C., Lotan, R., Valdés, G., & Cohen, E. (2005). Keeping content at the heart of content-based instruction: Access and support for transitional English learners. In J. Crandall & D. Kaufman (Eds.), *Content-based instruction in primary and secondary school settings* (pp. 11–25). Alexandria, VA: TESOL.

Commins, N. L., & Miramontes, O. B. (2006). Addressing linguistic diversity from the outset. *Journal of Teacher Education, 57*, 240–246.

de Carvalho, M. E. P. (2001). *Rethinking family-school relationships: A critique of parental involvement in schooling.* Mahwah, NJ: Lawrence Erlbaum.

de Tocqueville, A. (1969). *Democracy in America* (G. Lawrence, Trans.; J. P. Mayer, Ed.). New York: Harper & Row.

Echevarria, J. & Graves, A. (2003). *Sheltered content instruction: Teaching English language learners with diverse abilities* (2nd ed.). Boston: Allyn & Bacon.

Epstein, J. L. (2001). *School, family, and community partnerships: Preparing educators for improving schools.* Boulder, CO: Westview Press.

Epstein, J. L. (2002). *Improving school, family, and community partnerships in middle and high schools.* In J. L. Epstein, M. G. Sanders, B. S. Simon, K. C. Salinas, N. R. Jansorn, & F. L. Van Voorhis (Eds.), *School, family, and community partnerships: Your handbook for action* (2nd ed., pp. 220–234). Thousand Oaks, CA: Corwin Press.

Epstein, J. L., Sanders, M. G., Simon, B. S., Salinas, K. C., Jansorn, N. R., & Van Voorhis, F. L. (2002). *School, family, and community partnerships: Your handbook for action* (2nd ed.). Thousand Oaks, CA: Corwin Press.

Epstein, J. L., & Sheldon, S. B. (2002). Present and accounted for: Improving student attendance through family and community involvement. *Journal of Educational Research, 95*, 308–318.

ESCORT. (2001). Fostering home-school partnerships. In *The help!kit: A resource guide for secondary teachers of migrant English language learners* (pp. 173–190). Oneonta, NY: Author. Retrieved July 26, 2007, from http://escort.org/files/active/0/Chap9.pdf

Flaxman, E., & Inger, M. (1991). Parents and schooling in the 1990s. *The ERIC Review, 1*(3), 1–6.

González, N., Moll, L. C., & Amanti, C. (2005). *Funds of knowledge: Theorizing practices in households, communities, and classrooms.* Mahwah, NJ: Lawrence Erlbaum.

Grossman, P., Wineburg, S., & Woolworth, S. (2001). Toward a theory of teacher community. *Teachers College Record, 103*, 942–1012.

Inger, M. (1992). *Increasing the school involvement of Hispanic parents*. ERIC Digest. New York: ERIC Clearinghouse on Urban Education. (ERIC Document Reproduction Service No. ED350380)

Lareau, A. (1987). Social class differences in family-school relationships: The importance of cultural capital. *Sociology of Education, 60*(2), 73–85.

Lareau, A. (2000). *Home advantage: Social class and parental intervention in elementary school* (2nd ed.). Lanham, MD: Rowman & Littlefield.

Little, J. W. (1990). The persistency of privacy: Autonomy and initiative in teachers' professional relations. *Teachers College Record, 91*, 509–536.

Lopez, G. R. (2001). The value of hard work: Lessons on parent involvement from an (Im)migrant household. *Harvard Educational Review, 71*, 416–437.

Lortie, D. C. (1975). *Schoolteacher: A sociological study*. Chicago: University of Chicago Press.

McDonald, J., Mohr, N., Dichter, A., & McDonald, E. (2003). *The power of protocols: An educator's guide to better practice*. New York: Teachers College Press.

McLaughlin, M. W. (1993). What matters most in teachers' workplace context. In J. W. Little & M. W. McLaughlin (Eds.), *Teachers' work: Individuals, colleagues, and contexts* (pp. 79–103). New York: Teachers College Press.

McLaughlin, M. W., & Talbert, J. E. (2001). *Professional communities and the work of high school teaching*. Chicago: University of Chicago Press.

McLaughlin, M. W., & Talbert, J. E. (2006). *Building school-based teacher learning communities: Professional strategies to improve student achievement*. New York: Teachers College Press.

Moles, O. C. (1996). *Reaching all families: Creating family-friendly schools*. Washington, DC: U.S. Department of Education. Retrieved July 26, 2007, from http://www.ed.gov/pubs/ReachFam/index.html

Onikama, D., Hammond, O., & Koki, S. (1998). *Family involvement in education: A synthesis of research for Pacific educators*. Honolulu, HI: Pacific Resources for Education and Learning.

Pease-Alvarez, L., Angelillo, C., & Chavajay, P. (2005). Working through dilemmas about homework in an after-school program: Integrating theory, research, and practice. In L. Pease-Alvarez & S. P. Schecter (Eds.), *Learning, teaching, and community: Contributions of situated and participatory approaches to educational innovation* (pp. 131–150). Mahwah, NJ: Lawrence Erlbaum.

Rogoff, B. (2003). *The cultural nature of human development*. Oxford: Oxford University Press.

Schecter, S. R., & Bayley, R. (2002). *Language as cultural practice: Mexicanos en el Norte*. Mahwah, NJ: Lawrence Erlbaum.

Sosa, A. S. (1997). Involving Hispanic parents in educational activities through collaborative relationships. *Bilingual Research Journal, 21*, 285–293.

Téllez, K., & Waxman, H. C. (2006). A meta-synthesis of qualitative research on effective teaching practices for English learners. In J. M. Norris & L. Ortega (Eds.), *Synthesizing research on language learning and teaching* (pp. 245–277). Amsterdam: John Benjamins.

Trumbull, E., Rothstein-Fisch, C., Greenfield, P. M., & Quiroz, B. (2001). *Bridging cultures between home and school: A guide for teachers*. Mahwah, NJ: Lawrence Erlbaum.

U.S. Department of Education. (1995). *An invitation to your community: Building community partnerships for learning*. Washington, DC: Author.

U.S. Department of Education. (1997). *Family involvement in children's education—October 1997*. Retrieved July 26, 2007, from http://www.ed.gov/pubs/FamInvolve/execsumm.html

Valdés, G. (1996). *Con respeto: Bridging the distances between culturally diverse families and schools: An ethnographic portrait*. New York: Teachers College Press.

Valdés, G. (2003). *Expanding definitions of giftedness: The case of young interpreters from immigrant communities*. Mahwah, NJ: Lawrence Erlbaum.

Wilson, S. M., & Berne, J. (1999). Teacher learning and the acquisition of professional knowledge: An examination of research on contemporary professional development. In A. Iran-Nejad & D. P. Pearson (Eds.), *Review of research in education* (Vol. 24, pp. 173–209). Washington, DC: American Educational Research Association.

Yosso, T. J. (2005). Whose culture has capital? A critical race theory discussion of community cultural wealth. *Race, Ethnicity and Education, 8*(1), 69–91.

CHAPTER 8

Culture and Advocacy

Collaborating to Embrace Cultural Identities for Student Success

Raquel Oxford

$\big($ **CASE STUDY** $\big)$

Elizabeth is the deputy superintendent of curriculum for City View Independent School District (ISD), a small, rural but quickly growing district in northern Texas. In fact, City View is one of the fastest-growing districts in Texas, opening four campuses in the past 4 years to accommodate the growth of the community from just over 3,000 in 2000 to almost 20,000 in 2006. Elizabeth has lived in the region, taught in several area schools for many years, and now serves as an administrator. Though in the past the district has been low-incidence for English language learners (ELLs), in recent years Elizabeth has observed a marked increase in the number of ELLs in City View ISD. They have been almost exclusively children of immigrant, Spanish-speaking parents who are drawn by abundant job opportunities on local horse farms, in the booming construction industry, and in the overall healthy economy of the nearby Dallas/Ft. Worth metroplex. Elizabeth has a special interest in the success of all students and was motivated to approach a local university to jointly explore the needs and successes of the district in working with these immigrant children.

Nevertheless, Elizabeth struggled with finding the best approach to develop awareness and understanding of the students' backgrounds among members of the school community. She felt that the best way to advocate for the students was to immerse everyone in information about the students and their diverse circumstances. Additionally, Elizabeth wanted to develop awareness of current efforts already underway to assist ELLs, efforts that could be enhanced and further supported. Elizabeth therefore decided to undertake a collaborative research effort.

Prereading Questions

- Why do educators need to consider different cultures in the U.S. educational system?

- What is culture?

- What is multicultural education?

- What is culturally responsive teaching?

- What is effective for language learning students?

- What is advocacy?

- How do teachers collaborate to embrace culture and support advocacy?

WHY DO EDUCATORS NEED TO CONSIDER DIFFERENT CULTURES IN THE U.S. EDUCATIONAL SYSTEM?

According to U.S. Census data from 2002 (U.S. Census Bureau, 2003), the number of Hispanics in the United States has risen to 37.4 million people, accounting for more than 13% of the entire U.S. population. This figure exceeds the estimation of 31 million projected in 1995, and Latin Americans already accounted for 51% of the 28.4 million foreign-born people in the United States in March 2000. With this continued growth in the Hispanic population comes an increase in the number of limited-English-proficient students and ELLs in U.S. elementary and secondary public schools. Indeed, one third of Hispanics in the United States are under the age of 18 (U.S. Census Bureau, 2003), and 75% of children who need extra help learning English are native speakers of Spanish (Connell, 2004). Many other languages are also represented in ESL classrooms, creating a rich tapestry of culturally and linguistically diverse learners.

These students must be provided equal opportunity to learn through language assistance. They face not only language acquisition issues but complex differences in social and cultural structures as well. Responding to these students' needs should involve valuing their cultural identities and the strengths they bring to school (Violand-Sanchez, Sutton, & Ware, 1991), yet often teachers do not understand a student's home culture and the importance of linking to this resource. Indeed, cultural and social capital are often referred to as the richest untapped resources of diverse learners (Delpit, 1995) because teachers frequently underestimate students' funds of knowledge (Moll, Amanti, Neff, & Gonzalez, 1992). Understanding the complexity of culture is the first step in the journey to nurturing culturally responsive classroom communities.

WHAT IS CULTURE?

Culture is a complex, multifaceted construct that impacts students' learning and school experience in manifold ways. Indeed, language and culture are inextricably linked in powerful ways that impact classroom interactions with peers as well as teachers. Exploring the construct of culture is important if teachers of ELLs are to comprehend the depth of influence of culture and utilize students' cultures to maximize student achievement.

Culture is an intricate concept. It involves multiple and contested definitions including various perspectives from anthropology to psychology and sociology. For example, D'Andrade (1984) conceptualizes culture as "learned systems of meaning, communicated by means of natural language and other symbol systems, having representational, directive, and affective functions, and capable of creating cultural entities and particular senses of reality" (p. 116). Another seminal conception of culture defines it as a "historically transmitted pattern of meanings embodied in symbols, a system of inherited conceptions expressed in symbolic forms by means of which men communicate, perpetuate and develop their knowledge about and attitudes toward life" (Geertz, 1973, p. 89). Finally, the American Psychological Association (2003) recently defined culture as "the belief system and value orientations that influence customs, norms, practices, and social institutions, including psychological processes and organizations" (p. 380).

Thus, the range of what constitutes culture covers concepts such as patterns of behavior to items such as material objects. Culture affects verbal and nonverbal communication, which encompasses kinesics, proxemics, haptics, and patterns of participating and listening. Orientation modes, such as how individuals define their personal space or deal with the concept of time, as well as intellectual modes, including preferred ways of learning and the knowledge that is most valued and skills emphasized, are other ways in which culture subtly shapes all people (D'Andrade, 1984; LeVine, 1984). The often-referenced term *surface culture* refers to the tangible elements that are easy to describe, such as the arts, language, food, and holidays, while *deep culture* delves more into attitudes, perceptions, and values. All these aspects of culture are significant influences on the individual. As D'Andrade posits, "through these systems of meaning, groups of people adapt to their environment and structure interpersonal activities" (p. 116).

If culture is defined as the beliefs, traditions, values, attitudes, and behaviors of a group, then teachers need to understand how theirs is both similar and different from those of the students in their classrooms. Teachers themselves are influenced by their own culture, and this affects classroom interactions. Cochran-Smith (1995) asserts that,

> in order to teach in a society that is increasingly culturally and linguistically diverse, prospective teachers . . . need opportunities to examine much of what is usually unexamined in the tightly braided relationships of language, culture and power in schools and schooling. This kind of examination inevitably begins with our own histories as human beings and as educators; our own experiences as members of particular races, classes, and genders; and as children, parents, and teachers in the world. (p. 500)

If culture is a shared organization of ideas that includes the intellectual, moral, and aesthetic standards prevalent in a community and the meanings of communicative actions (LeVine, 1984), then indeed there are aspects that the teacher and student could share or compare. Bruner (1996) captures the connection: "Culture, then, though itself man-made, both forms and makes possible the working of a distinctively human mind. In this view, learning and thinking are always situated in a cultural setting and always dependent upon the utilization of cultural resources" (p. 4).

Learner-centered curriculum is a cornerstone of schools today, yet many do not fully consider the importance of tapping into a student's culture as a vital component of the way a student not only learns but establishes his or her identity. This is particularly important for middle and high school adolescent ELLs who may be recent immigrants grappling with reconciling their home culture with life in the United States. As teachers backload curriculum (Wiggins & McTighe, 2005), culture should be taken into account, and not simply at the superficial or surface level. One avenue to valuing culture is through multicultural education and culturally responsive teaching.

WHAT IS MULTICULTURAL EDUCATION?

The explicit link between understanding culture and engaging in the action of advocacy takes educators on the path of multicultural education. The journey begins with an understanding of Nieto's (1996) characteristics of multicultural education and Banks's (1995) dimensions of multicultural education, specifically equity pedagogy and an empowering school culture. Multicultural education is a thread running through the total curriculum, rather than a subject to be taught. Nieto provides the following comprehensive definition of multicultural education:

> Multicultural education permeates the curriculum and instructional strategies used in schools, as well as the interactions among teachers, students, and parents, and the very way that schools conceptualize the nature of teaching and learning. Because it uses critical pedagogy as its underlying philosophy and focuses on knowledge, reflection, and action (praxis) as the basis for social change, multicultural education promotes the democratic principles of social justice. (p. 307)

Therefore, multicultural education is education that is important for all students and connects knowledge and learning to social action and advocacy. As described by Nieto, it envelops the entire school from curriculum and instruction to policy and other practices.

The five dimensions of multicultural education identified by Banks (1995; content integration, knowledge construction, prejudice reduction, equity pedagogy, and empowering school culture) are excellent guidelines for an action plan to examine the environment of a school and propose change or encourage reform. Simple definitions provided by Banks and Banks (2003) show the connections to ELLs:

- Content integration: This deals with the extent to which teachers use examples from a variety of cultures in their teaching.

- Knowledge construction: Teachers need to help students understand, investigate, and determine how the implicit cultural assumptions, frames of reference, perspectives, and biases within a discipline influence how knowledge is constructed.

- Prejudice reduction: This focuses on the characteristics of students' racial attitudes and how they can be modified by teaching methods and materials.

- Equity pedagogy: This exists when teachers modify their teaching in ways that facilitate the academic achievement of students from diverse racial, cultural, gender, and social-class groups.

- Empowering school culture: Create a school culture that empowers students from diverse racial, ethnic, gender, and social-class groups by examining grouping and labeling practices, sports participation, disproportionality in achievement, and the interaction of the staff and the students across ethnic and racial lines. (p. 23)

Furthermore, Banks (1995) identifies four approaches (contributions, additive, transformation, and social action) used in content integration, starting from an approach that narrowly defines culture and moving up to more effective approaches to bring about real understanding of diverse groups that can lead to change. On the first level, the contributions approach, heroes, heroines, holidays, food, and discrete cultural elements are celebrated occasionally. Next, with the additive approach, content, concepts, lessons, and units are added to the curriculum without changing its structure. The structure of the curriculum is changed in the transformation approach to enable students to view concepts, issues, events, and themes from the perspectives of diverse ethnic and cultural groups. In the final level, the social action approach, students make decisions on important personal, social, and civic problems and take actions to help solve them. It is this top level that makes the link to cultivating a climate of advocacy in schools and communities.

WHAT IS CULTURALLY RESPONSIVE TEACHING?

The notion of culturally responsive teaching, or culturally relevant pedagogy, has gained popularity in recent years, especially in light of the dialogue in multicultural education and the work of Freire (1970) and Ladson-Billings (1994, 1995a, 1995b). Freire's critical pedagogy links the experiences, culture, and personal strengths of the learner to resolving problems in his or her everyday life. Ladson-Billings (1994) expounds on the notion of cultural relevance by stating that culturally relevant teaching "uses student culture in order to maintain it and to transcend the negative effects of the dominant culture" (p. 17). Furthermore, teachers with culturally relevant practices

- have high self-esteem and a high regard for others
- see themselves as part of the community, see teaching as giving back to the community, and encourage their students to do the same
- see teaching as an art and themselves as artists
- believe all students can succeed
- help students make connections between their community, national, and global identities

- see teaching as "digging knowledge out" of students (Ladson-Billings, 1994, pp. 33–53)

With these expectations for students, and taking their cultural backgrounds into consideration, teachers bridge the students' home and school cultures. A descriptor that has emerged from work in the area of culturally responsive teaching is *warm demander*. Warm demanders combine high expectations with caring about students' success and knowledge of effective pedagogy (Ware, 2006). These expectations, coupled with effective instruction, better empower students to navigate their worlds.

ESL teachers must be more aware of the worlds in which their students operate, including the linguistic, cultural, and sociopolitical realms. Minority students can be adversely impacted by the psychological stress of negative stereotypes aimed at their groups (Cohen, Garcia, Apfel, & Master, 2006), resulting in poor academic performance. An intervention as basic as allowing students to write about group characteristics or values important to them can halt downward trends in performance (Cohen et al., 2006), and this activity of speaking or writing from experience could certainly be applied to ELLs (Violand-Sanchez & Hainer-Violand, 2006).

There is consensus that being a culturally responsive teacher means doing whatever it takes for a student to be successful. The aim is excellence, and teachers assume the responsibility for their students to achieve it (Gay, 2000; Ladson-Billings, 1994). Valuing and knowing the students' cultural identity not only helps them succeed academically but also helps them to step out in broader arenas. Likewise, teachers can advocate a classroom and school climate of acceptance for linguistic and cultural diversity (Díaz-Rico, 2004) and move to develop a class culture that instills more intrinsic motivation in students (Wlodkowski & Ginsberg, 1995). Culturally responsive teaching strategies and techniques improve the behavior and achievement of students (Gay, 2000; Northeast and Islands Regional Educational Laboratory at Brown University, 2002), and everyone in the school community, from support staff to administrators to teachers and parents, must present a united front regarding high expectations.

WHAT IS EFFECTIVE FOR LANGUAGE LEARNING STUDENTS?

Linguistically and culturally diverse students face challenges in school, and in spite of the secondary school structure that tends to isolate teachers (Ruiz-de-Velasco, Fix, & Chu Clewell, 2000; see chapter 6), there is much that can be done in collaboration with colleagues to facilitate student success (Gray & Fleischman, 2004; Herrell & Jordan, 2004). To meet the needs of ELLs, however, all teachers must engage in pedagogy that supports these students (Short & Echevarria, 2004). Use of the native language and culture can help build classroom community (Baker, 2001), and maximizing the use of students' culture can increase self-esteem as well as improve access to academic material (Connell, 2004). It is access to academic content while learning language that is critical in order for students to move from basic interpersonal communication skills (BICS) acquired fairly quickly to cognitive academic language proficiency (CALP), something that can take considerable time but must, of necessity, occur as rapidly as possible so that learners don't fall even further behind their peers (Cummins, 1981;

Echevarria, Vogt, & Short, 2004). Following a constructivist view, by relating new content to students' culture and activating prior knowledge, teachers provide scaffolding and improve student learning and confidence (Gibbons, 2002; Vygotsky, 1978). Nurturing joint approaches to working with ELLs, such as cooperative learning, can accelerate achievement (Black, 2005; Padron, Waxman, & Rivera, 2002). Unfortunately, teachers seldom differentiate instruction, and few systematically instruct in ways that are culturally and racially sensitive (Tomlinson, 2005). Tomlinson asserts that, in order to be effective, teachers must consider a comprehensive set of factors including students' language, economic status, experience, views of the world, and so on. Seminal work from the Center for Research on Education, Diversity & Excellence (CREDE) outlined five standards for pedagogy that will be successful with all students (Dalton, 1998):

- Joint productive activity: Facilitate learning through joint productive activity among teachers and students.

- Language development: Develop students' competence in the language and literacy of instruction throughout all instructional activities.

- Contextualization: Contextualize teaching and curriculum using the experiences and skills of home and community.

- Challenging activities: Challenge students towards cognitive complexity.

- Instructional conversation: Engage students through dialogue.

These research-based standards can be considered foundational in instruction for culturally and linguistically diverse students in multiple settings. An excellent online resource for teachers and schools to explore is the Teaching Diverse Learners (n.d.) Web site. In addition to more accessible reviews of current topics, the site archives publications such as *The Teacher's Guide to Diversity: Building a Knowledge Base* (Trumbull & Pacheco, 2005), which invites readers to consider their own stances and viewpoints as they study diversity in education through reading and activities.

Walqui (2000) discusses strategies for successful engagement of immigrant students in secondary schools. Students must be able to strengthen their cultural and ethnic identities while developing the language they need for success. The following are basic principles of effective instruction for immigrant students that mirror other effectiveness research:

- The culture of the classroom fosters the development of a community of learners, and all students are part of that community.

- Good language teaching involves conceptual and academic development.

- Students' experiential backgrounds and prior knowledge provide a point of departure and an anchor in the exploration of new ideas.

- Teaching and learning focus on substantive ideas that are organized cyclically.

- New ideas and tasks are contextualized.

- Academic strategies, sociocultural expectations, and academic norms are taught explicitly.
- Tasks are relevant, meaningful, engaging, and varied.
- Complex and flexible forms of collaboration maximize learners' opportunities to interact while making sense of language and content.
- Students are given multiple opportunities to extend their understandings and apply their knowledge.
- Authentic assessment is an integral part of teaching and learning, and should be done by teachers and learners.

While using these principles, teachers must also keep in mind that ELLs are not a homogeneous group, even if they speak a common language (Suarez-Orozco & Suarez-Orozco, 2001). Much recent work examines the status of Hispanics in the United States. Tienda and Mitchell's (2006) report from the National Research Council examines the diverse assemblage encompassed by the term *Hispanic*, indicating that it represents immigrants and their children and grandchildren from nearly two dozen Spanish-speaking countries. It describes the trajectory of the younger generations and established residents, and it projects long-term trends in population aging, social disparities, and social mobility that have shaped and will shape the Hispanic experience. These more profound explorations of Hispanic culture can help inform teachers.

Despite the fact that students come from vastly different backgrounds, all teachers can ease the transition to a new school culture by pairing ELLs with English-speaking buddies, labeling classroom items in both English and the students' native languages, teaching English-speaking students some basic vocabulary in the ELLs' home language, incorporating classroom learning about the ELLs' culture and community into daily lessons, and providing translators for parents at school meetings and during home visits (Einhorn, 2002). That is, ELLs need time to acquire language and appropriate instruction from teachers who are equipped with the best strategies and knowledge concerning the various ELL cultures.

WHAT IS ADVOCACY?

Advocacy can be multifaceted, but empowering teachers and their students to speak up on important issues is central. Advocacy can be an umbrella for organized activism, but certainly it is the process of asserting oneself or interceding for someone else to affect policy, always toward a goal of self-empowerment through knowledge of one's rights. Advocacy is affected by attitudes toward culture and acceptance of diversity. Why should teachers be concerned with policy? Policy manifests itself as laws, programs, practices, and procedures. In education, policy ultimately affects a child and his or her learning, and this is especially true of ELLs (August & Garcia, 1988; August & Hakuta, 1997). The intersection of research and policy would optimistically be best practices; that is, in an ideal situation research reveals successful strategies that can become the focus of policy makers' mandates. Because that is not always the case, connections and collaboration between teachers, parents, researchers, administrators, and policy makers must be fostered.

An example of advocacy is teachers sharing with colleagues, school board members, parents of ELLs, and community members regarding bilingual-bicultural aid appropriations or other items of special interest to districts serving ELLs in order to continue to offer equal and equitable educational opportunities to all students. Teachers are advocates. All teachers must be more aware of their ability to influence students in positive and negative ways; this includes content area teachers who must be informed about the various standards for ELLs (e.g., Board of Regents of the University of Wisconsin System, 2007; TESOL, 1997). Teachers have access to resources and may understand the school and educational system in ways that parents and students cannot.

Another example of advocacy is teachers tapping into and discussing the many accounts shared in the media regarding students' personal lives and involvement, and channeling their energy into action and advocacy. For example, an English teacher led discussions on immigration, and the class's polemic resulted in a book of mostly personal immigrant experiences (Sanchez, 2006). Such projects give voice to students and allow them to play a part in facilitating understanding of themselves and others. So begins the road to cultivating self-advocacy in ELLs.

The following example of advocacy through a research team involves sharing information with teachers and increasing their awareness of efforts in their own school. The research team was necessary because teachers were fully immersed in daily teaching and too busy to undertake macro-level research. In addition, the team was necessary as a third-party voice whose credibility and impartiality could be relied upon.

HOW DO TEACHERS COLLABORATE TO EMBRACE CULTURE AND SUPPORT ADVOCACY?

As a rural district with previously low numbers of ELLs, City View ISD was trying to be proactive in its handling of a dramatic increase in the number of these students. District leaders admitted to not understanding the students' circumstances for migrating or having a complete picture of the students' cultures, their challenges, or their successes. Understanding culture deeply is a prerequisite for implementing tenets of multicultural education and culturally responsive teaching. District leaders also did not fully understand that the ESL and mainstream teachers as well as the support staff similarly struggled with gaps in their cultural knowledge of the students. When district leaders realized that the teachers were struggling to fill their knowledge gaps so that they could adequately educate more ELLs and advocate for their needs, they responded by suggesting a collaborative research project.

An overarching framework for collaboration is advocacy through collaborative research. This type of research is a form of responsive evaluation (Stake, 1975). It is a participatory and collaborative model that places value on insiders' perspectives and focuses on the stakeholders who have the most vested interests in the outcomes. The other principle of the research is that it is advocacy through the *flooding of information* to stakeholders who will then make their own decisions about the next steps to take.

Collaboration at the high school level took place among the superintendent, two university faculty members, a community liaison, one ESL teacher, one bilingual aide, and two content area teachers. The social studies and math teachers were the involved content area teachers because a large number of new ELL students were in their classes. The research was undertaken jointly through interviews conducted by the university faculty. The university research team volunteered to undertake the interviews so that teachers would not be burdened by setting aside time for the research that would otherwise be spent teaching. The university faculty and the teachers, however, came together for formal and informal information-sharing sessions during which the research findings were discussed and reflected upon.

The research brought to light students' cultural and linguistic challenges as well as the unacknowledged and unseen efforts of the ESL teacher to work with her colleagues. In addition, the information and recommendations provided by the university team aimed to give the ESL and mainstream teachers a stronger voice by providing them with the information they needed to advocate for themselves and for their students.

The Collaborative Research Process

The research team began its work during the 2001–2002 academic year to explore and document the needs of ELLs and the successful efforts of teachers and staff members in the school to assist the ELLs.

There were several steps to the research, discussed further below:

- brainstorming
- interviews with students
- information gathering with the ESL teacher
- meeting and making decisions
- sharing information

The first step was a brainstorming session between Elizabeth, the deputy superintendent, and the university group. Prior to the meeting, Elizabeth canvassed teachers' and staff's opinions about areas of critical interest. It was important for Elizabeth to take the lead in the discussions to demonstrate the commitment of leadership in undertaking the initiative to assist ELLs. The questions that emerged from the brainstorming were as follows: How were newly arrived immigrant students being introduced to the school culture? What were the students experiencing in their day-to-day routine? How did this differ from their previous experiences with school? How could teachers, the administration, the school, and the community in general be more receptive or welcoming to the newcomers? How could all parties begin to advocate for the students, including the students themselves and their families, in a more culturally responsive manner?

The second phase of the collaborative research was group and individual interviews with students, which were conducted by the researchers to explore issues from the students' cultural perspectives. Newcomers with less than 2 years in the district were selected to be interviewed in order to determine the perceptions of the district's cultural responsiveness and to be able to suggest advocacy needs for teachers and district staff. The following questions were used as a guide for interviews with the high school students:

- What difficulties or problems are faced by you/Spanish-speaking students when new to the district?
- What coping strategies do you/ESL students employ to deal with school-based difficulties? What do you/ESL students do to do well in school?
- How do the teachers and principals and your parents help you succeed in your studies? How do you help other ESL students to be successful in the school program?
- What seems to be most helpful in making you/ESL students successful in school?
- What are the most important needs you/ESL students are having now that interfere with school success?

Keeping the students' voices central to facilitating the collaboration between teachers was fundamental to a culturally responsive approach. The overarching belief was that the students' voices would help the content area teachers better understand ELLs' cultural and linguistic needs and, with help from the ESL teacher, begin to make culturally responsive curricular and instructional modifications for the students. Through the students' experiences, both ESL and mainstream teachers would be pushed to rethink how the learning environment is structured.

The third phase of the research was information gathering with the ESL teacher. She provided another perspective critical with regard not only to the ELLs she was working with but also the existing collaboration at the high school. Although there were several ESL-prepared teachers at the lower grade levels in City View ISD, Christine's position as the only ESL specialist at the high school—while also sharing her time and dedication with the middle school campus—was considered central to the development of any culturally responsive collaboration and advocacy at the high school. Interviewing Christine was critical in that it put the spotlight on her efforts and gave her the visibility that she needed in order to undertake the job. To assess the actual condition for collaboration, Christine was asked the following questions:

- How many regular content area teachers in your building have ESL preparation? Who are those teachers?
- Do you see teachers who have ESL preparation using what they have learned/ should know in their teaching?
- Do content area teachers ask you for strategies or resources for their non-English-speaking students? If so, what type of help do you provide most often?
- What kinds of resources and support do you believe regular teachers need in order to better serve the non-English-speaking students?

- Do parents of non-English-speaking students ask you for help in dealing with other teachers or school administrators?

- Specifically, how do you use the students' home cultures in your curriculum and instruction?

- What is your most difficult challenge in teaching non-English speaking students?

- What strategies or instruments do you use to assess whether your students are learning (i.e., how do you know when you have been successful)?

The fourth phase involved a meeting in which the research team made decisions about the information it had gathered. In line with the principles of responsive evaluation research and its promotion of participatory and collaborative ideals, the research team needed to determine how it could bring to light information that it had uncovered and encourage all involved to make their own decisions about the next best steps to take to improve ELL instruction and programming in their schools. The research team made the decision to disseminate this information through teacher roundtables throughout the year during which the research and its findings were discussed, informal conversations between school staff and members of the research team that occurred during the latter's observations of content area teacher classrooms, and direct consultation and discussion with the superintendent about the research findings.

The fifth phase of the collaborative research was the actual sharing of information as planned in the previous phase.

Data From the Research

Student Data

The interviews with the high school students were enlightening. The group of 10 students, though entirely Spanish-speaking, was not at all homogenous, with individuals coming from several Spanish-speaking countries. They included a brother and sister from Argentina, two sisters from Guatemala, another brother-sister pair from Honduras, and a handful of students from Mexico. The following is the information they provided:

- They discussed the reasons and circumstances of their immigration as well as aspects of their diverse cultures (e.g., country of origin, family structure). Some were still homesick for their countries, and situations of involuntary vs. voluntary immigration (Ogbu, 1987) impacted their feelings about school.

- The students came to school with different levels of school preparedness. Some students had missed periods of schooling, but others had attended private schools in their native countries and were notably ahead of their peers.

- The process of acculturation was different for everyone. The students agreed that they were in incredible shock in the first weeks without adequate language skills and that the major issue for them was becoming proficient in English. They reported that they often experienced issues of inferiority or insecurity within their ESL group due to differences such as accent or dialect, immigration or economic status, or simply being the newest student in a group.

- The students' coping strategies were also diverse and included using received cues and learned academic procedures such as following teacher directions or watching their classmates when they did not understand the oral English instructions given by the teacher. Depending on their English speaking ability, students asked classmates for help. Students with minimal English speaking abilities asked their more English-fluent, Spanish-speaking classmates; students who had more advanced English speaking abilities may have asked a native-English-speaking classmate for help.

- ELL parents are supportive of education. Parents are concerned that their children learn English in school, but they also want them to become fluent and literate in Spanish at home. Even when parents have minimal English literacy or fluency, they monitor and help their children in homework completion, to the extent that they are able, and praise their children when they demonstrate successful academic work.

- The students needed to see support from their principal, whom they considered absent from their lives as students in the school.

- The students cited a need for an intensive approach to academic English as important for their school success. This is one of the more interesting findings and as will be shown in the following section, served as an impetus for collaborative conversations between the ESL and content area teachers.

ESL Teacher Data

The interview with Christine, the ESL teacher, was meant to provide ground-level information about her perception of available resources and areas of possible improvement. She provided the following information:

- Classroom teachers did not have ESL preparation. Perhaps because high school teachers are generally content area specialists, Christine identified no regular classroom teachers with ESL preparation in the high school.

- All teachers needed support with modifications, materials and resources, and how to scaffold for the ELLs, particularly newcomers or others with lower levels of English proficiency.

- The ESL teacher's job involved providing cultural information to colleagues. As the lone high school ESL teacher, Christine felt like she needed to explain the ESL students' home situations to her colleagues. She felt that many teachers needed a better understanding about the fact that many migrant students do not have resources at home to do research or get certain materials. She said, "Sometimes parents will ask for help, but most of the time they are shy about coming to school. I think they may be embarrassed because of poor English skills."

- The ESL class was where students' home cultures were validated through the incorporation of literature from students' cultures and special projects that highlighted them.

- ESL and content area teacher collaboration existed informally. High school teachers are more autonomous but that does not mean that they do not relish time for professional interactions with fellow teachers and specialists in ESL. Through interviews with Christine, the research team learned that she had shared modifications with several content area teachers in the past. Christine reported that those teachers who collaborated with her to adapt lessons wanted affirmation that what they were doing was beneficial to the students who were learning English, not simply achieving in the content area. Many content area teachers felt that they did not know the students well enough to take ownership of modifications. However, scaffolding with visual aids and cooperative learning, a comfortable strategy for most of the ELLs at City View High School, was frequently employed. Finally, Christine also reported that, given limited time and opportunities, the teacher collaboration she undertook with colleagues did not include the sharing of students' cultural backgrounds.

Data Summary

The information garnered from student interviews made it readily apparent that the ESL students were already undertaking proactive steps in finding means to survive and achieve. The students demonstrated their sense of agency and their clear understanding of the pathways they needed to take to be successful. From the ESL teacher's interviews, it was apparent that there was a climate for collaboration. There were content area teachers at City View High School who were more than willing to make accommodations for new ELLs but often struggled with appropriate and effective strategies. However, the struggle may have led to these teachers' tendency to leave the students' progress in the hands of the ESL teacher, which would contradict the idea that welcoming and assuring the success of ELLs is the responsibility of the entire school community (Brisk & Harrington, 2000).

Several Successes in the Utilization of Data From Collaborative Research

The research project at City View High School was a first step in shifting this responsibility for ELL success from ESL teachers alone to the entire school. Individuals at several levels of the high school began to advocate for the success of ELL students.

The Deputy Superintendent's Advocacy

Once the information was gathered, Elizabeth, the deputy superintendent, encouraged interested parties to join the conversation to discuss and make joint decisions about steps that could be followed based on the information gathered. In addition, she advocated for the development of a newcomers' program in which the research findings would have a central focus.

In response to the information regarding the English language challenges that newcomer students were experiencing, the superintendent, upon consultation with teachers and the high school principal, agreed to enroll some of the ELLs in Spanish classes so that they could maintain and strengthen their native language as they learned English. This was a form of advocacy because it not only acknowledged the students' heritage but also allowed them to demonstrate their area of strength. The latter was especially significant because the Spanish language classes are traditionally scheduled for college-bound students who are native speakers. The ELLs in the class were able to demonstrate that they were on par with these college-bound students in regard to their ability to engage with and make sense of the world around them through the Spanish language.

The Principal's Advocacy

Another direct outcome of the collaborative research and participatory engagement in the results was that the high school principal was willing to play a more prominent role in facilitating the transition of new immigrant students. Christine, the researchers, and the principal developed a plan whereby the principal would personally greet the students and their families as well as make periodic visits to the ESL classroom. His mere presence reinforced the importance of education to the ELLs and how the school was moving in a direction of more collaborative cultural responsiveness and advocacy for the ELLs.

Teacher Advocacy

The collaborative research and the meetings that followed gave Christine prominence and a sense of professional affirmation and backing. With this new confidence, and with the knowledge that she had the backing of her administrators and the understanding of her colleagues, Christine targeted a couple of teachers, who had previously sought her advice in accommodating ELLs, for further collaborative conversations. This research empowered her to reach out to content area teachers and help them advocate for the success of ELLs.

The research findings strengthened existing collaborations between Christine and her content area colleagues. The findings added new dimensions to the collaboration to enhance cultural responsiveness in their instruction. For example, Kevin, the social studies teacher, reflected upon the research findings and decided to enlist Christine's help in incorporating cultural and heroic figures from his ELLs' heritage in his social studies instruction. With the realization that the Spanish-speaking students had unique details from their countries that they wanted to share, Kevin and Christine collaborated to create a task-based project culminating in an oral presentation with a visual complement; Kevin proposed the initial content knowledge framework of important figures, and Christine provided the cultural implications and means of improving various methods of instruction to ensure even better cultural responsiveness. Ultimately, by working together, the two created a project in which students were instructed to select a figure from their culture who represented qualities important to them or in some way was a hero to them. Students were given time to conduct research as part of one of their ESL periods, and they shared the work in both the ESL class and the social studies class. Kevin and Christine continued to collaborate so that that they could support each other through common learning activities.

Wanda, a math teacher at City View High School, often had a variety of ELLs in her classes during the course of the day. Before collaborative interviews and subsequent conversations with Christine, Wanda was somewhat hesitant to allow these students to use Spanish in the classroom, fearing that they might become tempted to provide each other with answers, not merely explanations. The research findings led her to reconsider her position on native language use in her classroom. She then conferred with Christine regarding the cultural implications of prohibiting any use of Spanish in her classrooms and decided to experiment. Now in an Algebra I class, two ESL students cluster at the back of the room with a bilingual, Mexican American student who has been enlisted as a peer translator. Wanda's discussions about this situation with Christine and the students have been positive and Wanda is secure in knowing that the students are doing good work. The use of their native language and culture, in fact, helped build classroom community, did not impede the acquisition of English (August & Hakuta, 1997), and was a good example of culturally responsive teaching.

Lessons Learned and Next Steps

It is clear from the discussion in this chapter that collaborative research can successfully use results to impact practice and policy in a school. However, teachers must have time to work together and discuss broad cultural and political issues such as immigration and how it impacts children in the classroom. Wanda's ELL students would have returned to their homes in Latin America behind in their studies if she had not had time to discuss with Christine the implications of students using Spanish in her classroom. Teachers must also have time to explore the theoretical and practical connections in curriculum and instruction and work together to develop meaningful classroom activities. Kevin's proposal to study history and geography by including cultural figures of importance to the ELLs would never have happened if he and Christine hadn't had time to collaborate in creating and refining the exercise. In the absence of time to plan together, teachers in middle and high schools must become creative in finding alternative venues for collaboration.

The experience at City View High School also affected the university researchers who helped gather the data used during the discussions. The research led them to rethink teacher preparation in the following ways: (a) content area teachers, in addition to taking a course on effective instructional strategies with ELLs, such as scaffolding, should be required to take classes that emphasize cultural competence and advocacy; (b) teacher educators must work toward building a professional community between ESL and content area preservice teachers based on collaboration; and (c) though it was more difficult to see emerging patterns of consistent curricular coplanning and collaborative conversations between ESL and content area teachers in City View High School, the research findings lend support to the inclusion of the practice in teacher preparation.

The question that remains is how the collaboration can be sustained. This chapter demonstrates that administrator leadership, from the deputy superintendent to building principals, has a significant impact on the climate in schools. In the case of City View ISD, Elizabeth's willingness as deputy superintendent to access and provide resources to smooth the progress of working with newcomers and their families sent a positive message that the district wanted to help teachers deal with the students in their classrooms and provide proper cultural responsiveness so that all students learned to the best of their abilities. City View ISD was under Elizabeth's leadership only a few years, so the force as well as the support to continue the collaboration research diminished significantly when she left her administrative role. Too little time had elapsed to have established systematic and self-sustaining cultural change through an ongoing collaboration between the ESL and content area teachers. Yet there is promise. During Elizabeth's tenure, a superintendent's student advisory council was formed, and today it includes students from each grade in high school. The body is multicultural and serves in an advisory capacity to the superintendent, which indicates that some self-advocacy may indeed have taken root. The walk together has begun, but it will need continued efforts by all involved to travel the road of diversity that leads to embracing differences and leaving no child and no teacher behind.

Questions for Discussion

Review the case study at the beginning of the chapter. Discuss the following questions that aim to extend the discussions included in the chapter.

1. If Elizabeth were your superintendent, and given the circumstances within your teaching context, where would you suggest she start in terms of the collaboration between ESL and content area teachers for the promotion of culturally relevant pedagogy and ELL advocacy?

2. How are newly arrived ELL students introduced to your school culture and community? How could this reception be more culturally responsive?

3. How might you begin to collaborate with colleagues to advocate for ELLs?

4. What resources would you need to sustain collaboration in your school?

Summary of Main Ideas

1. Educators need to consider different cultures in the U.S. educational system due to
   a) a dramatic increase in the number of Hispanics in the United States
   b) culturally and linguistically diverse ELLs
   c) the impact of culture on teaching and learning

2. Culture is
   a) a complex construct that can be defined from multiple perspectives
   b) the beliefs, traditions, values, attitudes, and behaviors of a group
   c) a vital resource in the teaching and learning of ELLs

3. The components of multicultural education include
   a) content integration
   b) knowledge construction
   c) prejudice reduction
   d) equity pedagogy
   e) empowering school culture

4. Culturally responsive teaching incorporates
   a) the student's culture
   b) having high self-esteem and a high regard for others
   c) being part of and giving back to the community
   d) the belief that all students can succeed
   e) helping students make connections between their community, national, and global identities

5. Advocacy is
   a) a concept rooted in critical pedagogy
   b) meeting the needs of ELLs in various venues, including the political arena
   c) giving students a voice for self-advocacy

6. Teachers collaborate effectively to embrace culture when they
   a) identify the unique cultural and linguistic background of each student
   b) vary instruction to connect to students' native language and culture
   c) use a variety of instructional activities that may include cooperative learning

7. Teachers collaborate effectively to support advocacy when they
   a) encourage students to use their native language in school settings
   b) give students contact and access to administration, such as the principal
   c) make known their professional development needs

References

American Psychological Association. (2003). Guidelines on multicultural education, training, research, practice, and organizational change for psychologists. *American Psychologist, 58*, 377–402.

August, D., & Garcia, E. (1988). *Language minority education in the United States: Research, policy and practice.* Springfield, IL: Charles C. Thomas.

August, D., & Hakuta, K. (1997). *Improving schooling for language-minority children: A research agenda.* Washington, DC: National Academy Press.

Baker, C. (2001). *Foundations of bilingual education and bilingualism* (3rd ed.). Tonawanda, NY: Multilingual Matters.

Banks, J. (1995). *Handbook of research on multicultural education.* New York: Macmillan.

Banks, J., & Banks, C. (Eds.). (2003). *Multicultural education: Issues and perspective* (4th ed.). New York: John Wiley & Sons.

Black, S. (2005, May). English spoken here. *American School Board Journal, 192*(5). Available from http://www.asbj.com/2005/05/0505research.html

Board of Regents of the University of Wisconsin System. (2007). *English language proficiency (ELP) standards.* Retrieved August 22, 2007, from http://www.wida.us/standards/elp.aspx

Brisk, M. E., & Harrington, M. M. (2000). *Literacy and bilingualism: A handbook for all teachers*. Mahwah, NJ: Lawrence Erlbaum.

Bruner, J. (1996). *The culture of education*. Cambridge, MA: Harvard University Press.

Cochran-Smith, M. (1995). Color blindness and basket making are not the answers: Confronting dilemmas of race, culture, and language diversity in teacher education. *American Educational Research Journal, 32*, 493–522.

Cohen, G. L., Garcia, J., Apfel, N., Master, A. (2006). Reducing the racial achievement gap: A social-psychological intervention. *Science, 313,* 1307–1310.

Connell, C. (2004). English language learners: Boosting academic achievement. *Research Points, 2*(1), 1–4.

Cummins, J. (1981). Age on arrival and immigrant second language learning in Canada: A reassessment. *Applied Linguistics, 2*, 132–149.

Dalton, S. S. (1998). *Pedagogy matters: Standards for effective teaching practice.* Santa Cruz, CA and Washington, DC: Center for Research on Education, Diversity & Excellence. Retrieved July 26, 2007, from http://crede.berkeley.edu/products/print /reports.html

D'Andrade, R. (1984). Cultural meaning systems. In R. A. Shweder & R. A. LeVine (Eds.), *Culture theory: Essays on mind, self, and emotion* (pp. 88–119). Cambridge: Cambridge University Press.

Delpit, L. (1995). *Other people's children: Cultural conflict in the classroom*. New York: New Press.

Díaz-Rico, T. L. (2004). *Teaching English learners: Strategies and methods*. Boston: Allyn & Bacon.

Echevarria, J., Vogt, M., & Short, D. (2004). *Making content comprehensible for English learners: The SIOP model* (2nd ed.). Boston: Allyn & Bacon.

Einhorn, K. (2002, September). Welcoming second-language learners: Terrific techniques to ease students from every nation into the school year. *Instructor, 111*(6), 54–55.

Freire, P. (1970). *Pedagogy of the oppressed*. New York: Continuum.

Gay, G. (2000). *Culturally responsive teaching: Theory, research, and practice*. New York: Teachers College Press.

Geertz, C. (1973). *The interpretation of cultures*. New York: Basic Books.

Gibbons, P. (2002). *Scaffolding language, scaffolding learning: Teaching second language learners in the mainstream classroom*. Portsmouth, NH: Heinemann.

Gray, T., & Fleischman, S. (2004). Successful strategies for English language learners. *Educational Leadership, 62*(4), 84–85.

Herrell, A. L., & Jordan, M. (2004). *Fifty strategies for teaching English language learners* (2nd ed.). Upper Saddle River, NJ: Pearson/Merrill Prentice Hall.

Ladson-Billings, G. (1994). *The dreamkeepers*. San Francisco: Jossey-Bass.

Ladson-Billings, G. (1995a). But that's just good teaching! The case for culturally relevant pedagogy. *Theory Into Practice, 34*(3), 159–165.

Ladson-Billings, G. (1995b). Toward a theory of culturally relevant pedagogy. *American Educational Research Journal, 32,* 465–491.

LeVine, R. A. (1984). Properties of culture: An ethnographic view. In R. A. Shweder & R. A. LeVine (Eds.), *Culture theory: Essays on mind, self, and emotion* (pp. 67–87). Cambridge: Cambridge University Press.

Moll, L. C., Amanti, C., Neff, D., & Gonzalez, N. (1992). Funds of knowledge for teaching: Using a qualitative approach to connect homes and classrooms. *Theory Into Practice, 31*(2), 132–141.

Nieto, S. (1996). *Affirming diversity: The sociopolitical context of multicultural education.* (2nd ed.). White Plains, NY: Longman.

Northeast and Islands Regional Educational Laboratory at Brown University. (2002). *The diversity kit: An introductory resource for social change in education.* Providence, RI: Brown University. Retrieved July 26, 2007, from http://www.alliance.brown .edu/tdl/diversitykitpdfs/diversitykit.pdf

Ogbu, J. (1987). Variability in minority school performance. *Anthropology & Education Quarterly, 18,* 312–334.

Padron, Y. N., Waxman, H. C., and Rivera, H. H. (2002). *Educating Hispanic students: Effective instructional practices* (Practitioner Brief #5). Retrieved July 26, 2007, from http://www.cal.org/crede/Pubs/PracBrief5.htm

Ruiz-de-Velasco, J., Fix, M., & Chu Clewell, B. (2000). *Overlooked and underserved: Immigrant students in U.S. secondary schools.* Retrieved July 26, 2007, from http:// www.urban.org/publications/310022.html

Sanchez, L. (2006, May 26). Instead of pickets, students grabbed their pencils. *Union Tribune.* Retrieved July 26, 2007, from http://www.signonsandiego.com/news /education/20060526-9999-7m26steele1.html

Short, D., & Echevarria, J. (2004). Teacher skills to support English language learners. *Educational Leadership, 62*(4), 8–13.

Stake, R. (1975). *Evaluating the arts in education.* Columbus, OH: Charles E. Merrill.

Suarez-Orozco, C., & Suarez-Orozco, M. (2001). *Children of immigration.* Cambridge, MA: Harvard University Press.

Teaching diverse learners. (n.d.). Retrieved July 10, 2007, from http://www.alliance .brown.edu/tdl/

TESOL. (1997). *ESL standards for pre-K–12 students*. Alexandria, VA: Author.

Tienda, M., & Mitchell, F. (2006). *Multiple origins, uncertain destinies: Hispanics and the American future. Panel on Hispanics in the United States*. Washington, DC: The National Academies Press.

Tomlinson, C. A. (2005). Traveling the road to differentiation in staff development. *Journal of Staff Development, 26*(4), 8–12.

Trumbull, E., & Pacheco, M. (2005). *The teacher's guide to diversity: Building a knowledge base. Volume II: Language*. Providence, RI: Education Alliance at Brown University. Retrieved July 26, 2007, from http://www.alliance.brown.edu/pubs/teach_guide_diversity/tgd_language.pdf

U.S. Census Bureau. (2003, May). *Census 2000 data*. Retrieved October 5, 2007, from http://www.census.gov/main/www/cen2000.html

Violand-Sanchez, E., & Hainer-Violand, J. (2006). The power of positive identity. *Educational Leadership, 64*(1), 36–40.

Violand-Sanchez, E., Sutton, C., & Ware, H. (1991). *Fostering home school cooperation: Involving language minorities families as partners in education*. Washington, DC: National Center for Bilingual Education.

Vygotsky, L. S. (1978). *Mind in society: The development of higher psychological processes*. (M. Cole, V. John-Steiner, S. Scribner, & E. Souberman, Eds. & Trans.). Cambridge, MA: Harvard University.

Walqui, A. (2000). *Access and engagement: Program design and instructional approaches for immigrant students in secondary schools*. McHenry, IL: Delta Systems; and Washington, DC: Center for Applied Linguistics.

Ware, F. (2006). Warm demander pedagogy: Culturally responsive teaching that supports a culture of achievement for African American students. *Urban Education, 41*, 427–456.

Wiggins, G., & McTighe, J. (2005). *Understanding by design* (2nd ed.). Upper Saddle River, NJ: Pearson Prentice Hall.

Wlodkowski, R., & Ginsberg, M. (1995). A framework for culturally responsive teaching. *Educational Leadership, 53*(1), 17–21.

CHAPTER 9

Extending Collaboration Into the Foreign Language Context

MOSAIC: Connecting Foreign Languages to Content Disciplines

Sally Hood

(**CASE STUDY**)

As usual, it is late afternoon when the MOSAIC team meets to review its work. It is a weekday and the four instructors have already put in a full day of teaching. Now they are gearing up for a 3- to 4-hour meeting during which they will continue their work on developing a unit that integrates geography content and the Spanish language. The two language specialists (LSs) have created six communicative activities to meet objectives (expressing location and describing geographical features) for a subtopic (places and regions in Spain and Oregon) of a unit the team named Immigration in Oregon. The two LSs wrote the activities together in a separate meeting the week before. They share the activities they developed with the social studies specialists, explaining the details as the social studies specialists peruse them. Discussions ensue.

"Well, how do you teach the geography of Oregon?" the LSs ask.

The geography teacher replies, "I give my students unlabeled maps and I talk about the various features while the students label the maps." The LSs are struck that they had not thought about how this would be an excellent way to provide comprehensible input for their students. The geography teacher then points to the list of geography terms that the LSs had provided in the activity and explains that he usually doesn't teach generic terms like *mountains, river,* and *lake*. Rather, he teaches proper names, such as Cascade Mountains, Willamette River, and Crater Lake (geographical features located in Oregon). The LSs begin rethinking their vocabulary list, keeping the objectives behind the subtopic in mind. This sliver of collaborative learning encourages them to alter their instructional practices toward the teaching of content via the Spanish language versus their accustomed way of focusing on the language specifically.

Prereading Questions

- Why are national foreign language standards important?
- What is content-based instruction?
- How do national foreign language standards call for the incorporation of content-based instruction?
- How can content specialists and foreign language specialists collaborate to undertake content-based instruction to address national foreign language standards?

WHY ARE NATIONAL FOREIGN LANGUAGE STANDARDS IMPORTANT?

Standards for Foreign Language Learning: Preparing for the Twenty-First Century (National Standards in Foreign Language Education Project, 1996), represents a collaborative project of nine groups: the American Council on the Teaching of Foreign Languages (ACTFL), the American Association of Teachers of French (AATF), the American Association of Teachers of German (AATG), the American Association of Teachers of Spanish and Portuguese (AATSP), the American Association of Teachers of Italian, the American Classical League, the American Council of Teachers of Russian, the Chinese Language Association of Secondary-Elementary Schools/Chinese Language Teachers Association, and the National Council of Japanese Language Teachers/Association of Teachers of Japanese. The task force that wrote the standards document consulted with a wide range of individuals in and outside of the foreign language teaching profession, resulting in a national consensus about the role of foreign language education. The standards writers' vision is one in which all students in the United States will become proficient in a language other than English. The standards document extends and more deeply defines changes that began in foreign language education more than two decades ago. Changes should progress from a "rigid, prescriptive system focused largely on language forms to a more flexible, descriptive, constructivist vision that recognizes developmental and creative aspects of second language acquisition with an emphasis on meaning" (p. 7). The standards document assumes and promotes communicative language teaching (CLT) as the philosophy guiding foreign language learning. Learning to use the language to function in diverse cultural contexts is paramount.

The national foreign language standards (NFLS) are organized within the following five goals that emphasize developing students' communicative skills:

1. Communication: participating appropriately in conversations with those who speak the foreign language; interpreting that society's concepts, ideas, and opinions; and presenting information, concepts, and ideas to an audience of listeners or readers on a variety of topics.

2. Cultures: understanding the relationship between the practices and products and the perspectives of the culture(s) studied

3. Connections: connecting knowledge to other disciplines and acquiring information through the foreign language

4. Comparisons: demonstrating an understanding of the nature of language and the concept of culture through comparisons of the language and culture studied and the student's own

5. Communities: using the language both within and beyond the school setting and showing evidence of becoming lifelong learners by using the language for personal enjoyment and enrichment (National Standards in Foreign Language Education Project, 1996)

Eleven standards, embedded within the five goals, define knowledge and abilities that all students should acquire by the end of a sequence of study. Each standard is then divided into sample progress indicators that specify student progress at various levels of instruction.

The Connections Goal (CG) was the organizing principle for this collaborative project, which is why this chapter focuses on a description of this goal and its implications. The CG addresses the interplay of language learning with other disciplines in the school curriculum, as students use a second language to learn other subjects, such as literature, social studies, science, or math. This implies that teaching and learning in the foreign language classroom are centered on learning information that is rooted in the various discipline areas through the language rather than on learning about the language per se. The assumption is that the language is learned through engagement with content. Examples of topics that teachers and students could explore within the disciplines range from weather, animals, and mathematical measurements to worldwide health issues, political issues, and scientific concepts. In addition, the premise of the CG extends learning content through the foreign language to acquiring this information through sources intended for native speakers of the language, providing opportunities for students to develop an awareness and, ideally, acceptance of different viewpoints. These native language sources might include, but are not limited to, songs, newspapers, a variety of genres of literature, Internet sites, and radio broadcasts. By exposure to information from a myriad of authentic sources, students studying another language and culture gain new and broader perspectives that they take outside the language classroom.

A curriculum that is designed around the CG fits within the realm of interdisciplinary approaches to teaching. Interdisciplinary curricula typically examine a particular theme, issue, problem, or topic through the lens of more than one discipline area (Jacobs, 1989). The benefits of teaching with an interdisciplinary curriculum are widely regarded. There is consensus in the literature that the relevance of ideas becomes clearer when viewed through multiple perspectives, the acquisition of knowledge becomes more meaningful because the topic is approached as a whole, learning becomes more personalized and interactive as students collaborate to solve problems and inquire into areas of interest, and instruction reflects how people operate in the "real world" (Jacobs, 1989; Met, 1999). From a conceptual standpoint, learning content in the foreign language classroom (e.g., a content-based approach to teaching the language) reinforces and extends knowledge students are learning in other disciplines, with the added benefit of thinking about the concepts in another language and with multiple perspectives.

WHAT IS CONTENT-BASED INSTRUCTION?

Content-based instruction (CBI) is defined as a philosophy, a methodology, a curriculum, or a framework (Stryker & Leaver, 1997). According to Stryker and Leaver, "CBI implies the total integration of language learning and content learning" (p. 5). A curriculum that is based on CBI should be developed from academic content standards in conjunction with academic language standards. In the foreign language classroom, this means that the content must go beyond topics that have traditionally been taught—family, travel, food—to those that are "cognitively engaging and demanding" (Met, 1999, p. 148). Met's assertion is connected with Cummins's (1981) communicative language framework, represented by a grid in Figure 1 to illustrate effective integration of language and content.

The grid includes two axes, one ranging from context-embedded instruction to context-reduced, and the other ranging from cognitively undemanding tasks to cognitively demanding. In context-embedded instruction, the teacher includes visuals or hands-on experiences to make the content more comprehensible. When instruction is context reduced, there is little to no support for the language learner. Cognitively demanding tasks should include work slightly above the learners' academic level and include higher level thinking skills. Cognitively undemanding tasks tend not to motivate learners to become engaged in the task. In CBI, tasks are focused on content and should be demanding and engaging; teachers should monitor the amount of context that they provide based on the students' levels of proficiency (Met, 1999). It is critical that information presented in CBI stem from subjects taught in school with academic content standards acting as the basis for instruction.

Crandall and Tucker (1990), Met (1999), and Stoller and Grabe (1997) outline several attributes of a CBI program. For example, activating or assessing schemata is an important technique that helps learners make connections between what they already know and new material that is presented. Student interaction is critical; lesson activities should be designed so that students talk to each other in the foreign language in pairs or small groups as they work together to solve a problem. In addition, teachers should provide students with a variety of materials and resources that they use to accomplish a task. Authentic materials are particularly useful for teaching language in context, especially in regard to meeting the second standard of the CG, which recommends using texts written for native speakers; these might include

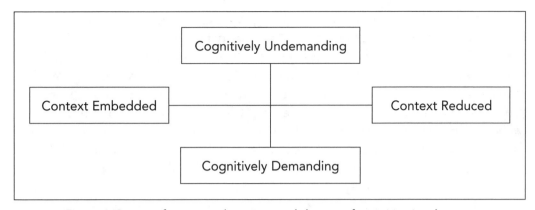

Figure 1. Range of contextual support and degree of cognitive involvement in communicative activities

Source: Cummins, 1981. Reprinted, with permission from the California Department of Education.

primary documents, poetry, maps, menus, timelines, charts, and tables. Learning in a CBI program should be experiential in nature, with students involved in hands-on projects, discovering new information in cooperation with their peers. Finally, writing is an integral part of daily activities in that it helps students reinforce and extend their learning. Students should be engaged in producing items typically written in content-specific classes, such as diagrams, math problems, letters, lab experiment procedures, and poetry. To summarize, learning in a content-based foreign language classroom is characterized by social interaction to accomplish a task using multiple resources that are found in the world outside of the classroom.

The instructional characteristics of CBI are congruent with a communicative language teaching (CLT) approach (pedagogy promoted in the NFLS), language learning theories that view language as communication, and social constructivist learning theory. CLT is distinguished by instructional features such as a focus on meaning making, learning language in context, student interaction, and an early development of reading and writing skills (Finocchiaro & Brumfit, 1983). The CLT approach came about through the work of language learning theorists who viewed language as communication. For example, Hymes (1972) created the term *communicative competence*, which highlights the integration of communication and cultural knowledge as an integral part of instruction. Halliday (1970) has built on Hymes's theory, emphasizing the functions of language, one of which describes using language to learn and discover. Richards and Rodgers (1986) claim that CLT pedagogy includes elements of a general learning theory because of its emphasis on activities that focus on authentic communication, meaningful language use, and the completion of specific tasks that promote learning. In particular, a relationship exists between CLT and Vygotsky's (1986) social constructivist learning theory of social development in which social interaction focused on accomplishing tasks is viewed as contributing to cognitive development. Stryker and Leaver (1997) support CBI's connection with CLT, stating that CBI is centered on developing communicative competency and fostering "the ability to communicate with native speakers in real-life situations" (p. 12).

According to Stoller and Grabe (1997), CBI has existed in the second language field for the past 25 years, but has increased in popularity just in the past decade. In step with the NFLS, foreign language teachers have begun to integrate content areas that have traditionally fallen outside the scope of foreign language classes. A range of CBI models in the United States have seen success in developing higher levels of language proficiency. According to Met (1999), these models lie along a continuum from total immersion programs (content driven) to language classes with frequent use of content for language practice (language driven). Bragger and Rice (1998) developed a CBI model that introduces progressively less familiar and more sophisticated content as students advance in language proficiency. Other researchers are designing courses and curriculum for integrating CBI across schools and proficiency levels. However, most language teachers in the United States teach in a "language-driven program model, in which their primary focus is on language outcomes" (Met, 1999, p. 150).

According to Crandall and Tucker (1990), the need for foreign language students to learn a language through CBI is critical. The reason for this is apparent: Most U.S. students only study a foreign language for 2 years, thus they rarely achieve a level of proficiency necessary for carrying on advanced-level conversations. There exists an acute need for individuals in the United States to develop advanced to superior proficiency ratings in a second language to establish both political and economic advantages. CBI may reduce attrition and help students cope with the progression from novice to advanced levels. A focus on CBI results in enhanced second language competence, increased subject matter knowledge, and increased self-confidence and motivation for further language study.

HOW DO NATIONAL FOREIGN LANGUAGE STANDARDS CALL FOR THE INCORPORATION OF CONTENT-BASED INSTRUCTION?

The literature supports a shared professional consensus that NFLS will not be realized without widespread and continuous professional development and that teachers must be actively involved in both its design and implementation (Bartz & Keefe Singer, 1996; Darling-Hammond, 1997; Glisan, 1996; Solomon, 1997). The profession calls for a collaborative approach to this professional development (Glisan, 1996; Phillips, 1998). Stryker and Leaver's (1997) work with CBI underlines the important role of collaboration to ensure CBI's effectiveness. They state that "instructors must be more than just good language teachers" (p. 22), they must also be knowledgeable about the specific content areas they are teaching within their CBI program. Stryker and Leaver recommend a team-teaching approach that involves a content specialist (CS) working with an LS. Phillips, referring to the Connections Goal (CG) in NFLS, believes that relying only on the language teacher to teach content is a narrow view of realizing the goal and recommends collaborative partnerships. Stryker and Leaver, referring to CBI, concur, claiming that expecting LSs to also teach content is a difficult challenge to overcome.

The call for more teacher-centered professional development includes recommendations designed to promote more in-depth teacher learning and change in teaching practices. Little (1993) developed general (not discipline-specific) professional development principles that emphasize collaboration. The principles suggest that teachers work interactively with the content of their discipline, exchanging new ideas and developing materials with a group of colleagues. This work should be structured so that it is a long-term project rather than the typical workshop format. Little highlights the importance of projects that allow teachers to focus on needs specific to their working context. Glisan (1996) specifically addresses NFLS, identifying areas of need with regard to professional development. Glisan discusses the need for foreign language teachers to have frequent opportunities to collaborate with colleagues and explains that teachers need substantial time to work together to decide on curricular components for different levels of instruction. She recommends that curricula should be "goal oriented" (p. 74), with a focus on meaningful content rather than grammar. Glisan's recommendations have implications in terms of meeting the CG because of the need for language teachers to work closely with content teachers and because of the focus on teaching content via the language rather than on teaching the language specifically. However, as Met (1999) and Glisan point out, collaboration among teachers creates a variety of challenges that the education field has only recently begun to experience.

HOW CAN CONTENT SPECIALISTS AND FOREIGN LANGUAGE SPECIALISTS COLLABORATE TO UNDERTAKE CONTENT-BASED INSTRUCTION TO ADDRESS NATIONAL FOREIGN LANGUAGE STANDARDS?

The Necessity of Social Trust and Teacher Efficacy in Teacher Collaboration

In a research study about teacher learning through a school-university partnership, Fisler and Firestone (2006) found that social trust and teacher efficacy played key roles in effective professional development partnerships. Social trust is defined by Coleman (as cited in Fisler & Firestone, 2006) as the confidence teachers have in the reliability and integrity of the individuals involved in a partnership and the extent to which teachers will make changes because of risks involved in the process. These risks include collaboration, observation, feedback, discussion of problems and solutions in the classroom, and the sharing of information and the acceptance of another's information as valid. Teacher efficacy is a personal belief that one can have a positive influence on student learning. Teachers who possess this belief are more willing to put forth an effort to make changes in their instruction and to persist in improving despite challenges (Fisler & Firestone, 2006). The combination of social trust and self-efficacy result in a strong belief that one is working with others to achieve a common goal, and thus the process of doing so is more successful and the resulting product is of higher quality.

Fisler and Firestone's (2006) research shows that teachers in the partnership who made the most instructional changes had the highest levels of social trust and were the ones who also improved their self-efficacy. Their 3-year study focused on five study groups facilitated by university faculty. Elementary teachers from a local school district were invited to participate in the groups, and study topics varied across the five groups depending on the needs of the teachers within them. The researchers interviewed the teachers and administrative staff, observed the study group meetings and classroom instruction, collected documents related to the study group meetings, and conducted several surveys with the teachers. Findings from the study showed that some teachers made positive instructional changes and improved their attitudes toward teaching and learning and their interactions with others in the school. However, the researchers' strongest findings were that the amount of learning varied considerably among all teacher participants and that social trust and self-efficacy were the two factors that influenced the variability. The teachers who exhibited the most professional development showed evidence of higher levels of social trust and self-efficacy, and the teachers who resisted making instructional changes were the ones who exhibited the least amount of social trust and self-efficacy. The researchers conclude that successful collaboration between schools and universities requires a strong sense of social trust and high levels of teacher self-efficacy in order for reforms to take place.

What This Type of Collaboration Looks Like

The Center for Applied Second Language Studies (CASLS), a national foreign language resource center at the University of Oregon, paired expertise from the university and local high schools to develop content-based thematic units, which are designed for use in high school and university language programs. Each thematic unit integrates the content areas of history or geography with continued language proficiency development in Spanish, Japanese, or French. This curriculum project, named MOSAIC, was carried out between 2003 and 2005 and resulted in four thematic units that integrate Spanish and geography, seven that integrate Japanese and history, and one that integrates French and earth science. MOSAIC was chosen as the name for this project because it conjures the image of a design in which an assembly of different pieces form a composite whole. Accordingly, the idea behind the MOSAIC project was to create units that include an assembly of language components and discipline-specific content that work together to form an integrated exploration of a particular theme. Each unit uses an array of interactive materials that include detailed lesson plans, instructions for teachers, handouts for students, performance assessments, and extension activities. The units are available free of charge on the CASLS Web site, and teachers are encouraged to adapt them to their individual needs.

This curriculum project involved a unique collaboration. For each thematic unit, teams of four worked together to create the materials. These teams comprised a university language teacher, a university content area scholar, a K–12 language teacher, and a high school content teacher. For example, a history professor, a Japanese professor, a high school social studies teacher, and a high school Japanese teacher developed a thematic unit on the history of the Edo period in Japan (1600–1868). In each team, the role of the CSs was to identify relevant content, texts, and source materials. The language specialists were responsible for assuring the pedagogical and linguistic quality of the materials and adapting the materials to the linguistic and cognitive level of their students. Each team worked together to conceptualize and plan each unit in detail. Team members used national and state standards documents as resources and as guides in the development of the units.

The Development of a Collaborative Unit: An Example

The first unit that was designed served as a protocol for the second one. In addition, the work that unfolded during the creation of the first unit brought out the highlights of this unique project and issues with which to contend. Sally, the research and development director at CASLS, agreed to codirect MOSAIC and collaborated in managing the project with Roger, a university professor of Spanish at the University of Oregon who had ties with faculty from various other university departments. Roger recruited the university participants for each team, and Sally, who had connections with local high school teachers, solicited their involvement.

The codirectors decided from the outset to allow team members to designate the theme of each unit. The project began with a Spanish-geography focus. Geography was chosen because Roger had a colleague who was a geography professor and, after learning about the MOSAIC project, was enthusiastic about participating in it. After the Spanish-geography team was established, the six members met for the initial work session. During this session, Roger and Sally laid out details of the project and solicited members' ideas. Sharon, the geography professor, suggested *immigration* as the theme of the unit during the first meeting. She had a myriad of ideas for instructional activities and possessed a variety of materials that she used in her teaching of geography at the University of Oregon. Sharon's strong expertise in this area, coupled with her interest in it, persuaded all of the team members that the topic of immigration would work well, especially because it was a current topic of critical national and local importance.

Proponents of CBI agree that an important attribute of a CBI program is a curriculum based on both second language and content area standards (Crandall & Tucker, 1990; Met, 1999; Stryker & Leaver, 1997). During this first work session, the team perused both the national geography standards and NFLS on which they would base the instructional activities and assessments. The team thought of the idea of using case studies from Oregon, a state with a substantial and growing Spanish-speaking population, so that students would learn some of the fundamentals of geographical analysis as they plotted growth and settlement patterns of Hispanic populations across the state. The team set up a scope and sequence for the unit by creating three guiding geographical questions. The team thought that each of these questions would draw students deeper into the issues surrounding immigration, and the customizable activities presented in the unit would allow teachers to personalize the topics for their students by examining their own local communities. At the same time, students would receive linguistic input and produce output on crucial advanced-level language functions such as detailed descriptions, comparisons, and past narration in addition to recycling lower level functions (e.g., asking information questions). Appendix A provides a global picture of the geography unit, including the standards and guiding questions that were chosen.

The immigration unit was divided into two smaller units. The team decided to structure the unit in this way to make it more manageable for teachers and to better organize the information in it. Appendix A displays the titles of the two smaller units, an abstract of the content explored in each, and a description of the performance assessment for each. The first small unit focuses on Basque immigration to the western United States. Basques from northern Spain came to the western United States in the late 19th and early 20th centuries and established stable communities that are still in existence today. The examination of this group serves as a case study, introducing students to the general phenomena that characterize human migration. Students learn about the basic *push* and *pull* factors that motivate migration and study details of the consequences of displacement on peoples and their communities.

The second small unit focuses on past and present immigrants from Mexico. It examines two waves of immigration from Mexico to Oregon. The first group arrived under the Bracero program in the years following the Second World War. The second group began arriving in the 1980s and continues to the present day. This unit allows students to gain a historical perspective through chronological ordering. Also, they investigate the specific demographic differences between groups, in terms of occupations held, settlement patterns, and cultural impact on the state.

Each small unit is organized in similar ways. Each lists guiding questions that serve as a scope and sequence, and each has a summative assessment that is performance based. The assessment for the small unit on Mexican immigrants requires students to prepare an illustrated genealogical tree of a Mexican family (hypothetical or based on interviews with an immigrant family in the community). An oral presentation based on the family tree elicits the language functions of past narration, extensive description, and comparisons between present and past time frames. The content of the presentation includes descriptions of family members and their origins, reasons for coming to the United States, and an explanation of why they ended up where they did. This task is designed so that students synthesize and personalize all they have learned about Mexican immigration to Oregon.

Each small unit contains six to eight activities and a list of Web and literature sources. Appendix B lists three activities in Unit 2 and illustrates a CBI curriculum that the team designed to meet the CG. The tasks reflect both standards of the CG.

The activities in the unit reflect CBI attributes outlined by Crandall and Tucker (1990) and Stryker and Leaver (1997). For example, authentic materials abound, and students use current information to complete activities. The Web and literature sources include maps, migration basics, country profiles, an online dictionary, and demographic information. Each source includes a Web address that is hyperlinked. In addition, all MOSAIC activities integrate at least two of the four skills (speaking, listening, reading, writing), and most of them three or all four. Student interaction and hands-on learning (two other attributes of CBI) characterize MOSAIC activities. Students talk to each other in pairs, work together in small groups, read individually, and listen as a whole class. Students play games, role-play television reporters, and participate in scavenger hunts in their local community. The characteristics of the MOSAIC activities reflect the purpose of the CG: Students use the language in student-centered pedagogical approaches to learn discipline-specific content.

The Scope and Sequence of Collaboration in Development of the Unit

The creation of each unit required a large time commitment from each team member, so team members were compensated for their work in the form of monthly stipends. Teams met two to three times per month for 2 to 4 hours. Work sessions were held in the late afternoon, evening, and at night to accommodate the teachers' schedules. In addition, team members worked outside the meeting times to write activities or gather resources, ideas for which were generated during meetings. The first Spanish unit on immigration took about 18 months to complete. Subsequent units took substantially less time, averaging 2 to 3 months from start to end. Some teams worked on more than one unit at a time in various stages of completion. The amount of time involved in the development of each unit depended on the individual personalities and working-learning style of each team member and the dynamics between the team members both during and outside meetings.

Different levels of collaboration occurred in the making of the first MOSAIC unit. Appendix C lays out these levels and the specific responsibilities that each team member assumed. These levels of collaboration evolved organically during the meetings; they were not planned a priori. Although Appendix C seems to illustrate the levels in a linear way, a constant interplay occurred between team members as needs arose and content was developed. The characteristics of CBI and the CG underlie the responsibilities listed. Specific CBI attributes, described by Crandall and Tucker (1990) and Stryker and Leaver (1997), are noted in Appendix C. In analysis, the collaboration that occurred between the various team members involved making decisions and exchanging ideas. The CSs located and provided materials and shared content-specific information. The LSs were the curriculum developers. As Appendix C illustrates, the LSs took on the most responsibilities and dedicated more time to the project than the CSs. The amount of time spent working outside the team meetings was one sign of how committed the LSs were to the project. This is a characteristic of social trust and of teacher efficacy; that is, the LSs persisted even in the face of strong time challenges (Fisler & Firestone, 2006).

Collaborative Conversations in the Development Process:
Toward Trust and Social Efficacy

The first meeting between the Spanish-geography team members focused on devising a work schedule and conceptualizing the unit. The codirectors spent time discussing the goals and intent of the project, overviewing the NFLS and the CG in particular; they also outlined general roles and responsibilities for each team member and a tentative timeline for completing the project. The team discussed logistical features of the work, including where, when, and for how long they all could meet together. It took some negotiation and compromise to establish meeting times and a projected project timeline in order to facilitate each team member's daily work schedule and long-term plans, such as vacations and work-related travel. As mentioned in the case study at the beginning of the chapter, Sharon, the university geography professor, suggested the unit topic of immigration during this first meeting because she already had information, resources, and activities at her disposal. The team discussed the fact that Oregon was experiencing a large increase in immigration, particularly Spanish-speaking immigrants, and that there was a local need to understand who the immigrants were and why they emigrated. Sharon educated the group on the historic waves of immigration in Oregon and how the members could make a connection between past waves and the current one. The team ended that first meeting with homework assignments involving research on the academic geography standards and NFLS. They would share this homework at the following meeting during which they planned to map out a scope and sequence for the unit.

With the topic of immigration, they spent the second meeting perusing the geography standards and NFLS for the ninth through twelfth grades. Brad, the high school social studies teacher, began a discussion by sharing geography standards with the team. They narrowed in on benchmarks focused on immigration concepts. As the team skimmed these standards during the meeting, the LSs developed a clearer understanding of them. It was interesting to note that Brad added to the breadth of the discussion by pointing out that the standards were very high and that he felt he did not or could not bring his students to the point of meeting them. He attributed this to his being held accountable to cover a range of topics from a given textbook in less depth. The team came to terms with this issue by deciding that MOSAIC units would be designed so that teachers could implement the unit as a whole or pick and choose activities within a unit that they could use to improve upon or extend their regularly taught curriculum. The fact that Brad was willing to admit that he was not addressing the standards was another indication of the social trust the group developed during this collaborative project (Fisler & Firestone, 2006).

The discussion about geography standards led to questions from the LSs about specific approaches, methods, and techniques that Brad and Susan included in their instructional practices. Brad began to identify geographic information he taught as a part of his regular curriculum. The team encouraged him to share not only what he taught, but how he taught it; they wanted details. As he talked, the team needed concrete explanations in order to visualize and understand the teaching and learning that occurred in his geography classes. This articulation took time; as Brad struggled to describe as specifically as possible his pedagogy, the team members asked clarifying questions about elements he knew implicitly. Brad pinpointed elements of his instruction, such as having students label maps with specific places and geographical features; identify areas in a country or region that are industrial, agricultural, tourist oriented, and so on; compare and contrast geographical features of two or more countries or regions under study; understand typical weather and climate conditions and the physical environment of a region; and learn about a region's economic activities and population. This discussion prompted Sharon to describe some of her curricula that complimented Brad's techniques: comparing and contrasting the Basque country of Spain with the area of Oregon to which Basques emigrated in the early 19th century (where there is still a substantial Basque population), understanding the principle waves of

Hispanic immigration to Oregon through the identification of push-pull factors, and analyzing census data for growth during different periods of Hispanic immigration to various regions of Oregon. The team took notes about these topics as the CSs talked; the LSs would use these ideas and turn them into language learning activities.

With the NFLS in mind and with a focus on communication and culture, the LSs shared activities in their repertoire related to geography. They discussed the fact that they, too, instructed students in the labeling of maps—labels such as mountains, rivers, deserts, seas, and so on. At one point, they asked Brad about the specific labels he required his students to use. He seemed surprised that the instructors did not always use the proper names of the geographical features, such as *Tajo River* versus *river*, or *Atlantic Ocean* versus *ocean*. This was an important insight because using specific proper names rather than generic terms (e.g., *lake* or *bay*) is in line with the NFLS that emphasize teaching in context and with real-life references and scenarios. This was one of the first insights that arose during this collaborative project; the LSs were struck that they had not considered something that made so much sense. As a result of this conversation, the team decided that the first couple of activities in the unit would address the labeling of maps of Spain and Oregon with specific geographical names in Spanish. This exchange of discourse and the subsequent action taken reflected characteristics of teacher efficacy (Fisler & Firestone, 2006); that is, the LSs were willing to experiment with new ways of teaching vocabulary with a desire to improve foreign language learning.

The team decided early on in the project that it was not feasible to spend team meetings creating specific activities for the units; rather it was best if they brainstormed subtopics, the sequencing of subtopics, and generic types of activities that could be done with those subtopics. The LSs would then use their notes from the team meetings to design activities in a separate meeting during which only the two of them would meet. The main focus of the team meetings became having the CSs bring in materials and resources they used in their own teaching or those they searched for in between meetings using sources from their field. During meetings, they shared these resources with the LSs and explained how they would be used in a geography class. Then, in a general manner, the team brainstormed how these resources could be adapted in a foreign language classroom and at a language proficiency level that would neither be too low nor too high for secondary or lower level university students. The team also brainstormed general types of activities that would exploit these resources to their fullest potential and remain interesting to the age level of secondary students or undergraduates. The fact that the LSs took extra time to meet, in addition to full-team meetings, was another indication of the social trust that had developed. They were willing to work together to develop new approaches to teaching, and they put forth a great amount of effort to do so (Fisler & Firestone, 2006).

Once the CSs shared techniques, the LSs compared the techniques to some of their practices. What normally ensued was a positive but sometimes difficult dialogue in which the CSs contributed ideas that improved upon the activities described by the LSs. Improvement involved taking a typical language learning activity and putting it more into context (a geographic one, in this case) and making it more specific to a concept (immigration, in this case). This type of conversation resulted in pushing the LSs to prioritize content over language. For example, the team decided that one of the first few activities in the unit would involve students comparing and contrasting geographical features in Spain with those in Oregon using maps the students had labeled during a previous activity. The focus of this type of activity in a geography class is on descriptions of the features themselves and their geographical location. In a foreign language class, the emphasis would primarily be on the grammatical structures required to make comparisons, such as *more . . . than, less . . . than, just like*, and verbs in the present subjunctive (e.g., the capital of Oregon is smaller than the capital of Spain). The final version of the activity would require the students to use those grammatical structures, but the focus would be on analyzing the geographical features themselves, not the structure of the sentences. As this first unit developed, the LSs increasingly used content to drive creation of activities and to use language as the vehicle to accomplish these activities. The LSs were willing to admit they could improve their language teaching, showed a desire to find better ways of teaching, and took the CSs' suggestions and revised activities—all of which were signs of both social trust and teacher efficacy (Fisler & Firestone, 2006).

According to Fisler and Firestone (2006), effective collaboration in education requires both of these concepts. By *effective*, the researchers refer to teachers' participation in decision making and openness and willingness to work with other educators to develop more innovative teaching practices. The MOSAIC team exhibited several attributes of social trust. First, the LSs were highly committed to the project. Second, the high school geography teacher and the LSs admitted to the team instructional practices that they did not implement. Third, the LSs were willing to learn geography content, which made the teaching of Spanish more complex. Finally, the LSs took time to work together to create activities. The MOSAIC team also demonstrated characteristics of teacher efficacy. First, all of them, especially the LSs, persisted with the project even in the face of time challenges. Second, they put forth an extraordinary amount of effort to make the project a success. Last, the LSs were willing to experiment with new ways of teaching because they had the desire to improve learning. As Fisler and Firestone note, the combination of teacher efficacy and social trust meant that the MOSAIC team was working toward a common goal and each member felt responsible for reaching it.

Successes

The MOSAIC project became a form of professional development for each team member. Both the CSs and the LSs experienced theoretical and practical shifts as they collaborated. For example, the project required team members to exchange their pedagogical content knowledge. Shulman (1987) describes teachers' pedagogical content knowledge as something that "represents the blending of content and pedagogy into an understanding of how particular topics, problems, or issues are organized, represented, and adapted to the diverse interests and abilities of learners, and presented for instruction" (p. 8). Through various exchanges, the LSs not only broadened their knowledge about social studies content, they specifically developed more expertise about content directly connected to their field: teaching Spanish. The LSs learned in a task-based manner by having to peruse resources, such as texts that provide information about the Basque region in Oregon, and deciding how to use those resources as organizing centers for activities in which students use Spanish to learn the information. In addition, the LSs had to make judgments about the level of language that students would use to accomplish each activity. The LSs often had to take resources provided by the CSs and translate them from English into Spanish. As a result, the LSs improved their Spanish language proficiency; in particular, their vocabulary increased as they began to think about social studies concepts in Spanish rather than in English.

The CS also learned about foreign language pedagogy. For example, as the LS sequenced activities so that learning was scaffolded, the CSs became more aware of both how language develops and how vocabulary is learned in a second language. The CSs also gained new knowledge about Mexican and Spanish cultures as the LSs discussed specific practices, products, and perspectives (per the Culture Goal of the NFLS) during their meetings and embedded them into activities. Further, many activities in the MOSAIC unit include components of sheltered instruction, which is promoted as an approach to teaching English language learners in mainstream classrooms (Echevarria, Vogt, & Short, 2004). These components are represented in various activities and include comprehensible input, building background knowledge, use of visuals, student interaction, graphic organizers, and ways to motivate students to become engaged in learning the language (e.g., games, role playing, information gap activities, jigsaw activities). Thus, the CSs were exposed to a more student-centered type of instruction characterized by accomplishing tasks in cooperative learning structures.

The LSs became increasingly aware of the benefits of teaching language in context. They needed a decreasing amount of input from the CSs as the MOSAIC project developed. Fewer meetings between all four team members were needed in the middle part of the unit's development. However, more meetings between the two LSs were increasingly required because once the LSs became familiar with geographical pedagogy and the CSs had provided them with a myriad of resources, their task became targeted on fleshing out activities. Their learning was scaffolded; once they had the background knowledge necessary to develop geography-based language activities, they relied less on the expertise of the CSs. It is important to note that the LSs brought activities they designed to full-team meetings so that the CSs could provide suggestions for improving them or correct any inaccuracies in the content. The LSs' instructional ideas also became increasingly more in line with standards-based teaching, especially with regard to the CG. The activities they created focused on content, were contextualized and task based, and reflected real-life applications of the language. For example, in one activity, students must synthesize information acquired throughout the unit about Basque history to communicate what life was like from a shepherd's point of view. The task integrates the use of technology, is meaningful because of the local context, and is performance-based through its subjective format in which students are able to inject their individual interpretations and creativity through structures of the language that they must form. This activity targets one of the sample progress indicators of the Connections Goal: "Through research projects, students expand on topics learned in other school subjects as they relate to the Spanish-speaking world, such as geographical information, historical facts and concepts, and ecological developments" (National Standards in Foreign Language Education Project, 1996, p. 450).

Another layer of professional development occurred between the institutional levels that the team members represented. Interestingly, Sharon, the geography professor, had been Brad's (the high school geography teacher) instructor for a geography course he took as part of his master's program. Sharon expressed on several occasions that she was impressed with Brad's developing expertise. In the MOSAIC project their role of sharing pedagogical content knowledge not only informed them of each other's instructional context, but also contributed to it by increasing the repertoire of ideas that could be adapted to their respective levels of instruction. This type of learning also occurred between the LSs; they learned how geographical topics could be incorporated into each of their levels of instruction by adapting them to different language proficiency levels. This type of learning between secondary teachers and university instructors resulted in a better understanding of each member's instructional needs and gave them a greater awareness of the need for careful articulation between high school classes and university courses.

Lessons Learned and Next Steps

Team members worked to overcome a number of challenges. The differences between teaching contexts in the university and in the high school were greater than originally expected. For example, at the secondary level language proficiency is generally lower (because students have only studied the language for 2 to 3 years), and the teams had to adapt authentic geography and history content so that it could be taught in Spanish. The second standard of the CG states that students should acquire information about other disciplines through resources created for native Spanish speakers (National Standards in Foreign Language Education Project, 1996). Resources written in Spanish and that centered on specific topics took time to locate and, once found, had to be analyzed for their difficulty level. Some of the resources used in the MOSAIC units were originally written in English, because Spanish versions were not available. This resulted in the LSs translating them into Spanish. According to the NFLS document, "translations, when available, may also be inaccurate or misleading in cultural perspective" (p. 450), and Stryker and Leaver (1997) concur in their description of CBI: "One of the major characteristics of CBI is the extensive (though not necessarily exclusive) use of materials taken directly from the culture being studied" (p. 8). Although resources written for native speakers may require higher levels of language proficiency than U.S. foreign language students possess, Stryker and Leaver claim that "the important issue is not so much what those texts are but what the teacher does with them" (p. 8). In other words, the teacher should be able to create tasks around authentic resources that make the content more accessible to students whose proficiency levels are below that of the text itself. Whether the LSs translated materials or adapted them so that students could work with them to accomplish a task, a substantial amount of time was required.

The biggest challenge of this collaboration was providing opportunities for the entire team to work together for extended periods of time. One part of this was scheduling a time during which they all could meet, and the other part involved the length of time it took to complete a unit. The codirectors, in charge of scheduling the meetings, found it occasionally impossible to find a mutual day and time that everyone could work together. Numerous e-mail messages and phone calls were often necessary just to arrange one meeting. Each team member worked full time, and the high school teachers often had afterschool commitments. Because this was the first unit created in the MOSAIC project, the organization, format, and process of integrating content and language across academic levels required more conversations and thought than had been imagined. This first unit, then, not only served as a template and a model for subsequent ones, but it was also, in a sense, an experiment. The results of the experiment resulted in a change in the type of collaboration that occurred in the creation of the subsequent units.

The modifications and future work of MOSAIC occurred on two levels. At the micro and MOSAIC project level, the level of collaboration changed. After the first unit, a lead writer took over many of the responsibilities that the LSs had had during the first unit. A foreign language consultant with several years of teaching experience was hired to write unit activities after the rest of the team brainstormed content and outlined a scope and sequence. The LSs and CSs worked together to suggest topics for the overall units and for lessons within each unit. The team acted as an editorial board, shaping the formation of the unit by meeting with the lead writer once a month. The change in the model evolved because of the fierce time commitment required for the LSs to work outside full-team meetings to write the activities. According to the current codirector of the MOSAIC project, Greg Hopper-Moore, the new model "improved the speed of unit creation significantly, with the average unit being almost complete after 2 months" (G. Hopper-Moore, personal communication, September 27, 2006). Although the model changed, the team members continued to learn from each other by gaining knowledge about the fields their counterparts represented and adapting topics to lower levels with hands-on application of the content in meaningful activities.

At the macro level, future steps include development of additional units in French and the ongoing piloting of all the units in secondary classrooms. Feedback from classroom pilots are incorporated to improve the quality of each unit. Final units are formatted online so that teachers can download them and adapt them to their specific needs. Web links to authentic materials used in conjunction with unit lessons are regularly checked and updated on the MOSAIC Web site. It is exciting to also note that, according to Robert Davis of the MOSAIC project, the Spanish immigration unit and a Japanese unit were recently published by the International Society for Technology in Education as one of several in a curriculum series. The MOSAIC units were featured (among two other curriculum projects) in the foreign-language-specific volume because of the unique manner in which they incorporate the national technology standards for teachers.

Questions for Discussion

Review the case study at the beginning of the chapter. Discuss the following questions that aim to extend the discussions included in the chapter.

1. What would you say is the underlying pedagogy of teaching geography from the perspective of the geography teacher? How does that pedagogy differ from that of the foreign language teachers' pedagogy?

2. In thinking about CBI and the CG, how do the roles and responsibilities of the LSs compare to those of the CSs in this collaborative model?

3. How can CBI be implemented with this type of collaborative model in such a way that time will not be a challenge?

4. How can CBI be implemented in a secondary setting with a similar model of collaboration involving only secondary CSs and LSs?

Summary of Main Ideas
1. Those that created the NFLS envision a future in which all students in the United States become proficient in a language other than English.
2. The NFLS include the CG, which emphasizes integrating content and language.
3. Meeting the CG implies developing a curriculum closely related to CBI.
4. CBI promotes using the language as a means of communication and implies the integration of language learning and content learning.
5. The greatest challenge in a CBI program is expecting language teachers to teach content.
6. Professional development that is long term, ongoing, collaborative, and teacher centered is necessary to attain the NFLS.
7. The MOSAIC project was a unique type of professional development and collaboration that focused on developing a content-based curriculum that met the two standards of the CG.

8. Collaboration in the MOSAIC project evolved organically.
    a) The roles and responsibilities for the CSs and LSs developed naturally as the team worked on the project.
    b) These roles and responsibilities were specific to the team as a whole and to the teams of two specialists, respectively.
    c) The LSs took on more responsibilities than the CSs.

9. The LSs benefited by
    a) learning social studies content
    b) improving their Spanish language proficiency
    c) becoming aware of the importance of teaching language in context
    d) improving their instructional ideas so that the ideas were more in line with the national standards for foreign language learning

10. The CSs benefited by
    a) learning about second language acquisition
    b) learning how vocabulary is developed in a foreign language
    c) expanding their knowledge about Mexican and Spanish culture
    d) being exposed to components of sheltered instruction

11. The time factor (time for collaboration) was overwhelming, and the collaborative model was altered to include a lead writer who took over many of the responsibilities of the LSs.

References

Bartz, W. H., & Keefe Singer, M. (1996). The programmatic implications of foreign language standards. In R. C. Lafayette (Ed.), *National standards: A catalyst for reform* (pp. 139–167). Lincolnwood, IL: National Textbook Company.

Bragger, J. D., & Rice, D. B. (1998). Connections: The national standards and a new paradigm for content-oriented materials and instruction. In J. Harper, M. Lively, & M. Williams (Eds.), *The coming of age of the profession* (pp. 191–217). Boston: Heinle & Heinle.

Crandall, J., & Tucker, G. R. (1990). Content-based language instruction in second and foreign languages. In A. Sarinee (Ed.), *Language teaching methodology for the nineties* (pp. 83–96). Newbury Park, CA: Sage.

Cummins, J. (1981). The role of primary language development in promoting educational success for language minority students. In California State Department of Education (Ed.), *Schooling and language minority students: A theoretical framework*. Sacramento: California State Department of Education.

Darling-Hammond, L. (1997, September). Quality teaching: The critical key to learning. *Principal, 77*(1), 5–11.

Echevarria, J., Vogt, M., & Short, D. (2004). *Making content comprehensible for English learners: The SIOP model.* Boston: Pearson Education.

Finocchiaro, M., & Brumfit, C. (1983). *The functional-notional approach: From theory to practice.* New York: Oxford University Press.

Fisler, J. L., & Firestone, W. A. (2006). Teacher learning in a school-university partnership: Exploring the role of social trust and teaching efficacy beliefs. *Teachers College Record, 108*, 1155–1185.

Glisan, E. W. (1996). Standards and foreign language teacher education: Developing new professionals during a time of reform. In R. C. Lafayette (Ed.), *National standards: A catalyst for reform* (pp. 57–95). Lincolnwood, IL: National Textbook Company.

Halliday, M. A. K. (1970). Language structure and language function. In J. Lyons (Ed.), *New horizons in linguistics* (pp. 140–165). Harmondsworth, England: Penguin.

Hymes, D. (1972). On communicative competence. In J. B. Pride and J. Homes (Eds.), *Sociolinguistics* (pp. 269–293). Harmondsworth, England: Penguin.

Jacobs, H. H. (1989). The growing need for interdisciplinary curriculum content. In H. H. Jacobs (Ed.), *Interdisciplinary curriculum: Design and implementation* (pp. 1–11). Alexandria, VA: Association for Supervision and Curriculum Development.

Little, J. W. (1993). Teachers' professional development in a climate of educational reform. *Educational Evaluation and Policy Analysis, 15*(2), 129–151.

Met, M. (1999). Making connections. In J. Phillips (Ed.), *Foreign language standards: Linking research, theories, and practices* (pp. 137–164). Lincolnwood, IL: National Textbook Company.

National Standards in Foreign Language Education Project. (1996). *Standards for foreign language learning: Preparing for the 21st century.* Yonkers, NY: Author.

Phillips, J. (1998). Changing teacher/learner roles in standards-driven contexts. In J. Harper, M. G. Lively, & M. K. Williams (Eds.), *The coming of age of the profession: Issues and emerging ideas for the teaching of foreign languages* (pp. 3–14). Boston: Heinle & Heinle.

Richards, J. C., & Rodgers, T. S. (1986). *Approaches and methods in language teaching: A description and analysis.* New York: Press Syndicate of the University of Cambridge.

Shulman, L. S. (1987). Knowledge and teaching: Foundations of the new reform. *Harvard Educational Review, 57*(1), 1–22.

Solomon, J. (1997, September). Language teachers align curricula with standards: Preliminary results of a national survey. *ERIC/CLL News Bulletin, 21*(1), 1–7.

Stoller, F. L., & Grabe, W. (1997). A six-T's approach to content-based instruction. In M. S. Snow & D. M. Brinton (Eds.), *The content-based classroom* (pp. 3–33). New York: Longman.

Stryker, S. B., & Leaver, B. L. (1997). Content-based instruction: From theory to practice. In S. B. Stryker & B. L. Leaver (Eds.), *Content-based instruction in foreign language education: Models and methods* (pp. 2–28). Washington, DC: Georgetown University Press.

Vygotsky, L. (1986). *Thought and language.* Boston: MIT Press.

Appendix A: A Global Picture of the Spanish-Geography Unit

Immigration: General Introduction

This unit is an integration of geography and Spanish on a topic of national and local importance: immigration. Using case studies from Oregon, students will learn fundamentals of geographical analysis as they plot the growth and settlement patterns of Hispanic populations across the state.

Why immigration?

Guiding Questions:

- What compels people to uproot themselves from their home culture and reestablish their lives somewhere else?
- What is the impact of immigration on the places that receive immigrant populations?
- What is the life of an immigrant like?

Standards

Geography Standards

- describe and compare the physical, human, and cultural characteristics of places
- describe the distribution of human populations and their changes over time
- use maps/charts to express spatial relations and to represent demographic and historical data

NFLS

- describe and compare location, physical characteristics of places and people
- narrate in past and present time frames
- ask information questions

Organization

Unit 1	Unit 2
Basque immigration to the western United States	**Past and present immigrants from Mexico**
This unit examines an interesting and little studied wave of immigration to Oregon: Basques from northern Spain. Examination of this group serves as a case study, introducing students to the general phenomena that characterize human migration.	This unit examines two waves of immigration from Mexico to Oregon . Students gain a historical perspective through chronological ordering and investigate specific demographic differences between groups.
Summative Assessment:	**Summative Assessment:**
Students integrate new information about Basque immigration into the personalized format of a letter from a recent immigrant to a friend back in the Basque country.	Students prepare an illustrated geneological tree of a Mexican family (hypothetical or based on interviews with an immigrant family in the community) and make an oral presentation.

Appendix B: MOSAIC Activities Representing CBI Attributes

	Activity 1	Activity 2	Activity 3
Title	Timeline/La línea cronológica	Mexican Population in Oregon: A Historical Perspective/La población mexicana en Oregon: Un vistazo histórico	Reading: The First Mexicans in Oregon/ Lectura: Los primeros mexicanos en Oregon
Content	Identifying important dates in Mexican and Mexican American history	Historical demographics	Migration, economic activity, cultural geography
Language Functions	Describing, narrating in past time frame, extracting details	Describing, comparing in past and present time frames	Describing, comparing, narrating in past and present time frames, extracting details
Task	Students read historical excerpts and match events with dates by gluing events on a timeline.	Students read tables of census data for Oregon from 1950 to 2000 and figure out percentages of Mexican-born residents in the past 4 census years.	Students read about the first wave of Mexican immigration to Oregon, answer comprehension questions, and participate in a discussion based on the reading.

Appendix C: Levels of Collaboration in the MOSAIC Project

Content specialists and language specialists together	Content specialists (only)	Language specialists (only)
Identifying topic and subtopic	Providing resources (CBI attribute)	Adapting resources (CBI attribute)
Developing scope and sequence	Locating resources	Integrating resources and activities
Discussing generic activities	Providing information	Identifying grammar structures and vocabulary needed to participate in activities
Developing unit structure	Gathering information	Deciding on types of activities and sequencing them appropriately (CBI attribute)
Identifying standards (CBI attribute)	Providing feedback	Scaffolding vocabulary and grammar structures (CBI attribute)
Developing guiding questions		Translating resources and information from English to Spanish
Creating performance assessments		Revising activities
		Embedding cultural elements
		Deciding on which skills to emphasize and integrating them (CBI attribute)
		Leveling activities

Glossary

A priori teaching approach—ESL teachers preteach key concepts, academic skills, and language that will be addressed by content area teachers in the mainstream classroom.

Academic Language Functions—Use and understanding of the vocabulary needed for academic tasks (e.g., *explain*, *compare*, *describe*).

Accommodation—Modification to or adaptation of classroom assignments, tasks, or assessments to meet the learning needs of an individual student or group of students.

Action research in education—Educational research conducted by one or more individuals to solve a problem or obtain information to inform educational practices. Researchers are often participants in the study.

Advisory—A class held between a faculty advisor and the subset of secondary students assigned to him or her; this course may focus on building study habits, social skills, career exploration, or more direct and individual coaching of individual students to promote their personal and academic growth.

Advocacy—The act of speaking out for or on the behalf of a person, issue, or concern. Teachers of ELLs can be advocates at the classroom, school, district, community, state, and national levels by sharing issues of concern for students.

Affective filter—The tendency of negative emotional states (e.g., low self-esteem or anxiety) to hinder language acquisition.

Assistive technology—Any item, piece of equipment, or product system that is used to increase, maintain, or improve functional capabilities of children with disabilities.

Basic interpersonal communication skills (BICS)—Social language used in informal contexts (e.g., school cafeterias, hallways, playgrounds). Research shows it can take second language learners up to 2 years to develop BICS.

Cognitive academic language approach (CALLA)—In CALLA, ESL teachers align their instruction with that of content area teachers through the incorporation of topics from content area subjects; the development of academic language skills necessary for the subjects and for academic performance in general (e.g., language skills to persuade and justify); and through explicit instuction in learning strategies for the simultaneous acquisition of language and content and the accomplishment of specific tasks in a content area.

Cognitive academic language proficiency (CALP)—Relatively formal language required to succeed in academic settings. Second language learners may require 5 or more years to attain this kind of fluency.

Cognitive coaching—A framework of professional development that questions and directs teachers toward understanding of their instruction.

Comprehensible input—When context, gestures, pictures, and background knowledge are used to complement language so that meaning is accessible for individuals learning that language.

Coteaching—A service delivery model in which a content area teacher and an ESL teacher collaborate to provide instruction to a linguistically diverse group of students.

Cultural contexts—Real-life contexts in which communication takes place (e.g., around family and in the home, during leisure time, and in academic settings).

Culturally-responsive teaching—A popular strand in curriculum and instruction today, culturally-responsive teaching involves a teacher building upon a student's culture and prior knowledge to ensure success in school. A culturally-responsive teacher who combines high expectations with caring about students' success and knowledge of effective pedagogy may be considered a warm demander.

Culture—A complex, multifaceted construct that involves multiple and contested definitions including various perspectives from anthropology to psychology and sociology. Culture can refer to attitudes, perceptions, and values within a group of people (deep culture) or to the tangible elements that are easy to describe, such as the arts, language, food, and holidays (surface culture).

Curriculum-based measurement—Brief, timed assessment exercises that use materials drawn directly from a student's academic program.

Differentiated instruction—The dynamic cycle of instruction and assessment that is inclusive of the myriad of needs within a classroom setting.

Dual discrepancy—An assessment term associated with the learning disability identification process included in the 2004 reauthorization of the Individuals with Disabilities Education Act known as RTI (see *response to intervention*). Specifically, dual discrepancy refers to a student who demonstrates low academic ability (not meeting grade-level benchmark curriculum expectations) and is making little or no progress over time.

Formal schema—Knowledge of the overall organization and conventional structures of specific types of text. Stories, fables, expositions, and scientific texts, for example, all require different formal schema.

Graphic organizer—A visual representation of content material designed to help students process or produce information that might otherwise be difficult to understand.

Immersion program—An educational curriculum that builds language learning by teaching all or part of its subject matter in the targeted (nonnative) language. In academic immersion programs, instructional planning is grounded in knowledge of language acquisition and integrates language with academic objectives.

Integrated curricula—Integrated and interdisciplinary curricula consist of the careful collaboration and planning among teachers of various subjects so that the content in each of their classrooms is continued, supported, and reiterated throughout the school day.

Knowledge about language (KAL)—An understanding of the elements and applications of linguistics for educational purposes. KAL is often transferred between university educators and K–12 educators working with English language learners.

Language minority families—Families who speak languages other than that used as the dominant language of instruction. While the home languages of such families may be spoken by the numerical majority of students in individual schools or communities, these families often are in the minority in terms of political power and social prestige.

Learning disability—A disorder in one or more of the basic psychological processes involved in understanding or using spoken or written language: oral expression, listening comprehension, math calculation, math problem solving, reading decoding, reading comprehension, reading fluency, and written language.

Low-incidence—Relatively small numbers of English language learners in a given area, according to demographic statistics.

Multicultural education—An idea or concept, an educational reform movement, and a process for teaching and learning based on equity and excellence and democratic beliefs and principles.

Multidisciplinary school teams—A group of school personnel who meets to discuss students' academic and assessment programming and makes recommendations about student disability classification and appropriate academic interventions. Also known as *in-school academic support*.

Problem-solving model—A response-to-intervention model in diagnosing learning disabilities in which Tier 2 interventions are completed with students in the general education classroom. (Tier 1 is classroom instruction.) The intervention is designed specifically for the student in question and student response to the intervention determines whether the student should be referred for more explicit assessments and consideration for learning disability classification (Tier 3).

Protocol—A conversational tool used by some teachers to structure and focus conversations about professional matters. A protocol's prompts, roles, and time limits may provide teachers with the permission and push to go beyond typical norms of autonomy and non-interference, helping them to provide colleagues with supportive and critical feedback about student learning and their own pedagogy in their work.

Pull-out ESL programs—For part of the school day, ELLs are pulled out of mainstream classrooms to receive specialized instruction in English by an ESL professional.

Reflective pedagogy—An ongoing process of analyzing one's own teaching experiences to inform and improve teaching practice. Often conducted under the guidance of facilitators, peer educators, or trainers.

Response to intervention (RTI)—An assessment model for classifying students with learning disabilities. Students who do not make good progress with the core/regular education curriculum are provided an intensive intervention. If little or no progress is made, an underlying learning disability is probable and further assessments are completed to assist the school in making its recommendation about classification.

Rhetorical organization—The sequencing or patterning of discourse to achieve specific purposes in a text, such as description, comparison-contrast, or persuasion. Rhetorical organizational patterns vary across cultures.

Scaffolding—Support for student learning that can come in various forms including linguistic, conceptual, procedural, and socio-cultural that can be gradually removed as students progress and develop their own effective learning strategies.

Scope and sequence—A curriculum plan in which a range of instructional objectives is organized according to the successive levels at which they are taught.

Sheltered instruction—Instruction for diverse learners in which content area teachers frequently use scaffolding techniques (e.g., visual support, focusing on vocabulary development through context and interaction, and building background knowledge and experiences).

Sheltered instruction observation protocol (SIOP)—provides concrete examples of the features of sheltered instruction. The SIOP protocol consists of 30 items (e.g., language and content objectives development; comprehensible input, building background) organized under three main sections: preparation, instruction, review/assessment.

Standard protocol model—A response-to-intervention model in diagnosing learning disabilities which in Tier 2 uses a standard set of procedures for students with similar characteristics of academic difficulty. (Tier 1 is classroom instruction; Tier 3 is explicit assessment.) The intervention includes predetermined activities that are not tailored to the individual needs of a student. If a student does not make good progress at first, additional intervention sessions can be provided.

Standards—Measurements of attainment in professional, academic, or linguistic development, established by departments of education, academic organizations, or other recognized authorities, and used as a basis for assessment.

Systemic reform—Planned, long-term improvement in educational policy or practice, involving all members of the institution or organization as participants.

Teacher professional community—The norms, attitudes, and practices that teachers develop together and that guide how teachers relate to colleagues and to students.

Tier—Refers to the (typically) three levels of intervention used in the response to intervention model: Tier 1 (classroom instruction), Tier 2 (an intensive intervention), and Tier 3 (formal assessment for classification of a student as having a learning disability and receiving long-term special education services).

Turfism—The problem of teachers having inflexible boundaries regarding the extent of their knowledge area expertise and responsibilities to students.

Zone of proximal development—The range of development between learners' ability to perform tasks independently and their ability to perform more advanced tasks with assistance from adults or more capable peers.

Contributors

George C. Bunch, a former high school ESL teacher, is assistant professor of education at the University of California, Santa Cruz, in the United States. His research explores the language demands of schooling; how students use their developing linguistic resources to meet these demands; and how students, teachers, school leaders, policy makers, language testers, and educational researchers view these demands and resources.

Michael W. Dunn has taught at the elementary level as a special education teacher in inclusive classrooms and as an ESL teacher in the Toronto, Canada area. As an assistant professor at Washington State University Vancouver, in the United States, since 2005, Michael's research interests include strategies for struggling readers and writers and response to intervention. He also teaches special education courses that have a literacy focus.

Heidi Goertzen is an ESL specialist with the Alabama State Department of Education, in the United States. She has taught content-based ESL and sheltered instruction in Texas, Indiana, and Alabama in grades Pre-K–8 and earned her master's degree in language education from Indiana University.

Sally Hood is an assistant professor in the School of Education at the University of Portland in Oregon, in the United States. She prepares ESL, foreign language, and reading teachers and supervises their student teaching. She received her doctorate in language education from Indiana University, Bloomington, in 2002. She taught French for 8 years in Indiana before doing her graduate work.

Susan Jenkins is a professor of TESOL at Saint Michael's College, in Vermont, in the United States, and has published in *TESOL Quarterly, English for Specific Purposes, The Journal of Second Language Writing,* and *The International Journal of Intercultural*

Relations. She is coprincipal investigator of a federal grant to provide professional development for content teachers working with English language learners.

Thomas H. Levine is an assistant professor of curriculum and instruction at the Neag School of Education, University of Connecticut, in the United States. He studies teacher collaboration and the conversion of high schools into smaller units. His dissertation research, which provides the empirical data for the chapter he coauthored, was generously supported by a Spencer Dissertation Fellowship and a McMurtry Stanford Graduate Fellowship.

Trish Morita-Mullaney serves as an ESL coach and coordinator in a Midwestern U.S. suburban/urban district. She was the primary editor for the English language proficiency standards for her state and serves on various statewide ESL taskforces. She has also developed an online professional development course for classroom/content area teachers within her district.

Mark Nigolian has a master's degree in TESOL and is an ESOL teacher in the Burlington School District in Vermont, in the United States. He was recently an ESOL specialist on a federal grant helping content teachers with sheltered instruction for English language learners in mainstream classrooms. He has presented at TESOL conventions and participated as a test-item writer for the WIDA Access test.

Mary Kay O'Brien is an ESL specialist in the Burlington School District in Vermont, in the United States, where she helps content teachers make their materials accessible to English language learners in mainstream classrooms. She has a master's degree in TESL, has presented at TESOL conventions, coauthored *Grammar One* with Jean Zukowski/Faust, and been on two successful grant-writing teams for Title VII grants.

Elizabeth O'Dowd is a professor of TESOL at Saint Michael's College in Vermont, in the United States. She is the author of *Prepositions and Particles in English* and coauthor of *GrammarLinks2*. She has published articles in *Lingua* and *Studies in Language*. She is coprincipal investigator of a federal grant to provide professional development for content teachers working with English language learners.

Raquel Oxford is assistant professor of second language education in curriculum and instruction at the University of Wisconsin-Milwaukee, in the United States, and program coordinator for World Languages. She has experience throughout the Pre-K–16 system and as a professional development school coordinator in Texas. Her research interests include second language teacher preparation and mentoring, technology integration, and multicultural education. She is an associate editor of *Hispania*.

Faridah Pawan is an assistant professor in the Language Education Department in the School of Education at Indiana University, Bloomington, in the United States. Her research areas are in teacher collaboration and computer-mediated communication. She is the principal investigator and director of three collaborative programs: the Interdisciplinary Collaborative Program, the Tandem Certification for Indiana Teachers Program, and the Interdisciplinary Collaboration for Content Area Teachers. She has published in several journals, including *TESOL Quarterly*, *Language Learning & Technology*, and *Journal of Ethnographic and Qualitative Research*.

Ginger B. Sietman is a doctoral student in language education at Indiana University in the United States. After graduating with a master's degree in communication from Purdue University, she taught public speaking and English language courses at Beijing Foreign Studies University, where she developed a passion for language education. She currently teaches in the Interdisciplinary Collaboration for Content Area Teachers program and has adapted a study skills course to meet the unique needs of international students at Indiana University.

Debra Suarez is associate professor of TESOL at the College of Notre Dame of Maryland in the United States. She teaches in the MA TESOL program and in the doctoral program, Educational Leadership for Changing Populations. Her areas of specialization are teacher education and heritage language learners. In addition to editing the Collaborative Partnership series for TESOL, she has contributed to *TESOL Journal*, *Journal of Multilingual and Multicultural Development*, *TESOL Quarterly*, and *Educational Horizons* and has coedited a special issue of *Heritage Language Journal*. A former ESL/EFL teacher, she has presented at TESOL conferences and taught graduate courses in countries around the world, including Korea, Guatemala, Venezuela, Ukraine, Mexico, Peru, and Syria.

Trenia Walker taught U.S. history and Texas history at the middle and high school levels for seven years in the Houston Independent School District. She is currently an assistant professor in social studies education at Washington State University Vancouver, in the United States. Her research interests include transformative learning theories and the implications for technology, popular culture, and globalization in social studies teaching and learning.

Linda Walsleben has an educational specialist's degree from Rutgers University, a master's degree from Marlboro College, and a master's degree in TESOL from State University of New York-Stony Brook. She has worked for 21 years as a foreign language and ESL teacher in New York, New Jersey, and Vermont, and is currently an ESL content specialist for the Burlington School District, in Vermont, in the United States.

Brenda Ward, ESL director for the Community Schools of Frankfort, Indiana, in the United States, received her bachelor's degree in elementary education with a secondary language arts endorsement from Purdue University and ESL certification from Indiana University. She is a teacher educator and an ESL consultant. She hopes to raise her two daughters with the same social justice ideology that she has embraced.

Index

Page references followed by *f* and *t* indicate figures and tables, respectively.

A

AATF. *See* American Association of Teachers of French

AATG. *See* American Association of Teachers of German

AATSP. *See* American Association of Teachers of Spanish and Portuguese

Academic achievement
  ability and, 106
  cognitive academic language proficiency and. *See* Cognitive academic language proficiency
  culturally responsive teaching and, 145–146, 148
  families and, 122, 124–125
  importance of English and, 153
  standards and. *See* Standards
  teachers' concerns with, 119
  time considerations and, 113, 114
Academic language. *See* Language
Access model of critical literacy, 6–7
Accountability, standards and, 62–63
ACTFL. *See* American Council on the Teaching of Foreign Languages
Active listening, assessment and, 96
Activism. *See* Advocacy

Activities
  learning disabilities and, 110–111
  teacher knowledge and, 1
Adaptation, culture and, 143
Additive approach to content integration, 145
Administrative support
  advocacy and, 155
  importance of, 2
  integrated curriculum and, 22, 27*t*
  professional development and, 36
Advisors, ESL teachers as, 128, 129, 136
Advocacy, 148–149, 158
Aesthetic standards, culture and, 143–144
Alabama, standards and, 62, 66, 76
American Association of Teachers of French, 164
American Association of Teachers of German, 164
American Association of Teachers of Italian, 164
American Association of Teachers of Spanish and Portuguese, 164
American Classical League, 164
American Council of Teachers of Russian, 164
American Council on the Teaching of Foreign Languages, 164
Anthropology, culture and, 143
Art, culture and, 143
Assessment
  case study, 85

Assessment *(continued)*
  classroom/large-scale assessment and, 71*f*,
    78
  collaboration and, 91–97
  differentiation of, 66, 90
  discussion, 98
  five qualities of, 86, 98
  framework for, 81–83*t*
  learning disabilities and. *See* Learning
    disabilities
  lessons learned/next steps for, 97–98
  reasons for, 86–91
  response to intervention and, 104–105
  responsibility and, 97*t*
  sample social studies unit and, 183
  standards and, 70
  summary of, 98–99
Assistive technology, learning disabilities and,
    111
Association of Teachers of Japanese, 164
Assumptions, culture and, 144
Attendance, grading and, 89–90
Attitudes, culture and, 143
Autonomy
  language issues and, 54
  professional development and, 36
  schools and, 12

B

Background knowledge
  assessment and, 95
  culturally responsive teaching and, 147
  integrated curriculum and, 20–21*t*
Backgrounds, student, 86, 91, 98
Barriers
  assessment and, 98
  to implementing integrated curriculum,
    11–13, 27*t*
  language issues and, 34–36, 53
Basic interpersonal communication skills, 47,
    65, 146
Behavior, grading and, 89–90
Bethune-Chavez Academy. *See* Communities
Bias, culture and, 144, 145
BICS. *See* Basic interpersonal communication
    skills
Burlington School District. *See* Language

C

CALLA model of instruction, 87–88
CALP. *See* Cognitive academic language
    proficiency
Cartesian dualism, 1
CASL. *See* Collaborative analysis of student
    learning
CASLS. *See* Center for Applied Second
    Language Studies
CBM. *See* Curriculum-based measurement
Center for Applied Second Language Studies,
    170, 171
Center for Research on Education, Diversity
    and Excellence, 38
Center on School, Family, and Community
    Partnership, 122
Certification, 64
CG. *See* Connections Goal
Challenge, culturally responsive teaching and,
    147
Chinese Language Association of Secondary-
    Elementary Schools, 164
Chinese Language Teachers Association, 164
City View Independent School. *See* Culture
Clarification, assessment and, 96
Classroom assessment, 71*f*
Classrooms. *See* Environment
CLIF framework, 41, 52–53
CLT. *See* Communicative language teaching
Coaching, vs. consulting, 91*t*
Cognitive academic language proficiency, 47,
    48, 65, 146. *See also* Language
Cognitive involvement in communicative
    activities, 167*f*
Collaboration
  advantages/challenges of, 135–136
  advocacy and, 149–156
  assessment and, 91–97, 99
  benefits of, 115
  community and. *See* Communities
  consulting vs. coaching and, 91*t*
  culturally responsive teaching and, 148,
    158. *See also* Culture
  with families, 126–128, 128–135, 134–135
  foreign languages and. *See* Foreign
    languages
  importance of, 1–2
  integrated curriculum and. *See* Integrated
    curriculum
  intentionally structured, 129–133, 137

language issues and. *See* Language
learning disabilities and, 106–112, 115
MOSAIC project and, 170–180, 185
standards and, 72–75, 76. *See also*
    Standards
time considerations and, 181
Collaborative analysis of student learning, 98
Colloquialisms, native speakers and, 39
Commitment, community and, 121
Common underlying proficiency, 88
Communication
    BICS and, 47
    CLIF framework and, 41
    families and, 122, 127
    foreign language standards and, 165
Communicative competence, 167
Communicative language teaching, 164, 167
Communities
    case study, 117–118
    collaboration with families and, 126–128,
        128–135
    culture and, 145, 157
    discussion, 136–137
    foreign language standards and, 165
    importance of, 119–121
    informal, 22–25, 27*t*
    lessons learned/next steps for, 135–136
    MOSAIC project and, 172
    schools as, 11–12
    successes in partnerships and, 134–135
    summary of, 136–137
    teacher professional community and, 119,
        137
    traditional views on, 122–126
    types of, 137
Comparisons, foreign language standards and,
    165
Competence, communicative, 167
Competencies. *See* Standards
Complexity, SIOP and, 39
Comprehension, checking for, 131
Comprehensive Inventory of Basic Skills, 105
Conflict
    community and, 122–123
    schools and, 11–12
Connected level of integrated curricula, 9*f*
Connections
    assessment and, 96
    foreign language standards and, 165
Connections Goal, 165–166, 168–169, 178,
    180

Consistency, integrated curriculum and, 27*t*
Constructivist approach
    integrated curriculum and, 10
    professional development and, 37
Consulting, vs. coaching, 91*t*
Content area teachers, 6
Content knowledge
    assessment and, 98
    assessment of. *See* Assessment
    culturally responsive teaching and. *See*
        Culture
    culture and, 144
    language issues and, 51–52*t*
    learning disabilities and. *See* Learning
        disabilities
    levels of proficiency and, 69*t*
    MOSAIC project and. *See* MOSAIC project
    standards and, 67–68. *See* Standards
Content stem, 69–70, 70*t*
Content-based instruction
    assessment and, 87. *See also* Assessment
    characteristics of, 172
    foreign languages and, 166–168, 168–169,
        178–179, 180, 184
    language and. *See* Language
    prevalence of, 1–2
Context
    cognitive involvement and, 167*f*
    MOSAIC project and, 177–178
    professional development and, 36
    SIOP and, 38
Contextualization, culturally responsive
    teaching and, 147
Contrastive analysis, 131
Contributions approach to content
    integration, 145
Conversation, culturally responsive teaching
    and, 147
Cooperative learning, SIOP and, 38
Coping strategies, culture and, 153
Costs. *See* Economic considerations
Coteaching. *See* Collaboration
CREDE. *See* Center for Research on Education,
    Diversity and Excellence
Credit accrual, standards and, 71
Critical literacy. *See* Literacy
Critical-friends protocol, 130*t*
Cultural considerations, effective practice for
    ELLs and, 146–148
Culture. *See also* Communities; Families
    advocacy and, 148–149, 158

Culture (*continued*)
  case study, 141
  CLIF framework and, 41
  collaboration and, 46
  defining, 142–144, 157
  discussion, 157
  foreign language standards and, 165
  language and. *See* Language
  lessons learned/next steps for, 156–157
  multicultural education and, 144–145, 157
  need for consideration of, 142, 157
  responsive teaching and, 145–146
  summary of, 157–158
  teachers and, 47
CUP. *See* Common underlying proficiency
Curriculum
  coherence and, 34
  culture and, 144. *See also* Culture
  integrated. *See* Integrated curriculum
Curriculum and Evaluation Standards for School Mathematics, 61
Curriculum-based measurement, 112

D

Debriefing, assessment and, 96
Decision making, families and, 122, 125
Deep culture, 143
Delaware, standards and, 66
Diagnosis, learning disabilities and, 106–107
Dialogue, culturally responsive teaching and, 147
Differences, language acquisition and, 65
Differentiation
  assessment and, 66, 89–90
  culturally responsive teaching and, 147
Disabilities, learning. *See* Learning disabilities
District of Columbia, standards and, 66
Dual discrepancy, defining, 113

E

Economic considerations
  accountability and, 63
  standards and, 61
Education, multicultural. *See* Culture
Educational Leadership, 32–33
Efficacy
  social, 173–176
  teacher, 169–170
Effort, grading and, 89–90

EFL. *See* English as a foreign language
ELLs. *See* English language learners
ELP standards. *See* Standards
E-mails, meetings and, 17
Emergent language acquisition, 50*t*, 66*t*
Energy, community and, 121
English
  as distinct from other languages, 39
  native speakers and, 39
English as a foreign language, 1. *See also* Foreign languages
English as a second language
  integrated curriculum and. *See* Integrated curriculum
  teacher knowledge and, 1
English language learners
  assessment of. *See* Assessment
  backgrounds of, 86, 91
  effective practice for, 146–148
  identification of, 105
  importance of collaboration and, 1
  integrated curriculum for. *See* Integrated curriculum
  language issues and. *See* Language
  sharing information about, 132–133
  standards and, 71. *See also* Standards
English language proficiency standards. *See* Standards
Enthusiasm, community and, 121
Environment, culture and, 143, 147
Equity pedagogy, culture and, 145
ESL. *See* English as a second language
Ethical considerations, utilization of children as interpreters and, 126
Evaluation, integrated curriculum and, 20–21*t*
Expression. *See* Speaking skills

F

Face-to-face communication, 127
Faculty. *See* Teachers
Families
  CLIF framework and, 41
  collaboration with, 128–135, 137
  communication with, 47
  community and, 121. *See also* Communities
  culture and, 153
  diagnosis learning disabilities and, 106–107
  native language of, 114
  parent workshops and, 127

parenting practices of, 123
support of, 122
support of for learning disabilities, 109–111
*Fifty Strategies for Teaching English Language
        Learners*, 47
Fluency
    language acquisition and, 50*t*
    length of time to gain, 33
    stages of language development and, 66*t*
    standards and, 94*t*
Focus topics, bonus period meetings and, 16*t*
Food, culture and, 143
Foreign languages
    case study, 163–164
    collaboration and, 169–178
    content-based instruction and, 166–169
    discussion, 180
    lessons learned/next steps for, 178–180
    standards and, 164–166
    summary of, 180–181
Fragmented level of integrated curricula, 9*f*
Frankfort High School. *See* Integrated
        curriculum
Front-loading vocabulary, 131
Funding. *See* Economic considerations

G

Games, MOSAIC project and, 172
Gatekeeping, access model and, 6–7
Georgia, standards and, 66
Goldstone High School. *See* Learning
        disabilities
Grading, as assessment, 89–90
Graduation, standards and, 71
Grammar
    language issues and, 47–48
    SIOP and, 39
Graphic organizers, 131
Group work, language and, 31
Guided practice, 131

H

Hands-on tasks
    content-based instruction and, 172
    standards and, 67–68
High school
    importance of integrated curricula and,
        10–11, 27*t*
    standards and, 61, 71

Holidays, culture and, 143
Home visits, 127–128, 129

I

ICP. *See* Interdisciplinary Collaborative
        Program
IDEA. *See* Individuals with Disabilities
        Education Improvement Act of 2004
Idioms, native speakers and, 39
Illinois, standards and, 66
Immersed level of integrated curricula, 9*f*
Immigrants. *See* English language learners
Imperial system, manipulatives and, 19
Independence, schools and, 12
Independent practice, 131
Indiana, ELLs and. *See* Integrated curriculum
Individuals with Disabilities Education
        Improvement Act of 2004, 104
Information gathering, learning disabilities
        and, 109–111
Input, integrated curriculum and, 20–21*t*
In-service. *See* Professional development
Instruction
    CLIF framework and, 41
    standards and, 67*t*, 95
    successes in improving, 133–134
Integrated curriculum
    barriers to, 11–13
    case study, 5–6
    defining, 8, 27*t*
    discussion, 26
    focus of, 8–10
    importance of inclusion of, 10–11
    lesson plans for, 20–21*t*
    lessons learned/next steps for, 21–26
    macrodynamics and, 14–18
    microdynamics and, 18–21
    sample, 24–25*t*
    scaffolding/content strategies and, 19*t*
    successful collaboration and, 13–14
    summary of, 27*t*
    ten levels of, 9*f*
    underlying issues regarding, 6–8
Integrated level of integrated curricula, 9*f*
Intellectual standards, culture and, 143–144
Interaction
    content-based instruction and, 172
    integrated curriculum and, 20–21*t*
Interdisciplinary Collaborative Program, 14

International School, 33
Interpreters, utilization of, 126
Intervention
    implementation of, 111–112
    learning disabilities and, 114
    parental support and, 110
    response to, 104, 108, 113–114
Isolation, integrated curriculum and, 27t

K

KAL. *See under* Knowledge
Kentucky, standards and, 66
Knowledge
    about language (KAL), 37–41, 54. *See also*
        Language
    background. *See* Background knowledge
    content area. *See* Content knowledge
    culture and, 144
    professional development and. *See*
        Professional development
    teacher, 1, 36

L

Language
    accessibility of, 32–34
    acquisition of. *See* Language acquisition
    case study, 31–32
    challenges in addressing issues of, 34–36
    collaboration and, 41–47, 43f, 44t
    communication with families and, 123–124
    culturally responsive teaching and, 146–148
    culture and, 143. *See also* Culture
    discussion, 53
    domains of, 68. *See also specific domains*
    function, 69–70, 70t
    lessons learned/next steps for, 47–53
    native. *See* Native languages
    professional development and, 36–38
    requisite knowledge of, 38–41
    stages of language development and, 64,
        65–66, 66t
    summary of, 53–54
Language acquisition
    CLIF framework and, 41
    collaboration and, 46
    KAL and, 38
    role of native language in, 65
    scope and sequence of, 50t
    stages of language development and, 64,
        65–66, 66t

Large-scale assessment, 71f
Leadership
    collaboration and, 72
    importance of, 2
    professional development and, 36
    teachers and, 25–26, 27t
Learning disabilities
    case study, 103
    collaboration and, 106–112
    defining, 104–105
    discussion, 114
    identification of, 106–107
    lessons learned/next steps for, 112–114
    summary of, 114–115
Lesson planning
    collaboration and, 74–75
    integrated curriculum and, 18–21, 20–21t
    language and, 33–34
Levels of language proficiency, 68–69, 81–83t
Liaisons, ESL teachers as, 128
Listening skills
    framework for classroom instruction/
        assessment and, 81–83t
    as language domain, 68
    learning disabilities and, 106
    standards and, 62
Literacy
    models of, 6–7
    standards and, 94

M

Macrodynamics, integrated curriculum and,
        14–18
Maine, standards and, 66
Manipulatives, integrated curriculum and, 19
Materials
    integrated curriculum and, 20–21t
    language issues and, 49
    professional development and, 37
Mathematics
    language issues and, 41–47
    standards and, 61, 67t
*Mathscape: Seeing and Thinking
        Mathematically*, 41
Measurement
    assessment and. *See* Assessment
    curriculum-based, 112
    manipulatives and, 19

Meetings
    collaboration and, 74–75
    coteaching and, 78
    integrated curriculum and, 14–16
    sample focus topics for, 16*t*
    sharing information about students and,
        132–133
Metric system, manipulatives and, 19
Microdynamics, integrated curriculum and,
    18–21
Middle school, importance of integrated
    curricula and, 10–11, 27*t*
Model performance indicators, 69–70, 70*t*, 78
Moral standards, culture and, 143–144
MOSAIC project, 170–180, 184, 185
Motivation, teachers and, 49
MPI. *See* Model performance indicators
Multicultural education, 144–145, 157. *See
    also* Culture

N

A Nation at Risk, 60–61, 71, 77
National Center for Education Statistics, 6
National Commission on Excellence in
    Education Report, 60–61
National Council of Japanese Language
    Teachers, 164
National Council of Teachers of English, 61
National Council of Teachers of Mathematics,
    61
National foreign language standards, 164–
    165, 168–169, 175, 178, 180, 183
Native languages
    assessment and, 93–95
    English acquisition and, 65
NCLB. *See* No Child Left Behind Act
NCTM. *See* National Council of Teachers of
    Mathematics
Nested level of integrated curricula, 9*f*
Networked level of integrated curricula, 9*f*
New Hampshire, standards and, 66
New Jersey, standards and, 66
NFLS. *See* National foreign language
    standards
No Child Left Behind Act
    integrated curriculum and, 6, 8, 27*t*
    professional development and, 33, 34
    standards and, 61–62, 64–65, 77
North Dakota, standards and, 66
Notetaking, 75

O

Oak Mountain High School. *See* Standards
Objectives, displaying, 132
Oklahoma, standards and, 66
Oral skills. *See* Speaking skills
Oregon, foreign languages and. *See* Foreign
    languages
Organizational resources
    graphic organizers and, 131
    importance of, 2
Outreach, 76

P

Parents. *See* Families
Patience, importance of, 136
Perceptions, culture and, 143
Perspective, culture and, 144
Planning
    integrated curriculum and, 21
    language issues and, 54
    lesson. *See* Lesson planning
Positive reinforcement, 131
Practice, teacher workshops and, 131
Prefixes, 131
Prejudice. *See* Bias
Preparation, integrated curriculum and,
    20–21*t*
Preproduction
    language acquisition and, 50*t*
    stages of language development and, 66*t*
Presentation, assessment and, 96
Privacy, schools and, 12
Problem-solving, standard protocol approach
    to, 114
Processing, learning disabilities and, 106
Production
    language acquisition and, 50*t*
    stages of language development and, 66*t*
Professional development
    community and, 119. *See also* Communities
    faculty share fairs and, 14, 18
    importance of collaboration and, 1
    integrated curriculum and, 14, 17
    linguistics training and, 40
    stages of language development and, 64
    university contributions and, 36–38
Proficiency standards. *See* Standards
Progress, standards and, 62
Protocols, reflection on instruction and,
    129–131

Psychology, culture and, 143
Pull-out programs, 10, 33, 53

Q

Quality Utilization of Education, Support and
    Training program (QUEST), 41, 52–53.
    See also Language
Questioning, assessment and, 96

R

Radio reading, 110
Reading
    framework for classroom instruction/
        assessment and, 81–83*t*
    as language domain, 68
    learning disabilities and, 106
    standards and, 61, 62, 74*t*, 94*t*
Reception, learning disabilities and, 106
Referral, collaboration and, 108–109
Reflection, use of protocols and, 129–131
Reflective listening, assessment and, 96
Refugees. *See* English language learners
Reinforcement, 131
Research
    collaboration and, 72–73
    professional development and, 36–37
Resources
    assessment and, 95
    culturally responsive teaching and, 157
    integrated curriculum and, 20–21*t*
    organizational. *See* Organizational resources
Respect, culturally responsive teaching and,
    145
Response to intervention, 104, 108, 113–114
Responses, assessment and, 96
Responsibility
    assessment and, 97*t*
    standards and, 63–65, 77
Review, integrated curriculum and, 20–21*t*
Rhode Island, standards and, 66
Riverview School District. *See* Learning
    disabilities
Role-play, MOSAIC project and, 172
RTI. *See* Response to intervention
Rural schools, ELLs and, 64

S

Saint Michael's College. *See* Language
Satisfaction, community and, 121
Scaffolding
    assessment and, 95
    culturally responsive teaching and, 153
    integrated curriculum and, 10, 19*t*
    language and, 31, 32, 53
    model performance indicators and, 70*t*
Scavenger hunts, MOSAIC project and, 172
Science, standards and, 67*t*
SEAs. *See* State educational agencies
Self-esteem, culturally responsive teaching
    and, 145
Sequenced level of integrated curricula, 9*f*
Sharing of information, teachers and,
    132–133
Sheltered Instruction Observation Protocol
    assessment and, 87–88
    collaborative approach to, 43*f*
    integrated curriculum and, 13, 19–20
    KAL and, 38–41
    language and, 32
SIOP. *See* Sheltered Instruction Observation
    Protocol
Social action approach to content integration,
    145
Social context, standards and, 67*t*
Social studies
    MOSAIC project and, 170–178
    sample unit for, 183
    standards and, 67*t*, 81–83*t*
Sociology, culture and, 143
Software, learning disabilities and, 111
Speaking skills
    framework for classroom instruction/
        assessment and, 81–83*t*
    as language domain, 68
    learning disabilities and, 106, 111
    standards and, 62, 68*t*
Special education. *See* Learning disabilities
Stages of language development, 64, 65–66,
    66*t*
Standard protocol approach, 114
Standardized testing. *See* Assessment; Testing
Standards
    alignment of, 87*t*
    assessment and, 98. *See also* Assessment
    as barrier, 12–13
    case study, 59–60

classroom/large-scale assessment and, 71*f*

collaboration and, 72–75, 92–97

combining content/ELP, 94*t*

discussion, 77

foreign languages and, 164–165, 168–169, 175, 178, 180, 183

implications of for students, 71

implications of for teachers, 62–66

importance of, 60–62

integration of, 74*t*

lessons learned/next steps for, 76–77

levels of proficiency and, 68–69, 69*t*

organization of, 66–71

summary of, 77–78

Standards for Foreign Language Learning: Preparing for the Twenty-First Century, 164

State educational agencies, standards and, 62

Story structure, 110*t*

Strategy instruction, integrated curriculum and, 25, 27*t*

Structure

collaboration and, 129–133

SIOP and, 39

Students. *See* English language learners

Summarization, 132

Support, level of, 69–70

Surface culture. *See* Culture

Synonyms, 131

Syntax, standards and, 75

T

Tasks, culturally responsive teaching and, 148

Teachers

advocacy and, 155–156

assessment and, 89–91, 95–97, 98–99

characteristics of, 128*t*

collaboration between ESL/content instruction and. *See* Collaboration

culturally responsive teaching and, 46, 47, 145–146, 153–154, 158

development of. *See* Professional development

diagnosis of learning disabilities and, 106–107

efficacy and, 169–170

encouragement of family collaboration and, 126–128

KAL and, 54

knowledge of, 1

as liaisons/advisors, 128

motivation and, 49

patience/time and, 136

professional community and, 119. *See also* Communities

requisite language knowledge of, 38–41

sharing information about students and, 132–133

standards and, 62–66, 72–75

strategy instruction and, 25

The Teacher's Guide to Diversity: Building a Knowledge Base, 147

Teachers of English to Speakers of Other Languages, 61–62, 67

Teaching, importance of collaboration and, 1

Technology, learning disabilities and, 111

TESOL. *See* Teachers of English to Speakers of Other Languages

Testing. *See also* Assessment

academic achievement and, 119

integrated curriculum and, 11

standards and. *See* Standards

Thematic units. *See* Integrated curriculum

Thinking skills, standards and, 61

Threaded level of integrated curricula, 9*f*

Time

academic achievement and, 113, 114

collaboration and, 45, 136, 181

importance of, 2

problems with lack of, 33

Training. *See* Professional development

Transformation approach to content integration, 145

Transformation model of critical literacy, 6–7

Translators, utilization of, 126

Trust, collaboration and, 169–170, 173–176

Turfism, 12

U

United Nations, 33

Units. *See* Integrated curriculum

Universities, professional development contributions and, 36–38

Urban schools, ELLs and, 64

V

Values, culture and, 143
Vermont
   language issues and. *See* Language
   standards and, 66
Vocabulary
   assessment and, 88
   collaboration and, 46
   language issues and, 48
   learning disabilities and, 110–111
   native speakers and, 39
   SIOP and, 38, 39
   standards and, 75, 94*t*
   teacher workshops and, 131
Volunteering
   families and, 122, 124
   interpreters/translators and, 126

W

Warm demanders, 146
Washington Language Proficiency Test, 105
WIDA. *See* World-Class Instructional Design
   and Assessment
Wisconsin, standards and, 66
WLPT. *See* Washington Language Proficiency
   Test
Word recognition, standards and, 94*t*
Workshops
   parent, 127
   teacher, 131–132
World-Class Instructional Design and
   Assessment, 34, 49, 65, 66–71, 67*t*,
   81–83*t*. *See also* Standards
Writing
   framework for classroom instruction/
   assessment and, 81–83*t*
   as language domain, 68
   learning disabilities and, 106, 111
   standards and, 61, 62, 74*t*
   teacher workshops and, 131

Also Available from TESOL

Bilingual Education
Donna Christian and Fred Genesee, Editors

Bridge to the Classroom: ESL Cases for Teacher Exploration
Joy Egbert and Gina Mikel Petrie

CALL Essentials
Joy Egbert

Communities of Supportive Professionals
Tim Murphey and Kazuyoshi Sato, Editors

Content-Based Instruction in Primary and Secondary School Settings
Dorit Kaufman and JoAnn Crandall, Editors

ESOL Tests and Testing
Stephen Stoynoff and Carol A. Chapelle

Gender and English Language Learners
Bonny Norton and Aneta Pavlenko, Editors

Language Teacher Research in Asia
Thomas S. C. Farrell, Editor

Literature in Language Teaching and Learning
Amos Paran, Editor

More Than a Native Speaker: An Introduction to Teaching English Abroad
revised edition
Don Snow

Perspectives on Community College ESL Series
Craig Machado, Series Editor
Volume 1: Pedagogy, Programs, Curricula, and Assessment
Marilynn Spaventa, Editor
Volume 2: Students, Mission, and Advocacy
Amy Blumenthal, Editor

PreK–12 English Language Proficiency Standards
Teachers of English to Speakers of Other Languages, Inc.

Planning and Teaching Creatively Within a Required Curriculum for School-Age Learners
Penny McKay, Editor

Professional Development of International Teaching Assistants
Dorit Kaufman and Barbara Brownworth, Editors

Teaching English as a Foreign Language in Primary School
Mary Lou McCloskey, Janet Orr, and Marlene Dolitsky, Editors

Teaching English From a Global Perspective
Anne Burns, Editor

Technology-Enhanced Learning Environments
Elizabeth Hanson-Smith, Editor

For more information, contact
Teachers of English to Speakers of Other Languages, Inc.
700 South Washington Street, Suite 200
Alexandria, Virginia 22314 USA
Toll Free: 888-547-3369   Fax on Demand: 800-329-4469
Publications Order Line: 888-891-0041
or 301-638-4427 or 4428
9 am to 5 pm, EST

ORDER ONLINE at www.tesol.org/

T E S O L